1993

The Roman empire of classical antiquity was a great power without any serious rivals. By contrast, the Roman empire of late antiquity faced another great power to the east, as well as increasingly troublesome barbarian tribes to the north. The ability of the empire to cope with these changed circumstances was affected in part by its access to reliable information and intelligence about these neighbours. This book offers the first systematic investigation of this dimension of late Roman foreign relations.

Adopting a comparative framework, it examines the theme of information in Roman relations with Sasanian Persia to the east and with a variety of northern peoples – Goths, Franks, Huns, and others. It aims to assess how well-informed the empire was about these peoples, and to account for differences in the availability of information between east and north. This involves consideration of institutional features of the empire and levels of organisational complexity among these neighbours, as well as variations in the socio-cultural character of the relevant frontier regions and their effect on the interchange of people and information. As a result, the book deals with a wide range of subjects beyond the traditional confines of military/diplomatic history, from geographical and ethno-graphical knowledge and assumptions, to levels of urbanisation and the role of religious and economic factors, and thereby helps to place late Roman foreign relations in a much broader context.

INFORMATION AND FRONTIERS

INFORMATION
AND FRONTIERS

ROMAN FOREIGN RELATIONS
IN LATE ANTIQUITY

A. D. LEE

CAMBRIDGE
UNIVERSITY PRESS

Published by the Press Syndicate of the University of Cambridge
The Pitt Building, Trumpington Street, Cambridge CB2 1RP
40 West 20th Street, New York, NY 10011–4211, USA
10 Stamford Road, Oakleigh, Victoria 3166, Australia

© Cambridge University Press 1993

First published 1993

Printed in Great Britain at the University Press, Cambridge

Library of Congress cataloguing in publication data
Lee, A. D.
Information and frontiers: Roman foreign relations in late antiquity /
A. D. Lee.
p.   cm.
Includes bibliographical references and index.
ISBN 0 521 39256 X
1. Rome – Foreign relations – 284–620. 1. Title.
DG312.L44 1993
327.37'009'015 dc20   92–34199   CIP

ISBN 0 521 39256 X hardback

To my parents

CONTENTS

PREFACE

THE preface is traditionally the place where one offers a justification for the writing of a book. In this case, however, the question was not whether the subject was one worth writing about, but rather whether it was feasible, given the limitations of the available sources. The role of information in Roman foreign relations during late antiquity is a field of enquiry whose importance should be self-evident, yet, perhaps because of the apparent dearth of relevant material, it has not previously been investigated in a systematic manner. I hope to have shown that greater progress can be made than might otherwise have been thought possible, even if many pertinent questions have had to be left without satisfactory answers.

It will be readily apparent from the footnotes how much this book owes to the labours of numerous late Roman and early Byzantine scholars, especially in recent decades and in the elucidation of the literary sources. I have endeavoured to acquaint myself with as much of the relevant modern literature as possible, but in so vast a field I am bound to have overlooked items; some publications have appeared too late for me to use, notably the volume on *Byzantine Diplomacy* edited by Simon Franklin and Jonathon Shepard which includes a number of papers dealing with late antiquity.

Various debts for help with specific problems are acknowledged at the appropriate points in the body of the study, but it is a pleasure to be able at last to thank here a number of people who have played particularly important parts in bringing this project to completion. Rosamond McKitterick has given sane advice and consistent encouragement throughout, and John Matthews cheerfully allowed himself to become a regular point of reference, especially on eastern matters. Earlier versions of the whole or parts have also benefited greatly from the constructive criticism of Averil Cameron, Peter Garnsey, Keith Hopkins and Jonathon Shepard. Larry Epstein and Jonathon Shepard kindly agreed to read the final typescript, and their detailed comments have been

of inestimable value. Finally, I owe a special debt of gratitude to Robert
Browning for his interest in and support of my work.

Two institutions have given generous financial assistance without which this
research could not have been undertaken – the Association of Commonwealth
Universities, through the award of a Commonwealth Overseas Scholarship, and
Trinity College, Cambridge, through electing me to a Research Fellowship.
I am very grateful to both bodies. Access to the resources of the University
Library, Cambridge, has been of fundamental importance, and I would
especially like to thank the staff in the Reading Room and the West Room
for their ever-courteous help. The faculty libraries in Classics, History, and
Oriental Studies have provided valuable supplementary services.

On a more personal note, I am especially grateful to my wife Anna for her
patient support and loving encouragement, particularly during the past eighteen
months. I would also like to thank my aunt Ruth for her lively interest and help
in my academic endeavours over the years. Finally, this book is dedicated to my
parents – one small way of saying thank you for so much.

CHRONOLOGICAL LIST OF SELECTED ROMAN EMPERORS (EARLY THIRD TO EARLY SEVENTH CENTURY AD)

For purposes of orientation, this list presents the chronological details of emperors mentioned in this study; the frequent overlapping of dates is due to the common late Roman practice of having co-emperors.

Severus Alexander (222–35)
Maximinus Thrax (235–8)
Gordian III (238–44)
Aemilianus (253)
Valerian (253–60)
Gallienus (253–68)
Aurelian (270–5)
Probus (276–82)
Carus (282–3)
Diocletian (284–305)
Galerius (305–11)
Constantine (306–37)
Constantius II (337–61)
Constans (337–50)
Julian (361–3)
Valentinian I (364–75)
Valens (364–78)
Gratian (375–83)
Theodosius I (379–95)
Arcadius (395–408)
Honorius (395–423)
Theodosius II (408–50)
Valentinian III (425–55)
Marcian (450–7)
Leo I (457–74)

Zeno (474–91)
Anastasius (491–518)
Justin I (518–27)
Justinian (527–65)
Justin II (565–78)
Tiberius II (578–82)
Maurice (582–602)
Phocas (602–10)
Heraclius (610–41)

CHRONOLOGICAL LIST OF SASANIAN KINGS

(220s–628)

Ardashir I (226?–241?)
Shapur I (241–272?)
Hormizd Ardashir (272–3)
Vahram I (273–6)
Vahram II (276–93)
Vahram III (293)
Narseh (293–302)
Hormizd II (302–9)
Shapur II (309–79)
Ardashir II (379–83)
Shapur III (383–8)
Vahram IV (388–99)
Yazdgerd I (399–420)
Vahram V (420–39)
Yazdgerd II (439–57)
Hormizd III (457–9)
Peroz (459–84)
Valash (484–8)
Kavad (488–531)
Zamasp (496–8)
Khusro I (531–79)
Hormizd IV (579–90)
Vahram Chobin (590–1)
Khusro II (590–628)

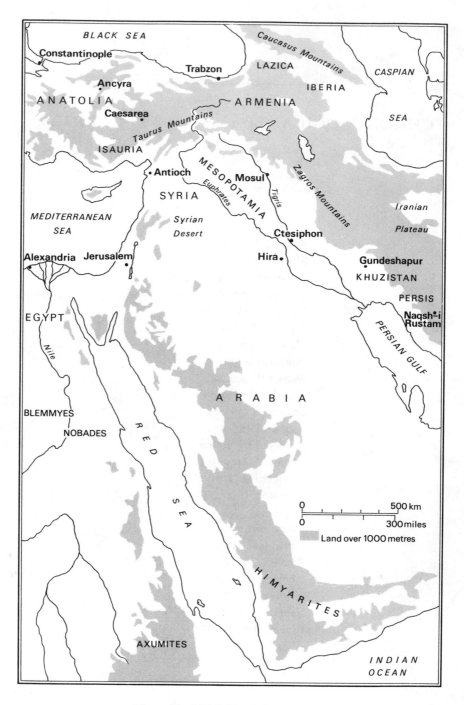

Map 1 The Middle East in late antiquity

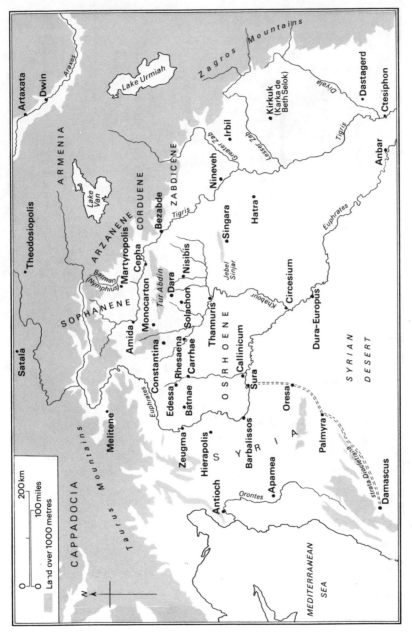

Map 2 Northern Mesopotamia and adjacent regions

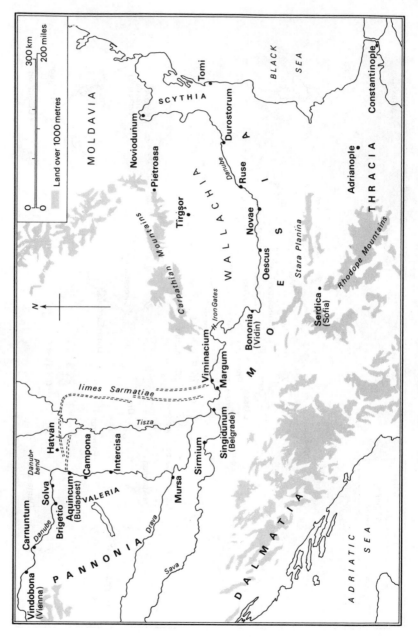

Map 3 The middle and lower Danube and adjacent regions

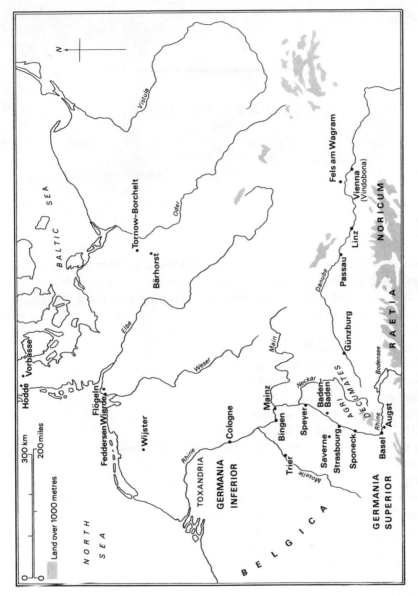

Map 4 The Rhine and upper Danube and adjacent regions

ABBREVIATIONS

(Details of editions used can be found in the Bibliography. Note the convention that a slash followed by Arabic numbers in a source reference indicates line numbers in the relevant text: e.g., Men. fr. 6,1/203-4 = lines 203–4 in fragment 6,1 of Menander Protector.)

Agath.	Agathias
Amm. Marc.	Ammianus Marcellinus
Chr. Pasch.	*Chronicon Paschale*
Chr. Seert	*Chronicle of Seert*
CJ	*Codex Justinianus*
CTh	*Codex Theodosianus*
De Caer.	Constantine Porphyrogenitus, *De Caerimoniis*
Eunap.	Eunapius
Evag.	Evagrius
Expos.	*Expositio Totius Mundi et Gentium*
Greg. Tur. *HF*	Gregory of Tours, *Historia Francorum*
HA	*Historia Augusta*
HE	*Historia Ecclesiastica*
Herod.	Herodian
John Eph.	John of Ephesus (*Lives* = *Lives of the Eastern Saints*)
John Epiph.	John of Epiphania
J. Styl.	Ps.-Joshua Stylites
Lib.	Libanius
Mal.	Malalas
Men.	Menander Protector
ND Or./Occ.	*Notitia Dignitatum, pars Orientis/Occidentis*
Pan.Lat.	*Panegyrici Latini*

Pet. Pat.	Peter the Patrician
Proc.	Procopius (*Bld.* = *Buildings*, *SH* = *Secret History*)
Soc.	Socrates Scholasticus
Tac.	Tacitus (*Ann.* = *Annals*, *Ger.* = *Germania*)
Theod.	Theodoret (*HR* = *Historia Religiosa*)
Theoph.	Theophanes
Th. Sim.	Theophylact Simocatta
Veg.	Vegetius, *Epitoma Rei Militaris*
Zach.	Ps.-Zacharias Rhetor
Zos.	Zosimus

OTHERS

AA	*American Anthropologist*
AB	*Analecta Bollandiana*
AE	*L'Année epigraphique*
AHR	*American Historical Review*
ANRW	*Aufstieg und Niedergang der römischen Welt*
BAR	British Archaeological Reports (Oxford)
BMGS	*Byzantine and Modern Greek Studies*
BS	*Byzantinoslavica*
BZ	*Byzantinische Zeitschrift*
CCSL	Corpus Christianorum Series Latina
CHI	*Cambridge History of Iran*
CIL	*Corpus Inscriptionum Latinarum*
CQ	*Classical Quarterly*
CRAI	*Comptes rendus de l'Académie des Inscriptions et Belles-lettres*
CSCO	Corpus Scriptorum Christianorum Orientalium (Scr. Syr. = Scriptores Syri)
DOP	*Dumbarton Oaks Papers*
DS	Daremberg-Saglio, *Dictionnaire des antiquités*
EHR	*English Historical Review*
FHG	*Fragmenta Historicorum Graecorum*, ed. C. Müller
GGM	*Geographi Graeci Minores*, ed. C. Müller
GLM	*Geographi Latini Minores*, ed. A. Riese
GRBS	*Greek, Roman and Byzantine Studies*
ILS	*Inscriptiones Latinae Selectae*, ed. H. Dessau
JEH	*Journal of Ecclesiastical History*
JNES	*Journal of Near Eastern Studies*
JRA	*Journal of Roman Archaeology*
JRS	*Journal of Roman Studies*
MBAH	*Münstersche Beiträge zur antiken Handelsgeschichte*

MGH	*Monumenta Germaniae Historica*
OJA	*Oxford Journal of Archaeology*
PG	*Patrologia Graeca*
PL	*Patrologia Latina*
PLRE	*Prosopography of the Later Roman Empire*
PO	*Patrologia Orientalis*
PrG	*Progress in Geography*
RAC	*Reallexikon für Altertum und Christentum*
RE	Pauly-Wissowa(-Kroll), *Realencyclopädie der classischen Altertumswissenschaft*
RH	*Revue historique*
RIDA	*Revue internationale des droits de l'antiquité*
SC	Sources chrétiennes
StIr	*Studia Iranica*
TCRPGA	Travaux du Centre de Recherche sur le Proche-Orient et le Grèce antiques (Strasbourg)
TM	*Travaux et mémoires*

INTRODUCTION

SCOPE AND AIMS

THIS study is concerned with the foreign relations of the Roman empire during late antiquity, defined here as the period from the early third to the early seventh century AD. It is not, however, a general history of late Roman foreign relations. In the first place, it pursues a particular theme within that field – the role of information. And secondly, it focuses on late Roman relations with two particular regions – Sasanian Persia in the east, and the areas adjacent to the empire's northern Continental frontier, occupied by a number of different peoples of Germanic and central Asiatic origin during the course of late antiquity. At the same time, this study deals with much more than just military and diplomatic affairs: the particular questions it pursues entail consideration of the broader context within which relations were played out, notably the socio-cultural character of the relevant frontier regions, and the differing levels of organisational complexity among the empire's neighbours.

Numerous studies have been devoted to elucidating various aspects of the history and conduct of late Roman foreign relations, but the role of information has received little systematic attention. Yet there can be no doubt as to its importance. Access to information is a crucial determinant of political power generally,[1] and the amount of information available to a government concerning the institutions, activities and affairs of potentially hostile neighbours exercises a decisive influence on the ability of a state to conduct its foreign relations effectively, whether in warding off aggression, or in taking advantage of opportunities to enhance its position.

Information is of course a broad term. This study is concerned with two categories of information relevant to foreign relations – background knowledge

---

[1] R. Wirsing, 'Political power and information: a cross-cultural study', *AA* 75 (1973), 153–70, at 155–6.

and strategic intelligence. Background knowledge comprises long-term stocks of information (and assumptions) about the geography, environment, and socio-political character of neighbouring states and peoples. It constitutes the mental frame of reference within which decisions about foreign relations are worked out, though admittedly it is hard to reconstruct and its impact on foreign affairs is not readily perceptible. Strategic intelligence is information about the current activities and affairs of potentially hostile neighbours of direct strategic significance – information indicating the possibility of aggressive action by neighbours, or alternatively a favourable opportunity to gain an advantage against them through military or diplomatic action. It has the potential to exert a more direct influence on the course of events than background knowledge, but is also to be distinguished from tactical intelligence (with which this study is not concerned) – that is, very short-term information of immediate relevance to a particular military engagement (such as the positions of enemy units before a battle).

It is natural to think of information primarily in positive terms, as items of definite knowledge, which is after all the dictionary definition. But there is value in also giving consideration to an alternative, 'negative' definition derived from the discipline of information theory: information as 'the reduction of uncertainty, the elimination of possibilities'.[2] Although uncertainty is clearly not a problem unique to antiquity, the scope for uncertainty then was clearly much greater than in the modern world. This alternative definition serves as a useful reminder of the broader context of uncertainty and ignorance which forms the backdrop to the following investigation of information. This study will argue that late Roman government had more information relevant to foreign relations at its disposal than has usually been recognised, but it is important to acknowledge at the outset the overall environment of uncertainty within which it had to operate.[3]

There are undoubtedly many questions that one would like to be able to answer about the role of information in late Roman foreign relations, which the limitations of the available evidence render unrealistic propositions. It would,

[2] F. I. Dretske, *Knowledge and the Flow of Information* (Oxford, 1981), 4. Cf. D. M. MacKay, *Information, Mechanism and Meaning* (Cambridge, Mass., 1969), 11 ('one of the most important technical senses of the term 'information' [is] that which enables us to make a *selection* from a set of possibilities or to *narrow the range* of possibilities about which we are ignorant'); E. M. Rogers and R. Agarwala-Rogers, *Communication in Organizations* (New York, 1976), 64–5 ('Information is a change in the probability that some alternative will occur in a given situation. Information thus represents a reduction in uncertainty').

[3] In this respect this study shares a broad common concern with recent work on the problems of uncertainty in ancient economic life: P. Halstead and J. O'Shea (eds.), *Bad Year Economics: Cultural Responses to Risk and Uncertainty* (Cambridge, 1989); P. Garnsey, *Famine and Food Supply in the Graeco-Roman World: Responses to Risk and Crisis* (Cambridge, 1988); T. W. Gallant, *Risk and Survival in Ancient Greece: Reconstructing the Rural Domestic Economy* (Cambridge, 1991).

for example, be very illuminating to know how decisions on foreign relations were reached, but the non-survival of minutes from the imperial consistory means that little can be said on this subject in any systematic manner. This study therefore addresses itself to two broad questions which lie within the realm of the possible, which is not to say they do not pose problems of their own. The first question concerns the availability of information, not in any strictly quantitative sense, but rather in terms of the general reliability of background knowledge and the broad frequency with which strategic intelligence moved between the empire and its neighbours. The second concerns the means by which this information was acquired. This question in particular requires examination of the organisation of the states and peoples involved, and of the character of the frontier regions across which relations were conducted. In this way, this study places late Roman military and diplomatic affairs within a wider social and institutional context.

The east and the north form the geographical focus of the study because these were the two most important spheres of late Roman foreign involvement, as a result of which the sources are more plentiful and, in particular, contain sufficient material for a meaningful exploration of the theme of information. The foundation of a new capital at Constantinople, with its closer proximity to the eastern frontier and the Danube, has often been seen as reflecting these strategic priorities. In the 220s one of the great Persian noble families, the Sasanians, overthrew a weak and fragmented Parthian regime and promptly adopted a much more aggressive stance towards the Roman empire. Ruling the regions comprising modern-day Iraq and Iran for the next four centuries, the Sasanians developed a centralising state comparable to the Roman empire in political and military organisation; as such, the Persian empire posed the most serious potential threat to the security of the Roman empire during late antiquity.

The third century also witnessed serious developments to the north of the empire, as Germanic tribes along the Rhine and upper Danube combined into the larger confederations of the Franks and the Alamanni, while the Goths emerged as a challenge to the empire on the lower Danube. Though not yet as well organised as Persia, these peoples were in the process of state-formation and by the fifth century some of them had established independent kingdoms in the western provinces of the empire. Moreover, during the fifth and sixth centuries the lands north of the lower Danube were occupied by Huns and then Avars, both nomadic pastoral peoples of central Asiatic origin. Although neither of these peoples ever developed into genuine states, their military prowess, especially as cavalry, enabled them to establish temporary dominance over the Danubian plains from where they posed serious threats to imperial security.

The other frontiers of the empire during this same period demanded less attention. The fate of Britain was not decisive for the survival of the empire, and when control of the island was lost in the fifth century, it was not primarily to northern Picts but to Germanic invaders from across the North Sea. Similarly, the tribal peoples living near the empire's southern frontiers, in Egypt and north Africa, were not untroublesome, but the seriousness of the threat from this quarter may be gauged by the fact that Roman control in most of north Africa succumbed early in the fifth century, not to these provinces' long-time neighbours, but to the Vandals, newly arrived from Europe; only the province of Tripolitania fell to an indigenous threat, referred to variously in the sources as the Austuriani or the Laguatan.[4] Indeed the Romans *perceived* this region as being less threatened: for centuries only one legion (together with auxiliaries) was permanently stationed there, and the units which replaced this force in the late third century are thought to have been only slightly larger in numbers.[5] And when Egypt was permanently lost in the seventh century, it was not to the Blemmyes or Nobades, enemies of old from the upper reaches of the Nile, but to the unexpected forces issuing forth from Arabia and the east under the standard of Islam.

PREVIOUS WORK

Although a number of studies have been devoted to late Roman foreign relations during particular periods, or with particular states or peoples,[6] the role of information and intelligence has received little attention. One exception is Francis Dvornik's *Origins of Intelligence Services* (1974), which includes chapters on Rome and Byzantium in which he brings together some of the evidence relating to communications, internal policing, and military and diplomatic intelligence during late antiquity. Unfortunately, his approach tends towards the anecdotal, and the ambitious scope of the book means that there is little detailed or systematic analysis of particular periods.[7] The only sophisticated treatment of the subject known to me is an important and stimulating paper by Fergus Millar which deals with what might be called 'structural' aspects of Roman foreign relations during the first four centuries AD. By focusing attention on issues such as the significance of conceptual frameworks, problems of communication, and the character of decision-making, this paper makes major contributions on a number of fronts. It does, however, argue that Roman

---

[4] D. J. Mattingly, 'The Laguatan: a Libyan tribal confederation in the late Roman empire', *Libyan Studies* 14 (1983), 96–108.

[5] B. H. Warmington, *The North African Provinces from Diocletian to the Vandal Conquest* (Cambridge, 1954), 15.

[6] E.g., B. Stallknecht, *Untersuchungen zur römischen Aussenpolitik in der Spätantike (306–395 n. Chr.)* (Bonn, 1969); P. A. Barceló, *Roms auswärtige Beziehungen unter der constantinischen Dynastie (306–363)* (Regensburg, 1981).

[7] E.g., he notes the existence of the so-called Peutinger Table (113), important evidence for late Roman cartographic knowledge, without even hinting at the problems which this item poses.

decision-makers had to function largely without access to reliable information
about the empire's neighbours, and at one point even suggests that the empire's
frontiers constituted 'an information barrier'.[8]

If the present study reaches a less pessimistic conclusion than Professor
Millar, it is at least partly due to the fact that the four centuries spanned in this
book overlap with only one and a half of the four centuries on which he focuses.
But there are also differences of approach to general issues, two of which may
be noted briefly. The suggestion that the empire's frontiers constituted an
information barrier is, in my view, unfortunate: it is rare for frontiers in any
historical context to act as hermetic seals preventing all human interaction,[9] and
so long as there is some degree of human interaction, there will be some
transfer of information.[10] And I would endorse the view that Millar's emphasis
on the apparent lack of formal institutions for the conduct of Roman foreign
relations and acquisition of information underestimates the potential for long-
standing informal processes to fulfil the functions of formal institutions, and so
obviate the necessity for the latter's evolution.[11]

SOURCES

Confronted with our subject, one of the first questions a historian of modern
international relations might ask is what source material is available in the way
of government archives and reports. The answer is a dispiriting nothing. There
is certainly evidence for the existence of archives concerned with foreign
relations during the late Roman period (see pp. 35–40), but nothing from these
has survived, at least in direct documentary form. There are also references in
the literary sources to reports (*relationes*) which contained strategic intelligence
(e.g., Amm. Marc. xxvi.6.11), and it is apparent that a *relatio* could take a
written and not just an oral form (e.g., Amm. Marc. xxviii.6.22; xix.5.2); but

8 'Emperors, frontiers and foreign relations, 31 BC to AD 378', *Britannia* 13 (1982), 1–25, at 19.
   These conclusions have been endorsed by C. R. Whittaker, *Les Frontières de l'empire romain*
   (Paris, 1989), 28, and (in more detail) B. Isaac, *The Limits of Empire: the Roman Army in the East*
   (Oxford, 1990), Chapter 9.
9 'A frontier . . . is not always a barrier: it is usually a zone of contact and interchange' (P. Lemerle,
   'Invasions et migrations dans les Balkans depuis la fin de l'époque romaine jusqu'au VIIIe
   siècle', *RH* 211 (1954), 265–308, at 273); 'the existence of a *limes* always in practice generates
   social intercourse – and that in both directions – between the parties whom the barrier is
   designed to insulate from one another' (A. Toynbee, quoted in D. Obolensky, 'Byzantine
   frontier zones and cultural exchanges' in *Actes du XIVe congrès international des études byzantines*
   (Bucharest, 1974), 301–13, at 308).
10 'All interactions imply information flow' (C. Renfrew, 'Trade as action at a distance: questions
   of integration and communication' in J. A. Sabloff and & C. C. Lamberg-Karlovsky (eds.),
   Ancient Civilization and Trade (Albuquerque, 1975), 3–59, at 53.
11 J. Matthews, 'Hostages, philosophers, pilgrims, and the diffusion of ideas in the late Roman
   Mediterranean and Near East' in F. M. Clover and R. S. Humphreys (eds.), *Tradition and
   Innovation in Late Antiquity* (Madison, Wis., 1989), 29–49, at 35–6.

again none of these – or almost none – has been preserved. The only known possibility is one of the recently discovered Vindolanda writing tablets which appears to give a few details about the tactics of mounted Britons: 'our best guess is that it is an intelligence report in the form of a brief memorandum'.[12] However, its uniqueness, brevity and early second-century date mean that its value for the purposes of this study is minimal.

If direct documentary evidence is thin on the ground, a wide variety of sources nevertheless provides a considerable amount of indirect material about the role of information in late Roman foreign relations, much of which has not previously been subjected to systematic analysis.[13] These include classicising histories, ecclesiastical histories, and chronicles. Many of these sources contribute something at only one or two points in this study, and it will be more convenient for any necessary background about them to be presented at those points; but a number of classicising historians from late antiquity will be referred to with sufficient frequency to warrant making some comments about their character now. The epithet 'classicising' refers to the way in which these writers sought to emulate classical models of historical writing such as Thucydides. This aspiration is important because it imposed certain constraints on the way they wrote, such as a studied avoidance of technical language and the 'invention' of speeches – conventions which obviously need to be taken into account when using these sources.

The most consistently valuable of these sources is the history of Ammianus Marcellinus, by virtue of both its geographical breadth and the attention to detail which characterises the work. The surviving (latter) half of his history provides a very full narrative of events throughout the empire from 354 to 378. During the earlier part of this period Ammianus himself held the rank of *protector domesticus* in the army, acting as a staff officer to the general Ursicinus. In this capacity he was closely involved in events on the eastern frontier prior to and during Shapur's invasion of 359. He also accompanied Ursicinus to Gaul a few years before these events, and he later joined Julian's Persian expedition in 363. As a result, he gained personal experience of both the east (including Persian territory as far as the capital Ctesiphon) and part of the north during a period of momentous events, and his relationship with Ursicinus gave him an intimate knowledge of the making of decisions affecting military and diplomatic affairs and their implementation. His proximity to Ursicinus

---

[12] A. K. Bowman and J. D. Thomas, 'Vindolanda 1985: the new writing tablets', *JRS* 76 (1986), 120–3, at 122. This tablet is one of those now on display in the British Museum's Wolfson Gallery. The authoritative collection by R. O. Fink, *Roman Military Records on Papyrus* (Case Western Reserve, 1971) contains nothing resembling an intelligence report.

[13] A notable exception, dealing with one major source, is N. J. E. Austin, *Ammianus on Warfare* (Brussels, 1979) which, despite its title, focuses specifically on the question of military intelligence in Ammianus.

could also sometimes result in his misunderstanding imperial decisions,[14] but the value of his position for his history far outweighs its disadvantages. His years in the army allowed him to build up a network of relationships on which he could draw when writing the portion of his history concerning affairs after 363, for his account of these years shows him continuing to be well-informed about a wide range of events.[15]

Procopius of Caesarea's history of Justinian's wars in the sixth century likewise benefited from his having spent many years as secretary to Justinian's most successful commander, Belisarius. Much of Procopius' *Wars* is of minimal relevance to the concerns of this study, for Books iii–iv and v–vii deal respectively with the reconquest of Africa from the Vandals and of Italy from the Goths. It is unfortunate that amongst all this Procopius provides only incidental commentary on events along the Danube. But the first two books, supplemented by portions of Book viii, provide a detailed account of Roman–Persian relations during the first half of the sixth century. As stressed by Averil Cameron in her study of Procopius, however, this account requires careful handling, particularly as it is these early parts of the *Wars*, written when Procopius retained a strong admiration for Belisarius and a consequent reluctance to criticise, which must be specially scrutinised for possible bias.[16] Moreover the existence of Procopius' *Secret History*, in which this reluctance to criticise is entirely absent, complicates interpretation of the *Wars* where the *Secret History* provides an alternative version of specific episodes.[17] When using the *Wars*, therefore, it is necessary 'to examine the credentials of every individual passage'[18] – a daunting task for someone grappling with the work as a whole, but feasible in a study such as this where only selected passages are relevant. Such strictures, though necessary, should not, however, be allowed to detract from the fact that Procopius was in one of the best possible positions to provide a detailed account of military and diplomatic affairs on the eastern frontier for this period. As such, his account must not be dismissed too readily without being given the serious consideration it warrants. He may not have been the great historian which his reputation suggests, but he was at least 'an excellent reporter'.[19]

---

[14] E. A. Thompson, *The Historical Work of Ammianus Marcellinus* (Cambridge, 1947), Chapter 3; J. Matthews, 'Ammianus and the eastern frontier in the fourth century: a participant's view' in P. M. Freeman and D. L. Kennedy (eds.), *The Defence of the Roman and Byzantine East* (BAR S297, 1986), 549–64, at 553–6.

[15] For full discussion of Ammianus as a historian, see J. Matthews, *The Roman Empire of Ammianus* (London, 1989); for detailed analysis of his sources, see G. Sabbah, *La Méthode d'Ammien Marcellin* (Paris, 1978), Part 3.

[16] *Procopius and the Sixth Century* (London, 1985), 152.

[17] For discussion of one such case, see A. D. Lee, 'Procopius, Justinian and the *kataskopoi*', *CQ* 39 (1989), 569–72.

[18] Cameron, *Procopius*, 136.

[19] *Ibid.*, 151.

Relations with Persia during the fifth century were virtually free from armed conflict, which perhaps accounts for the lack of a contemporary history focusing on those relations, while also making such a lack less serious. For much of the fifth century the empire was preoccupied with the Huns on the lower Danube. Although no continuous narrative has survived, major excerpts from the account of Priscus of Panium were preserved by the scribes of the emperor Constantine Porphyrogenitus in the tenth century. Because Constantine's concern was to provide a handbook of exempla on diplomacy, these excerpts contain much detail about Roman–Hun relations. Furthermore, some of Priscus' knowledge was gained at first hand through his participation in an important embassy to Attila in 449. He was obviously a man with connections to those in positions of influence at the imperial court and so was well placed to know the background to events. He was certainly prepared to express his own views on how best to handle the Huns, but this does not diminish his undoubted value as a source for the foreign relations of this period.[20]

The history of Menander Protector has also survived only as excerpts in Constantine Porphyrogenitus' compilation. Again the excerpts focus on diplomacy and warfare, this time ranging from the final years of Justinian's reign to the end of the reign of Tiberius (582). Much of this material concerns the eastern frontier, including the 570s when war between the empire and Persia was renewed, and the lower Danube, where the Avars now posed a major threat. Unlike Priscus, Menander does not seem to have actively taken part in any of the events he describes, but he clearly knew some of the participants in the more recent episodes he narrates, while he also had access to documentary evidence, both official and private.[21]

The history of Theophylact Simocatta covers the reign of the emperor Maurice (582–602), with some commentary on the 570s. Its focus is firmly on warfare and diplomacy, in both the east and the north. However, Theophylact was never personally involved in any of the events he describes, and since he was probably writing in the late 620s, he is unlikely to have had the opportunity to draw on the recollections of eye-witnesses for the greater part of the period with which he deals.[22] The trustworthiness of his account is therefore dependent on the reliability of his sources. For Persian affairs he drew heavily on the history of John of Epiphania (only one fragment of which survives: *FHG* iv.273–6), who in turn relied on earlier accounts for the 570s and much of the 580s, but had access to knowledgeable contacts for the late 580s and had

---

[20] For discussion of Priscus as a historian, see R. C. Blockley, *The Fragmentary Classicising Historians of the Later Roman Empire* vol. I (Liverpool, 1981), 48–70.

[21] See the brief discussion in R. C. Blockley, *The History of Menander the Guardsman* (Liverpool, 1985), 18–20.

[22] M. Whitby, *The Emperor Maurice and his Historian: Theophylact Simocatta on Persian and Balkan Warfare* (Oxford, 1988), 40–51, 92–109, 222–42.

himself been involved in the events surrounding the restoration of Khusro II in 591.[23] Theophylact's narrative of the conflict on the Danube with the Avars and Slavs during the last two decades of the sixth century reveals a consistent bias in favour of the general Priscus at the expense of the other commanders, probably reflecting Theophylact's use of an account by a partisan of Priscus.[24] However, this bias is sufficiently clear for Theophylact's account still to be of use. Despite his defects as a historian, it is unfortunate that he did not continue his history beyond the overthrow of Maurice by Phocas in 602, for the final decades of Roman–Persian relations during which warfare on a major scale was resumed are poorly documented.

The indirect nature of the evidence which writers such as these contain may be illustrated by some remarks apropos of strategic intelligence. First, they often make explicit remarks to the effect that the emperor or his officers received information about affairs outside the empire. This does not of course necessarily prove that the information in question was actually received; a series of further questions needs to be asked to establish the reliability of such testimony – such as, was the writer in a position to know what he states, and is there perhaps some underlying polemic in his work which might have caused him to embroider his account in this way? Such questions will be considered at appropriate points in Chapter 4, but the cases of Ammianus and Procopius may serve as a preliminary illustration. Both men were contemporaries of the events that form the main subject matter of their histories, and both served in positions of responsibility close to commanders who were at the centre of many of the incidents described and who would have been the obvious recipients of any information that became available about enemy activities. Further questions about possible bias need to be considered in relation to each specific incident, but statements about strategic intelligence in these authors deserve *prima facie* to be given serious consideration.

The starting-point for the second type of indirect evidence is the assumption that information of strategic importance will produce reactions. One may not be able to follow the 'path' of the information directly in the sources, but one can look for the responses it provoked, and in this way establish that information was in fact received. The best illustration of this is the despatch of embassies seeking to forestall aggression, as occurred a number of times in the course of Roman–Persian relations. The literary sources do not usually state anything about the acquisition of information as such in these cases, but the despatch of such embassies presupposes the receipt of intelligence about enemy preparations.[25]

---

[23] *Ibid.*, 222–4.   [24] *Ibid.*, 98–105.

[25] This line of argument has been presented in greater detail in A. D. Lee, 'Embassies as evidence for the movement of military intelligence between the Roman and Sasanian empires' in Freeman and Kennedy, *Defence*, 455–61.

The emphasis thus far has been on the way in which the sources can be used to establish that transfer of information did actually occur. The other major area for investigation is the means by which information was acquired. The historical writers already discussed contain much material of value about the role of information-gathering agencies such as embassies and spies, and can be supplemented by reference to military treatises, such as the *Strategikon* attributed to the emperor Maurice.[26] In using such sources there is the problem of knowing to what extent they are descriptive, and to what extent prescriptive, but if one accepts that the *Strategikon* 'attempted to regulate a conscious reform',[27] then one will have greater confidence in its descriptive value, even if reforms are rarely successful in every detail.

Information was also acquired as a result of the informal diffusion of news by word of mouth. A major determinant of the level at which information circulated in this way was the movement of people, particularly in frontier regions. Hence, an attempt must be made to assess the volume of cross-frontier traffic in the east and the north. Again, the major literary sources contain much incidental evidence relevant to this subject, but for the eastern frontier much light is also shed on the nature of society and interchange in northern Mesopotamia by the substantial body of indigenous Syriac literature, comprising chronicles, church histories and saints' lives;[28] it is greatly to be regretted that almost nothing comparable exists for the northern frontier.[29] Since levels of urbanisation also provide an index of human interaction, archaeological evidence concerning settlement density in the vicinity of the relevant frontiers is also germane, though of course the amount of work which has been done on this question by archaeologists varies considerably from region to region.

The broad structure of the study is straightforward: Part I provides essential background detail, Part II assesses the reliability of background knowledge and availability of strategic intelligence, and Part III examines the means, formal and informal, by which information was acquired. An underlying theme through-out the study is the comparison of east and north. Chapters 1 and 2 highlight the differing levels of organisational complexity among the empire's neighbours, and the distinctive socio-cultural character of the respective frontier regions. Chapter 3 argues that Roman background knowledge about Persia during late

---

[26] For brief discussion of the problems of authorship and date, see Whitby, *Maurice*, 130–2.

[27] J. F. Haldon, 'Some aspects of Byzantine military technology from the sixth to the tenth centuries', *BMGS* 1 (1975), 11–47, at 45, where other pertinent remarks on this problem are made.

[28] For succinct overviews of this literature, see the two surveys by S. P. Brock, 'An introduction to Syriac studies' in J. H. Eaton (ed.), *Horizons in Semitic Studies* (Birmingham, 1980), 1–33, and 'Syriac historical writing: a survey of the main sources', *Journal of the Iraqi Academy (Syriac Corporation)* 5 (1979/80), 1–30.

[29] A notable exception is the anonymous *Passion of St Saba the Goth* (for which see p. 75).

antiquity was generally better than that about northern peoples, and Chapter 4 that strategic intelligence moved across the eastern frontier with significantly greater frequency than across the northern. Chapters 5 and 6 endeavour to account for these differences with regard to information by relating them back to the organisational and socio-cultural differences discussed in the first two chapters, and it is to these that we now turn.

PART I

CONTEXTS

I

THE PROTAGONISTS

SASANIAN PERSIA

Organisational character

IN the mid-220s[1] the Parthian Arsacid dynasty, rulers of a state which for the past three centuries had been the Roman empire's largest eastern neighbour, was overthrown by the revolt of one of the nobility, Ardashir, lord of Persis (Fars). During the preceding years Ardashir and his father had exploited the turmoil arising from Roman invasion and disputed succession within the royal family to expand their domain to a point where Ardashir was able to challenge for the rulership of all Persia.[2] The success of that challenge marked the establishment of the new Sasanian dynasty, an event which was to have fundamental repercussions for the Roman empire. In place of the increasingly weak and fragmented state with which it had dealt in the second century, the empire soon found itself confronted by a regime intent on controlling more closely the territories it had inherited and enlarging them.

Given the experience of the Parthians, it was clearly in the interests of the new dynasty to try to restrict as much as possible the power and independence of the other noble families in Persia and to expand centralised royal control. There can be no doubt that overall the Sasanians achieved greater success in this realm than the Arsacids had done. Indicative of their aspirations is the more pronounced royal support of the Zoroastrian religion,[3] which was no doubt seen as possessing unifying potential while also serving as a counter-weight

---

[1] For the debate about the precise year, see *CHI* vol. 3, 118–19 (R. N. Frye).

[2] For further detail, see R. N. Frye, *The History of Ancient Iran* (Munich, 1984), 291ff.

[3] For reservations about the common assumption that the new dynasty established Zoroastrianism as the 'state religion', see P. Gignoux, 'Church–state relations in the Sasanian period' in T. Mikasa (ed.), *Monarchies and Socio-religious Traditions in the Ancient Near East* (Wiesbaden, 1984), 72–80.

to the nobility.[4] But the most powerful testimony to the actual growth of centralising control is the vast network of systematically laid-out irrigation canals and accompanying engineering projects which archaeologists have found in southern Iraq and Iran and have dated to the Sasanian period. The Parthians had certainly been responsible for important improvements in irrigation, but developments during the Sasanian period facilitated a doubling of the area under cultivation to the point where virtually all available land in the regions surveyed was being exploited – an unprecedented feat not matched again until this present century.[5]

However, while there is no doubt as to the Sasanian achievement as a whole, one would not expect Sasanian administrative institutions to have appeared in fully developed form at the advent of the new regime, nor to have been monolithic and unchanging over four centuries. A more carefully nuanced picture of the rate and effectiveness with which royal control was extended is obviously desirable, but large gaps in the evidence make it difficult to trace developments with precision. The most detailed information for Sasanian administrative history pertains to the reign of Khusro I in the sixth century, when a centralised bureaucracy of some complexity functioned in the capital Ctesiphon, comprising 'departments' responsible for taxation, the army, correspondence, and registration of documents, overseeing an empire organised into a hierarchy of provinces, districts and sub-districts.[6] However, since this structure was the result of reforms initiated by Khusro, it is clearly illegitimate to assume that such a level of organisation was characteristic of earlier centuries of Sasanian rule (except for the important institution of the government courier system).[7] In the absence of comparable evidence for earlier periods, one must resort to various indirect, inferential approaches to the evolution of Sasanian administration.

The famous trilingual inscription of Shapur I from the mid-third century, referred to by modern scholars as the *Res Gestae Divi Saporis* ('the achievements of the divine Shapur'), gives some insight into the situation at the very begin-

---

[4] This latter point is emphasised by N. Pigulevskaja, *Les Villes de l'état iranien aux époques parthe et sassanide* (Paris, 1963), 121–2.

[5] See the various studies by R. M. Adams: 'Agriculture and urban life in early southwestern Iran', *Science* 136 (1962), 109–22; *Land behind Baghdad: a History of Settlement on the Diyala Plains* (Chicago and London, 1965), Chapter 7; *Heartland of Cities: Surveys of Ancient Settlement and Land Use on the Central Floodplain of the Euphrates* (Chicago and London, 1981), Chapter 5.

[6] The most detailed discussion is (despite its title) M. G. Morony, *Iraq after the Muslim Conquest* (Princeton 1984), Chapters 1–3, though scepticism has recently been expressed about the usual assumption (accepted by Morony) that Khusro divided the empire into four geographical 'quarters' for administrative purposes: P. Gignoux, 'L'organisation administrative sasanide', *Jerusalem Studies in Arabic and Islam* 4 (1984), 1–29, at 4–5.

[7] Concerning which, see Morony, *Iraq*, 90.

ning of the new dynasty.[8] The inscription includes a description of the court of the first king, Ardashir. His courtiers do include various administrative officials, such as 'chief of the scribes' and 'chief of the arsenal', though even these were no doubt inherited from the Parthians, and they are outnumbered by sub-kings, lords and nobles. Some of the latter seem to be members of Ardashir's own family appointed to govern parts of the empire, which is indicative of some movement towards centralisation of authority,[9] but the overall picture is one of initial continuity with the predominantly feudal arrangements of the Parthians.[10]

Nevertheless, the situation did not remain static until Khusro's reforms, and there are in fact various indications that the Sasanian monarchs achieved some success in developing a bureaucracy and reducing the power of the nobility prior to the sixth century. Shapur's inscription includes a description of his own court which marks a clear advance over that of his father. The number of courtiers is larger, and while the feudal element is still strongly represented, new officials account for a greater proportion of the increase. Similarly, the inscription of Narseh at Paikuli, from the end of the third century, 'seems to indicate a growing complexity of the Sasanian state and bureaucracy'.[11] Numismatic evidence for the organisation of minting provides a further important indication: 'strict central control is discernible from the outset', while, significantly, 'after the seizure of power, the Sasanians suppressed all mintings from semi-independent regions which had survived under the Arsacids'.[12]

The policy of founding royal cities, familiar to Roman historians chiefly because the cities were often peopled with captives from the Roman empire, also has relevance to the position of the king *vis-à-vis* the nobility:

> The Sasanian economic landscape divides itself into two parts: on the one side the domain directly under royal rule, and on the other the domain of the landowning nobility in which central power operated only indirectly. It was in the interest of powerful, far-reaching royal control to increase the number of royal cities, and their attendant rural districts. This had the effect of converting indirectly-ruled into directly-ruled districts, and only partly-taxed districts into fully-covered ones. The history of the royal founding of cities thus also concerns the struggle between royal power and that of the nobility.[13]

---

[8] For an English translation based mainly on the Parthian and Middle Persian texts, see Frye, *Ancient Iran*, 371–3 (Appendix 4).

[9] *Ibid.*, 295.

[10] R. N. Frye, 'Notes on the early Sasanian state and church' in *Studi orientalisci in onore di G. Levi della Vida* (Rome, 1956) vol. 1, 314–35; M. A. R. Colledge, *The Parthians* (London, 1967), 64.

[11] R. N. Frye, 'History and Sasanian inscriptions' in *La Persia nel medioevo* (Accad. Naz. dei Lincei, Quaderno n. 160: Rome, 1971), 215–23, at 219.

[12] *CHI* vol. 3, 331 and 334 (R. Göbl).

[13] F. Altheim, quoted in Adams, *Heartland of Cities*, 200–1. Interestingly, Procopius remarks that the Roman prisoners in the royal city of Veh-Antioch, founded in the sixth century by Khusro I, were regarded as subordinate to the king himself and not to the Persian nobility (*Wars* ii.14.3).

This policy was particularly pursued by the first two kings, Ardashir and Shapur I, while Shapur II in the fourth century also founded a number of royal cities,[14] and so constitutes grounds for assuming enhancement of royal power well before the sixth century (though of course this was not an irreversible process). Finally, there is the evidence of the irrigation schemes referred to earlier, which reflect a high degree of government control and organisation. The Katul al-Kisrawi, the giant feeder-canal associated with Khusro I which drew water from the Tigris into the Diyala system, supports the assumption that the irrigation network can only have reached its full extent in the sixth century when a well-developed bureaucratic apparatus was in place.[15] Nevertheless, Shapur I is known to have been responsible for some of the major engineering projects which facilitated earlier expansion of the irrigation network,[16] providing another indirect indication of the existence of a central administration of considerable competence in the early Sasanian period.[17]

The overall picture, then, would appear to be one of gradual steps towards tighter centralised authority and the formation of a bureaucracy in the first centuries of Sasanian rule. The power of the nobility was never completely broken, as evidenced by periods of instability in the late third and fifth centuries; nevertheless, the empire of the Sasanians was generally much more cohesive than that of the Arsacids had been. Concomitant with this was an expansion of urban settlement, especially in the Persian heartlands. Archaeological surveys have demonstrated this for the Diyala basin and the Euphrates floodplains to the east and south of Ctesiphon respectively,[18] while a recent gazetteer of Jewish communities in Sasanian Persia, drawn from the Babylonian Talmud, lists over 150 locations, the bulk of which lay within the area to the west and north of Ctesiphon.[19] In the midst of all this lay the capital itself, part of a vast urban sprawl covering an area of approximately 15 square kilometres, the result of successive Hellenistic, Parthian and Sasanian foundations[20] – hence the Arabic name for the Sasanian capital, Mada'in, 'the cities'.

A particularly important dimension of Persian state organisation for this study

[14] Frye, *Ancient Iran*, 312.
[15] Adams, *Land behind Baghdad*, 76–7.
[16] Adams, 'Agriculture and urban life', 116 (great weirs built across the Karkheh, Diz and Karun rivers in Khuzistan); Adams, *Land behind Baghdad*, 76 (large canal near 'Ukbara).
[17] Use of surface ceramics for dating development of the irrigation system *within* the Sasanian period is problematic. Adams does state that they suggest a preponderance of activity in the late rather than the early period, 'insofar as the surface collections allow us to differentiate early and late sub-periods' (*Heartland of Cities*, 183). This is an important qualification, for elsewhere he acknowledges the limitations of this method for discriminating with precision between sub-periods within the Sasanian period as a whole (*ibid.*, 232).
[18] Adams, *Land behind Baghdad*; *Heartland of Cities*. This evidence is discussed in more detail on pp. 156–60.
[19] A. Oppenheimer, *Babylonia Judaica in the Talmudic Period* (Wiesbaden, 1983).
[20] *Ibid.*, 179–235; Matthews, *Ammianus*, 140–3.

is that of the army.[21] Knowledge of the detailed organisation of the Persian army during late antiquity is limited, but it is clear that it was based on a levy system, with the nobility providing the cavalry and their tenants the foot-soldiers.[22] The existence of the king's personal bodyguard of 10,000 mounted troops[23] and the need for permanent forces to man frontier forts[24] meant that Sasanian monarchs were not without any troops in continuous service, but it was only in the sixth century that Khusro I set about creating a central standing army on a large scale. By providing for the regular payment and equipping of the lesser, impoverished nobility (dehkans), he ensured the dependence on and loyalty to himself of a substantial force and lessened his reliance on the levies of the great Persian noble houses.[25] This served as the core of expeditionary forces thenceforth, but the levy nevertheless continued as the source of the remainder of the Persian army until the end of the Sasanian dynasty.[26] The use of a levy system throughout the Sasanian period presupposes the organisational ability to co-ordinate the assembling of forces prior to campaigns, but will also have meant that the Persian kings could never expect to mount campaigns without allowing for a significant time lag between deciding on war and actually setting off.[27]

A telling feature in any military organisation is that of logistical infrastructure. The Parthian kings apparently made no provision for the supplying of their troops when on campaign (Dio xl.15.6), so when the Roman historian Herodian, writing in the very early years of the Sasanian dynasty, maintained that Persian soldiers were responsible for providing their own food on campaign (vi.7.1), it is possible that he was simply assuming a continuation of Parthian practice. But if he was reliably informed concerning early Sasanian procedure, it is apparent from oriental sources that this practice was soon abandoned. The Babylonian Talmud of the Jewish communities in Persia indicates that the government was responsible for the provision of food for soldiers,[28] while

[21] The following two paragraphs are based on A. D. Lee, 'Campaign preparations in late Roman–Persian warfare' in D. H. French and C. S. Lightfoot (eds.), *The Eastern Frontier of the Roman Empire* (BAR s553, 1989), 257–65, where further detail on a number of points may be found.

[22] A. Christensen, *L'Iran sous les Sassanides*, 2nd edn (Copenhagen, 1944), 206ff.

[23] M.-L. Chaumont, 'Chiliarque et curopalate à la cour des Sassanides', *Iranica Antiqua* 10 (1973), 139–65, at 152–4. For the use of these troops on campaign before Khusro's reforms, see Proc. *Wars* i.14.31, 44ff. (530).

[24] R. N. Frye, 'The Sasanian system of walls for defence' in M. Rosen-Ayalon (ed.), *Studies in memory of Gaston Wiet* (Jerusalem, 1977), 7–15.

[25] Christensen, *Les Sassanides*, 367ff.; *CHI* vol. 3, 154 (Frye).

[26] G. Widengren, 'Iran, der grosse Gegner Roms: Königsgewalt, Feudalismus, Militärwesen', *ANRW* II.9.1 (1976), 219–306, at 285ff.

[27] It is worth also noting that, like the Romans but unlike northern peoples, the Persians produced military treatises, on which see C. A. Inostracev, 'The Sasanian military theory', *Journal of the K. R. Cama Oriental Institute* 7 (1926), 7–52.

[28] J. Newman, *The Agricultural Life of the Jews in Babylonia between the years 200 CE and 500 CE* (London, 1932), 184–5.

the *Artestaristan*, the Sasanian warrior code, included instructions about 'the proportion of daily provisions for two warriors, the meat and milk and bread thereof. . . [and] the reason of verifying its distribution and weighing'.[29] Roman sources provide corroboration. On capturing the fortress of Anbar in 363 Julian's troops found within 'a vast store of arms and provisions' (Amm. Marc. xxiv.2.22), whose quantity points to government initiative, while Persian war preparations in 579/80 included the collection and stockpiling of food in Nisibis, Dara and other frontier forts (Men. fr. 23,9/52-5).[30] The fact that the Persian land tax was collected in kind[31] is also consistent with the provision of military supplies by the government, and there are many references to the presence of pack-animals and baggage-trains on a substantial scale in Persian armies.[32] The Persian ability to conduct sustained sieges for months on end also presupposes the ability to organise logistical support.[33] The limited evidence does not permit more detailed understanding of the mechanics of the provisioning of Persian armies, but it is apparent that some sort of system existed and functioned.

These, then, in brief outline were the salient characteristics of the Roman empire's major eastern neighbour during late antiquity. No other state or people with whom the Romans had dealings in this period achieved anything like a comparable degree of urban development or governmental organisation, which must in part explain the Romans' willingness in due course to concede to Sasanian Persia, uniquely among foreign peoples, recognition of parity of status. This is reflected most obviously in developing diplomatic practices,[34] but also in other expressions of attitude such as the emperor Julian's dismissal of advice to attack the Goths with the statement that he was seeking 'better enemies' (Amm. Marc. xxii.7.8), by which he clearly meant the Persians. Julian's comment encapsulates nicely the way in which Sasanian Persia was seen as a power to be both respected and feared, and directs our attention to the important issue of Persian and Roman aims regarding one another.

[29] *Denkard* viii.26.10, tr. E. W. West, *Pahlavi Texts* vol. 4 (Oxford, 1892), 87.

[30] Note the convention adopted in this study, that a slash followed by Arabic numbers in a source reference indicates line numbers in the relevant text – in this case, lines 52–5 in fragment 23,9 of Menander Protector.

[31] Newman, *Agricultural Life*, 166–8; Morony, *Iraq*, 61–2.

[32] References in Lee, 'Campaign preparations', 259–60, to which add Faustus of Buzand iii.21 (tr. Garsoïan): the Persian king 'collected his entire army together with his own baggage, the entire large *karawan* and a multitude of elephants; he came – with innumerable supplies, his own royal pavilions, all his women and the queen-of-queens – to the confines of Armenia'.

[33] Cf. J. G. Crow, 'The function of Hadrian's wall and the comparative evidence of late Roman long walls' in *Studien zu den Militärgrenzen Roms III* (Stuttgart, 1986), 724–9, at 728.

[34] On which see A. D. Lee, 'The role of hostages in Roman diplomacy with Sasanian Persia', *Historia* 39 (1991), 366–74, where further references will be found.

Aims

There are of course considerable difficulties in ascertaining Persian aims *vis-à-vis* the Roman empire because of the general dearth of contemporary literary sources from the Persian perspective. The most explicit statements regarding Persian aims are found in Roman literary sources which, by virtue of deriving from the opposition, require careful evaluation.[35] Dio reports the first Sasanian ruler, Ardashir, as 'threatening to recover everything which the Persians of old once used to possess as far as the Hellenic sea, as his rightful inheritance from his forebears' (lxxx.4.1).[36] Herodian has the Persian king making the same claim, adding that Ardashir 'alleged that from the rule of Cyrus, who first transferred the kingdom from the Medes to the Persians, up to Darius, the last of the Persian kings, whose kingdom Alexander of Macedon destroyed, the whole country as far as Ionia and Caria had been under the government of Persian satraps' (vi.2.2, tr. Whittaker). In the mid-fourth century, Shapur II maintained, in a letter to Constantius II, that 'even your ancient records acknowledge that my forefathers held sway as far as the river Strymon and the borders of Macedonia, and it is appropriate that I demand this territory' (Amm. Marc. xvii.5.5).[37]

Scholars in Iranian studies have expressed some reservations about the accuracy of these reports in classical sources and some of the deductions which have been made from them by classical scholars, since there is no independent oriental evidence that the Sasanians retained detailed knowledge of the Achaemenid period, including elementary facts such as the very name of a king as important as Cyrus.[38] Instead, the Sasanian historical tradition spoke of 'a great empire, that of the Kayanians, which Alexander had dismembered and plundered, and which the Arsacids had mismanaged'.[39] This means, of course, that Herodian's reference to Cyrus in his report of Ardashir's claims is

---

[35] Cf. Isaac, *Limits of Empire*, 21ff.

[36] Dio's statement has recently been impugned in the following terms: 'The source for his information concerning the inner cogitations of the Sassanid monarch must remain a matter for conjecture' (D. S. Potter, *Prophecy and History in the Crisis of the Roman Empire* (Oxford, 1990), 370–1). Certainly Dio does not indicate his source, but since he does say that Ardashir made threats, it is unfair to imply that Dio could only have acquired the information by a feat of mind-reading.

[37] As Matthews has noted (*Ammianus*, 485 n. 12), Ammianus does not claim to preserve the actual text of Shapur's letter.

[38] E. Yar-Shater, 'Were the Sasanians heirs to the Achaemenids?' in *La Persia nel medioevo*, 517–31; E. Kettenhofen, 'Die Einforderung des Achämenidenerbes durch Ardashir: eine Interpretatio Romana', *Orientalia Lovaniensia Periodica* 15 (1984), 177–90.

[39] *CHI* vol. 3, 409 (E. Yar-Shater).

spurious,[40] but clearly it does not invalidate the more general import of the classical sources that the early Sasanian rulers proclaimed themselves heirs to a great Persian empire of the past.[41] For this, independent confirmation does exist. Even if they thought in terms of Kayanians rather than Achaemenids and credited the former with exploits of a legendary nature, Sasanian identification with past Persian greatness is readily apparent in, for example, their choice of Naqsh-i Rustam, site of the impressive Achaemenid royal tombs, as one of the places in which they proclaimed their own achievements through similarly impressive rock-carved reliefs.[42]

It therefore remains striking that Sasanian kings did not make greater territorial demands than they did on occasions when the Romans were vulnerable – when Shapur I captured the emperor Valerian in the mid-third century, when Shapur II had Julian's defeated army at his mercy in 363, and when Khusro I was free to roam through Syria in 540. Once control of the eastern half of the north Mesopotamian plain had been wrested from Roman hands in 363, the Persians seemed content to abide by the status quo with respect to major territorial aggrandisement. Only Khusro II exploited his opportunity after 602 to occupy vast tracts of the Roman empire (without, interestingly, any suggestion in the sources that he tried to justify his aggression in terms of reclaiming his Achaemenid inheritance).

This overall restraint suggests that Sasanian aims were more limited than their proclaimed ambitions indicated.[43] No doubt, the early emphasis on their undertaking a revival of Iranian fortunes and greatness was important in the internal legitimation of the new dynasty, particularly *vis-à-vis* the nobility. Khusro II, on the other hand, had been restored to his throne by the Romans, and so needed to prove emphatically that he was not just a puppet.

But it is not sufficient to leave the matter here, to say that Sasanian claims

---

[40] It has been suggested that 'the Roman governors whom Herodian quotes were drawing on their own knowledge of the Persian past as preserved in Greek sources, rather than quoting Ardashir literally' (Yar-Shater, 'Heirs?', 525). This 'amplification' might equally well have been the work of Herodian himself. The status of Herodian's reference to Darius is less certain, however, since the Sasanian tradition did have as the final Kayanian ruler a Dara who was overthrown by Alexander (*CHI* vol. 3, 377 (Yar-Shater)).

[41] Cf. Frye, *Ancient Iran*, 293.

[42] Cf. *CHI* vol. 3, 120 (Frye). Scepticism has recently been expressed about the significance of this association on the basis that Shapur I's great trilingual inscription, the *Res Gestae Divi Saporis*, and one by the priest Kartir, were inscribed on the tower at Naqsh-i Rustam known as the Ka'bah-i Zardusht or 'Cube of Zoroaster', rather than on the adjacent cliff faces which display the facades of the Achaemenid tombs: 'both Kartir and Sapor appear to have been more interested in the Ka'bah than in the cliffs opposite it' (Potter, *Prophecy and History*, 373). However, this suggestion overlooks the fact that the cliffs bear a number of Sasanian reliefs including one of Shapur I triumphing over the emperor Valerian, as well as a bust and further inscription of Kartir, both positioned below and to the left of the tomb of Darius I. See E. F. Schmidt, *Persepolis* vol. 3, *The Royal Tombs and Other Monuments* (Chicago, 1970), 13, with Fig. 2 (Item 12).

[43] Cf. Isaac, *Limits of Empire*, 21ff.

were mere rhetoric. The crucial question is how the Romans *perceived* Persian intentions. Certainly, Dio is dismissive of Ardashir as posing no serious threat in his own right,[44] but at this stage the Romans had no experience of warfare with Persian forces under Sasanian command and so no reason to expect anything different from the inadequacies of Parthian-led forces. Shapur's campaigns in the 250s, and especially his capture of the emperor Valerian and the sacking of Antioch, must have shattered such complacency and replaced it with cons-iderable and enduring apprehension. Valerian's fate, for example, was still remembered with horror and indignation in the mid-sixth century.[45] The Persians may indeed only have reached Antioch on two occasions prior to the seventh century,[46] but Antioch was thought to have been Shapur II's goal in 359 (Lib. *Or.* xii.74), and the conquest of Syria the aim of the same king through-out the reigns of Constantine and Constantius II (Julian *Or.* i.22 [27a]). In these cases, the Persians became entangled in lengthy sieges of fortress cities near the frontier, but even if these were in fact the Persian objectives from the outset, to the Romans the protracted sieges could easily have seemed like fortuitous diversions of Persian energies away from what were thought to be their real objectives. Narseh was believed to have attacked the Roman empire in the late third century out of a desire to emulate the exploits of Shapur I and with a view to gaining control of Syria (Lactantius *De Mortibus Persecutorum* ix.5). Likewise, Procopius took it for granted that Khusro's aim in Syria was permanent occupation, in which he had only been thwarted by his inability to sack all the fortified cities of the region (*Wars* viii.7.10–11), and John Lydus assumed that, but for the Roman fort at Dara, the Persians would have taken possession of more Roman territory (*De Magistratibus* iii.47).

Similar fears were expressed concerning Khusro's intentions in Caucasian Lazica. In outlining the background to the Persian invasion of that region in 541, Procopius includes among the inducements used by the Lazian envoys to persuade Khusro to undertake the expedition the argument that control of Lazica will give the Persians access to the Black Sea: 'after you have constructed boats on this sea, you will be able without difficulty to reach the palace in Constantinople' (*Wars* ii.15.27). The point here is not whether the Lazian envoys actually held out this possibility to Khusro, or if they did, whether Khusro really believed it to be feasible, but rather that a Roman writer presented it as a plausible reason for the Persian invasion of Lazica. This concern is reiterated on a number of subsequent occasions by Procopius himself (*Wars* ii.28.23, viii.7.12), and also by Agathias, who attributes to Justinian great alarm

---

[44] He is only concerned because of the mutinous behaviour of Roman troops in the east, as stressed by Isaac, *Limits of Empire*, 22.

[45] Pet. Pat. fr. 13 (*FHG* iv.188). Agathias (iv.23.7) recalls the incident with similar distaste, though his information may have derived from the Persian royal archives (iv.30.2–4).

[46] Emphasised by Isaac, *Limits of Empire*, 32, 250.

over the potential consequences of the Persians gaining undisputed control of
the region: 'there would be no obstacle to them sailing freely up the Black Sea
and delving into the innermost parts of the Roman empire' (ii.18.7). These
anxieties will have gained substance from Khusro's evident determination to
continue fighting in Lazica after the conclusion of a truce in Mesopotamia in
545, and from the great trouble the Persians took in constructing a good road
from Iberia to Lazica in spite of the enormous difficulties involved in over-
coming the rugged terrain (Proc. *Wars* viii.13.5). Indeed, Procopius even
claimed that Khusro conveyed ship-building timber to Lazica only to have his
efforts thwarted by natural disaster (*Wars* ii.29.1–3).[47] Certainly, Roman
concern to have their suzerainty over Lazica recognised in the peace of 561/2
supports the idea that these fears were genuine. Later in the century, and on a
more general level again, Menander reports Khusro's successor, Hormizd IV, as
declaring to Roman envoys his intention to enlarge Persian territory at Roman
expense (fr. 23,9/84), and John of Ephesus has the Persian general Tamkhusro
avowing his intention in 582 to 'conquer all Roman lands' and winter in
Antioch (*HE* vi.26); the important point about both these instances is not
whether the individuals in question actually said what is reported, but the fact
that Roman writers thought such sentiments appropriate in the mouths of
Persian leaders. Whatever Persian aims may in practice have been, then, it
appears to have been a fairly consistent Roman assumption that the Sasanian
kings were intent on expanding into the eastern provinces of the Roman
empire.

A similar misunderstanding is likely to have characterised Persian thinking
regarding Roman aims. Certainly, the Romans never seem to have considered
extending control far beyond the Tigris during late antiquity, as they could
perhaps have done in 298/9, nor should Julian's expedition be seen as an attempt
to conquer Persia. As has been observed by a number of scholars,[48] a chance
remark in Ammianus' account (xxiii.2.5) indicates his intention to return to
Roman territory at the end of the campaigning season in 363, implying a
limited aim – presumably that of regaining the initiative in the east after Shapur's recent successes by striking at the heart of the Persian empire and forcing
him back onto the defensive.

It is doubtful, however, that the Persians will have appreciated this,
particularly when Julian was accompanied by the fugitive Sasanian prince
Hormizd whom, according to some reports current at the time, he planned to
place on the Persian throne (Lib. *Ep.* 1402). For them, the memory of Trajan's

---

[47] The likelihood of Khusro having to transport timber to a region rich in forests has been queried
      by D. C. Braund, *CQ* 41 (1991), 223, which does not, however, affect the point being made
      here about Roman perceptions of Persian intentions.
[48] O. Seeck, *Geschichte des Untergangs der antiken Welt* (Berlin and Stuttgart, 1895–1921), vol. 4,
      341–2; R. T. Ridley, 'Notes on Julian's Persian expedition', *Historia* 22 (1973), 317–30, at 326.

annexations in the second century, and subsequent Roman advances on Ctesiphon – by Avidius Cassius, Septimius Severus, Carus, Galerius,[49] and Julian – must have exercised a powerful influence on their perception of Roman intentions. Nor were some later Roman emperors particularly concerned to disabuse the Persians of such ideas. In 572, Justin II dismissed a Persian envoy with the threat that he would overthrow Khusro and place a king of his own choice on the Persian throne (Men. fr. 16,1/55–6), and is also reported to have believed that a Roman alliance with the Turks would enable him to destroy Persian power (Men. fr. 13,4). Indeed, an oriental source from the early seventh century presents Khusro as expressing considerable alarm about the Roman–Turkish *rapprochement*.[50] Similarly, Procopius presents Khusro's invasion of Syria in 540 as being motivated in the first instance by fear that Justinian's successes in the west would augment Roman power to a point where Persia would be unable to resist (*Wars* ii.1–3), and the welcome Justinian extended in the early 530s to the fugitive Persian prince Kavad, son of Zames, or at least someone claiming to be him (i.23.23–4), can only have served to arouse Persian suspicions about Roman intentions.

I would therefore argue that Roman–Persian relations were pervaded by mutual suspicion and fear of one another's intentions. From this perspective, major invasions (as well as smaller-scale raids) by both powers should be seen primarily as pre-emptive in aim, as attempts to keep one another off-balance and on the defensive. This is not to deny the role of subsidiary motives such as the economic benefits arising from booty and prisoners, nor is it inconsistent with the development of mutual recognition of parity of status.[51] Respect need not entail trust, and conceding equality to one another in diplomatic protocol would have served, if anything, to reinforce recognition of the potential threat which they posed to each other, rather than to assuage fears. So while neither power seems in fact to have had ambitions to acquire territory beyond the strategically crucial north Mesopotamian plain, the failure of both to appreciate this meant that there remained considerable potential for warfare in the region.

THE EMPIRE'S NORTHERN NEIGHBOURS

During late antiquity the Roman empire had dealings with many different northern peoples with varying degrees of intensity, but the ancient sources provide background information of sufficient detail only about some of these,

---

[49] As argued by T D. Barnes, 'Imperial campaigns, AD 285–311', *Phoenix* 30 (1976), 174–93, at 183–4.

[50] The *Life of Anushirwan*, in M. Grignaschi, 'Quelques spécimens de la littérature sassanide conservés dans les bibliothèques d'Istanbul', *Journal asiatique* 254 (1966), 1–142, at 16–28, quoted and discussed by Whitby, *Maurice*, 218.

[51] Cf. N. G. Garsoïan, 'Byzantium and the Sasanians', *CHI* vol. 3, 568–92, at 591.

notably the Alamanni and Franks on the Rhine, and the Goths, the Huns, and the Avars on the Danube. It is appropriate to consider the first three of these peoples together, since they were all characterised by a settled mode of existence, while the Huns and Avars were predominantly nomadic in their way of life.[52]

The origins of the peoples known to the Romans as 'Alamanni' and 'Franci' are obscure, but it is generally thought that both were the outcome of processes of confederation which took place during the late second and early third century among the smaller, more fragmented Germanic tribes which feature in Tacitus' *Germania*.[53] In the course of the third century, the Franks expanded their territory westwards to the middle and lower Rhine, and the Alamanni into the salient defined by the upper reaches of the Rhine and Danube (the so-called *agri decumates*), as the Romans withdrew to the line formed by these rivers.[54] The origin of the Goths is even more obscure. In recent decades, the traditional view that their ancestral home lay in Scandinavia has encountered greater scepticism about the possibility of secure knowledge concerning their early history.[55] But the appearance of the Goths in the vicinity of the empire's northern frontier by the third century is certain, on the basis of both the presence of a Gothic unit in the Roman army as early as the first decade of the third century,[56] and the extensive archaeological remains referred to as the 'Sîntana de Mureş/ Černjachov' culture which have been associated with Gothic occupation of the regions north of the lower Danube and Black Sea.[57]

All three peoples pursued a settled way of life based on agriculture and animal husbandry, supplemented by handicraft production in pottery and bone.[58] The typical unit of settlement was the village, comprising a usually random configuration of huts or 'long-houses', and, on the admittedly limited

---

[52] J. H. W. G. Liebeschuetz, *Barbarians and Bishops: Army, Church and State in the Age of Arcadius and Chrysostom* (Oxford, 1990), 83–5, has, however, recently queried whether the Goths were as settled as is usually assumed.

[53] L. Musset, *The Germanic Invasions: the Making of Europe AD 400–600*, tr. E. and C. James (London, 1975), 68–9, 80–1; B. Krüger (ed.), *Die Germanen: Geschichte und Kultur der germanischen Stämme in Mitteleuropa* vol. 2 (Berlin, 1983), 336–7, 381.

[54] For a geographical overview of fourth-century 'Alamannia', with references to the archaeological literature, see Matthews, *Ammianus*, 306–8, 523 n. 4.

[55] R. Hachmann, *Die Goten und Skandinavien* (Berlin, 1970); W. Goffart, *Barbarians and Romans, AD 418–584: the Techniques of Accommodation* (Princeton, 1980), Chapter 1. H. Wolfram, *History of the Goths*, tr. T. Dunlap (Berkeley, 1989) still accepts that there is a kernel of truth in the stories of a Scandinavian origin.

[56] M. Speidel, 'The Roman army in Arabia', *ANRW* II.8 (1977), 687–730, at 712–16.

[57] For a very useful guide to the archaeological literature on this subject, see P. Heather and J. Matthews, *The Goths in the Fourth Century* (Liverpool, 1991), Chapter 3.

[58] M. Todd, *The Northern Barbarians, 100 BC–AD 300*, rev. edn (London, 1987), Chapters 3–4; Matthews, *Ammianus*, Chapter 14.1. This is not to deny the existence of important differences between the three peoples discussed here. E.g., Matthews notes superior Gothic pottery techniques – the Goths used a wheel, whereas the Alamanni still formed theirs by hand (312, 321–2).

available archaeological evidence, generally covering an area of less than 10 hectares.[59] This stands in rather dramatic contrast to the numerous Sasanian sites ranging from 20 to 200 hectares in area – 34 sites in the central Euphrates floodplain and 48 in the lower Diyala valley.[60]

Within this context, significant social and political changes were occurring, at least partly as a result of interaction with the Roman empire through diplomacy, trade, and the service of individuals in the Roman army. A social system based on kinship relations had given way to differentiation between a commons and an aristocracy with its own military retinues supported by agricultural production from their property. A decision-making council of aristocrats had replaced the general assembly of warriors typical of earlier periods, and the office of king was beginning to emerge.[61] These peoples were therefore gradually acquiring the characteristics of states, or perhaps more appropriately 'proto-states',[62] and were developing the ability to organise themselves so as to pose more serious threats to the Roman empire than had been the case prior to the third century.[63]

Having acknowledged this, one has only to compare them with Sasanian Persia, even in its early phase, to appreciate that they still had a considerable way to go before they could be described as fully fledged states. Plurality of kingship generally remained the rule throughout the fourth century,[64] and one continues to find tribal sub-groupings within the Alamanni (e.g., Juthungi, Bucinobantes), Franks (Chamavi, Salii) and Goths (Tervingi, Greuthungi) acting independently. Moreover, all three peoples still lacked even the most rudimentary administrative apparatus. The prerequisite for the development of such an

---

[59] For the detailed evidence, see pp. 159–61.

[60] Adams, *Land behind Baghdad*, 72 (Table 19) and *Heartland of Cities*, 179 (Table 17).

[61] J. H. F. Bloemers, 'Acculturation in the Rhine/Meuse basin in the Roman period' in R. Brandt and J. Slofstra (eds.), *Roman and Native in the Low Countries: Spheres of Interaction* (BAR s184, 1983), 159–209, especially 201–2; L. Hedeager, 'Empire, frontier and the barbarian hinterland: Rome and northern Europe from AD 1–400' in M. Rowlands, M. Larsen and K. Kristiansen (eds.), *Centre and Periphery in the Ancient World* (Cambridge, 1987), 125–40; E. A. Thompson, *The Visigoths in the Time of Ulfila* (Oxford, 1966), 43–55. P. Heather, *Goths and Romans 332–489* (Oxford, 1991), 97–107, sees this process as having progressed further among the Gothic Tervingi than Thompson allows.

[62] Cf. W. G. Runciman, 'Origins of states', *Comparative Studies in Society and History* 24 (1982), 351–77, especially 354–5. On the need to keep the extent of these changes in perspective, note M. G. Fulford, 'Roman material in barbarian society, c. 200 BC–c. AD 400' in T. C. Champion and J. V. S. Megaw (eds.), *Settlement and Society* (Leicester, 1985), 91–108, at 103–6.

[63] The considerable but short-lived power of the Marcomannic confederation in the latter half of the second century had foreshadowed third-century developments.

[64] Matthews, *Ammianus*, 314 (on the Alamanni); E. Zöllner, *Geschichte der Franken* (Munich, 1970), 110–11; Thompson, *Visigoths*, 43ff. As already noted, Heather has recently argued for the existence of a permanent ruler among the Gothic Tervingi in the fourth century, though he also acknowledges that the authority of this ruler was inevitably restricted to some degree by the power of lower-level leaders (*Goths and Romans*, 97–107, especially 105–7).

apparatus was the acquisition of some degree of literacy,[65] which would seem to have been lacking among any northern people until the late fourth century at the earliest:

> There is no certain evidence that the literary arts were practised among them until after their settlement in the Roman provinces. German chiefs and other leaders did, it is true, send letters on various occasions to Roman emperors and commanders, and these letters were written in Latin. But not a single word of them need have been penned by a literate German. Roman travellers, merchants, prisoners, slaves and, later, Christian priests will usually have been called on to do this.[66]

It was, for example, the Christian bishop Ulfila who developed a script for the Gothic language in order to provide the Goths with direct access to the Bible, but 'there is no reason to believe that by the middle of the fourth century more than a handful of Goths were literate. It would be easy to exaggerate the use which they made of writing even after Ulfila had invented his alphabet.'[67] While these conditions persisted, anything resembling administrative organisation must have been virtually non-existent.[68] Other obvious indications of this are the lack of indigenous coinages, and the absence of any central urban settlement which might have been designated a 'capital'.[69] Indeed, the general lack of cities or

---

[65] See J. Goody, *The Logic of Writing and the Organisation of Society* (Cambridge, 1986), with the comments of M. T. Larsen, 'Literacy and social complexity' in J. Gledhill, B. Bender and M. T. Larsen (eds.), *State and Society: the Emergence and Development of Social Hierarchy and Political Centralisation* (London, 1988), 173–91.

[66] Todd, *Northern Barbarians*, 9–10. The early Germans did, of course, make some limited use of runes, but 'runic script . . . served almost no practical purpose' (Musset, *Germanic Invasions*, 204).

[67] Thompson, *Visigoths*, 32.

[68] In the light of this, claims that have been made for the existence of a Gothic chancellery in the mid-fourth century must be regarded with scepticism (e.g., G. Diaconu, 'On the socio-economic relations of natives and Goths in Dacia' in M. Constantinescu, S. Pascu and P. Diaconu (eds.), *Relations between the Autochthonous Population and the Migratory Populations on the Territory of Romania* (Bucharest, 1975), 65–75, at 73, where the passages adduced from Ammianus do not support the assertions made).

[69] It would seem, however, that the Goths had progressed further towards this than the Alamanni or Franks, for Soviet archaeologists have identified a number of sites in the Ukraine and Moldavia which appear to have functioned as tribal centres of some sort (A. V. Kropotkin, 'On the centres of the Chernyakhovo culture tribes', *Sovetskaya Arkheologiya* (1984) fasc. 3, 35–47 (in Russian with English summary)); the settlement at Pietroasa in Romania may have functioned in the same way (Heather and Matthews, *Goths*, 57), while a large cemetery like that at Tîrgşor (286 graves: G. Diaconu, *Tîrgşor: Necropola din secolele III-IV n.e.* (Bucharest, 1965)) might have been associated with a large settlement. Significantly, however, 'no Sîntana de Mureş/ Černjachov site with any fortification has yet been discovered' (Heather and Matthews, *Goths*, 57). Diaconu ('Socio-economic relations', 73–4) has claimed the existence of large tribal centres along the lower Danube on the basis of the evidence for cemeteries in B. Mitrea and C. Preda, *Necropole din secolul al IV–lea e.n. în Muntenia* (Bucharest, 1966), but most of the cemeteries along the lower Danube contained less than 10 graves, while the handful with higher figures (20–40 graves: Independenţa, Izvorul, Odobescu; around 70: Oinac, Spanţov) still fall well short of the total at Tîrgşor (which lies well north of the Danube).

towns is significant, for urbanisation is usually (though not always) a con-comitant of state-formation.[70] In short, then, centralisation of political power had begun, but was as yet far from complete.

As for the more specific question of military organisation, the evidence is very thin, but the traditional Germanic emphasis on personal ties of loyalty between warriors and individual leaders will have militated against the development of well-organised and cohesive armies comparable to those of the Romans or Persians. 'Individual kings and war-leaders rarely enjoyed the authority that would enable them to train an army and hold it together in pursuit of some clearly defined aim.'[71] Nor is there anything to suggest that they were ever capable of organising in advance the necessary logistical support for sustained campaigns. The literary sources suggest that they relied on living off the land,[72] a conclusion which finds indirect support in their inability to conduct sieges. This inability was not just a reflection of lack of technological know-how, but also of the way in which the continual need to be off foraging for supplies inhibited the sort of sustained effort in one location which a siege required.[73] However, it is important to note that while the lack of a formal system of logistical support was in this and other respects a handicap, it did also give Germanic peoples the important advantage of speed. When an attack was decided upon, they were not delayed by the need to wait for the accumulation of supplies and their mobility *en route* was enhanced by the lack of a supply train. This contrasts with the practice of the Romans and Persians, who could take months preparing for campaigns, and whose armies moved more slowly the larger they were.[74] Lack of organisation had some compen-sations.

The Huns and the Avars differed from the Germanic peoples in several respects. The Huns were a central Asiatic people, though it is doubtful that they should be identified with the Hsiung-nu of Chinese records.[75] They began moving from the Eurasian steppe into the lower Danube basin in the late fourth century, compelling large numbers of Goths to seek admission to the empire in the 370s. Those Goths who remained outside the empire had to submit to the Hunnic rule exercised over Wallachia throughout much of the fifth century. A similar pattern was repeated in the second half of the sixth century when the Avars, another people of Asiatic extraction, occupied the plains to the north of

---

[70] H. J. M. Claessen, 'The early state: a structural approach' in H. J. M. Claessen and P. Skalník (eds.), *The Early State* (The Hague, 1978), 533–96, at 541.

[71] Todd, *Northern Barbarians*, 162.

[72] E. A. Thompson, *The Early Germans* (Oxford, 1965), 140ff. Cf. Todd, *Northern Barbarians*, 162 ('Any form of commissariat was probably rarely organised').

[73] Crow, 'Function', 728.

[74] Lee, 'Campaign preparations'.

[75] O. Maenchen-Helfen, 'Huns and Hsiung-nu', *Byzantion* 17 (1944–5), 222–43.

the lower Danube as far west as Hungary and established hegemony over the inhabitants they found there.[76]

The crucial distinguishing characteristic of the Huns and Avars was that they were nomadic pastoralists. This had far-reaching consequences with respect to their social, economic and political development, which diverged significantly from that of other northern peoples who pursued more settled modes of existence. The economic imperatives of nomadic society, based as it was on the herding of animals rather than on agriculture, had significant implications for social and political structures. Under the normal conditions of movement between pastures, the emergence of an organised state was highly unlikely.[77] Dispersal in small groups over large areas, absence of permanent settlements, and minimal social differentiation usually inhibited any such development. It was only when a nomadic people was able to use its military skills, notably horsemanship and archery, to establish dominance over a settled agricultural population from which they then exacted tribute that some degree of central-ising authority emerged. Resources became more predictable, permitting the possibility of planning. It was, however, an authority whose tenure was charac-teristically unstable and short-lived.[78]

These features are evident in Hunnic and Avar society between the fourth and early seventh centuries in so far as available evidence permits observation. In the late fourth century, the Huns comprised disparate tribal groupings, with certain leading men (*primates*) able to exercise some influence over decisions.[79] By the mid-fifth century they had established hegemony over the agricultural population of the Danubian plains. The inflow of tribute from these subjects and of booty from successful wars facilitated the emergence of Attila as sole ruler, together with an upper stratum of *logades* (λογάδες), 'prominent men', though it seems unlikely that these leading men had a formal role in the administering of Attila's empire.[80] Although, significantly for a nomadic ruler, Attila had what appears to have been at least semi-permanent 'headquarters' north of the Danube,[81] any attempt at more than the most elementary forms of governmental organisation will have been impossible in the absence of literacy. Attila relied on

[76] For detailed treatment of the Avars, see W. Pohl, *Die Awaren: Ein Steppenvolk in Mitteleuropa, 567–822 n. Chr.* (Munich, 1988).

[77] For detailed discussion from the point of view of nomadic societies in general, see A. M. Khazanov, *Nomads and the Outside World*, tr. J. Crookenden (Cambridge, 1984), Chapter 5.

[78] P. Anderson, *Passages from Antiquity to Feudalism* (London, 1974), 219–26. Cf. J. J. Saunders, 'The nomad as empire builder', *Diogenes* 52 (1965), 79–103.

[79] E. A. Thompson, *A History of Attila and the Huns* (Oxford, 1948), 43–5.

[80] O. Maenchen-Helfen, *The World of the Huns* (Berkeley, 1973), 192–5, *contra* Thompson, *Attila*, 161–7.

[81] The wooden structures which comprised Attila's 'palace' and the houses of other leading Huns (as well as a bath-house of imported stone in the Roman style) were observed by Roman envoys in 449 (Priscus fr. 11,2/356–72).

Romans, acquired either as prisoners or as 'gifts' from leading imperial officials, to act as secretaries for him, and the documents which the sources show these men drawing up were letters to the emperor, not commands to subordinates.[82] The fragility of this nomadic empire became all too apparent with the death of Attila, which precipitated a crisis that gave the subject peoples the opportunity to revolt successfully.

The Asiatic phase of the Avars is, like that of the Huns, the subject of much scholarly debate,[83] but by the mid-sixth century they in turn dominated the settled population of the Danubian plains, with a single ruler, the khagan, and an aristocracy of some sort: Menander speaks of *archontes* (ἄρχοντες) (lit. 'those in charge': fr. 15,1/7,13), Theophylact of *dunatotatoi* (δυνατώτατοι), 'the most influential men', and *logades* (i.6.3, vi.11.6).[84] More archaeological evidence is available for the Avars than the Huns, principally considerable numbers of graves. Few graves datable before about 600 have been found in the large cemeteries, which has been taken to indicate the absence of permanent Avar winter quarters until about that time, while their increasing incidence from then onwards has been seen as marking a transition to a more sedentary style of life. Grave goods show the continuing importance of cattle breeding and other pastoral concerns, but items such as sickles have also been found, indicating some degree of more settled agricultural activity.[85]

The tenuous nature of the khagan's control is illustrated in a number of incidents arising from his dealings with the Romans. For example, in the late 560s the khagan's envoys agreed to certain Roman conditions but requested some small gifts so that their ruler would not lose face before the other peoples of his confederation (Men. fr. 12,5/56–63). In 602, Roman attacks on Avar territory caused large numbers of Avar subjects to desert the khagan and go over to the Romans (Th. Sim. viii.6.1; cf. Maurice *Strat.* xi.2/74–8). Finally, the failure of the Avar siege of Constantinople in 626 precipitated a revolt by the subject populations which effectively ended the Avar empire.

Virtually nothing is known about the military organisation of either the Huns or the Avars,[86] although the latter are described as giving thought to such matters (φροντίζουσι τάξεως πολεμικῆς), and used a baggage-train (τοῦλδον: Maurice *Strat.* xi.2/6,46). The greater facility of both peoples at siege warfare, compared with the various Germanic peoples of the third and fourth

---

[82] See, e.g., Rusticius and Constantius in Priscus fr.11,2/145–8 and 320–1; fr. 14/5–8.

[83] For discussion of which, see Pohl, *Awaren*, 31–7.

[84] The difficulties of trying to reconstruct Avar social organisation from the archaeological evidence are discussed by Pohl, *Awaren*, 188–9, who also observes (186) that the literary sources leave it 'unclear whether the Avar "logades" were tribal leaders or personal agents of the khagan and to what extent they owed their position to him'.

[85] S. Szadeczky-Kardoss, 'The Avars' in D. Sinor (ed.), *The Cambridge History of Early Inner Asia* (Cambridge, 1990), 206–28, at 226–7.

[86] Cf. Pohl, *Awaren*, 174.

centuries,[87] might perhaps reflect better organisation of food supplies, but Avar success in this field, at least, was usually achieved by surprise,[88] and the mobility of their chief sources of food – their herds of horses and cattle (cf. Maurice *Strat.* xi.2/31-2) – offered a simple solution to logistical problems (though of course the animals in turn required forage and must have hindered speed of Avar movement to some degree).[89]

Although a greater degree of (short-lived) political centralisation is apparent among both peoples, compared with the Franks, Alamanni and Goths, there are still clear differences again between these nomadic empires and Sasanian Persia – in degree of administrative organisation, urbanisation, and permanence of central authority. These differences, and those between Persia and the settled northern peoples of the third and fourth centuries, had paradoxical implications for the empire's relations with east and north. On the one hand, these differences made Persia a more formidable enemy than the empire's northern neighbours, for example in so far as the Sasanians possessed the organisational infrastructure to mount and sustain large expeditions. On the other hand, this very organisational complexity could become a handicap from the perspective of information and intelligence: preparation of expeditions took time and made it more difficult to conceal intentions. Northern peoples' relative lack of organ-isational structures certainly imposed constraints on their ability to support sustained campaigns, but it did have compensating advantages in terms of greater speed and unpredictability, while their lack of large political central places comparable to Persian Ctesiphon made it more difficult for Roman military planners to formulate clear objectives. The significance of these differences for the theme of information will become apparent as this study progresses.

ROMAN RESOURCES FOR FOREIGN RELATIONS

The main non-Roman protagonists in this study have been introduced; it remains to make some remarks about the late Roman empire itself. The organisational sophistication of the empire hardly needs discussion, but a few brief observations may be made by way of comparison, before turning to other matters. The empire of this period was a centralised state with a substantial bureaucracy through which the empire's resources were taxed and a large standing army maintained.[90] The level of administrative complexity attained can

---

87 *Ibid.*, 173; Whitby, *Maurice*, 67–8 (Huns), 84–5, 172–3 (Avars).
88 *Ibid.*, 173.
89 Whitby (*ibid.*, 172) notes their practice of sending advance parties to achieve surprise.
90 For succinct overviews of the late Roman army and bureaucracy, see R. S. O. Tomlin, 'The army in the late empire' and J. H. W. G. Liebeschuetz, 'Government and administration in the late empire', both in J. Wacher (ed.), *The Roman World* (London, 1987), 107–20, 455–69, and for greater detail, the fundamental work of A. H. M. Jones, *The Later Roman Empire 284–602* (Oxford, 1964), Chapters 11-17.

be illustrated by the arrangements for the supply of rations to units of the field armies during peacetime:

> Supplies were issued to the regiments . . . by *delegatoriae*, or warrants from the praetorian prefect entitling them to draw specified quantities of foodstuffs from the revenues of a given province . . . The actuary of the unit applied to the *officium* of the provincial governor, who issued an order to certain villages . . . to supply specified quantities of foodstuffs, against a receipt (*formaria*) given by the actuary, which would entitle them to deduct the amounts supplied against their assessed tax.[91]

Actual campaigns, of course, placed additional demands on the system in terms of the assembling of troops and the supply of additional provisions, in which organisational matters the Romans were clearly superior to their northern neighbours. Yet as has been emphasised already, organisational complexity had its costs: preparations of this sort were not easily disguised, and they took time. The emperor Valentinian, for example, spent three months organising arms and logistic support for his campaign against the Quadi in 375; it hardly seems surprising that when he finally did cross the Danube, most of the enemy had already withdrawn into the mountains (Amm. Marc. xxx.5.11–13).[92]

This theme does not require further elaboration, and in fact the main aim of this section is to take up some rather different questions which nevertheless bear on the organisational dimension of imperial foreign relations. They focus on the issue of the resources, documentary and human, available to late Roman government in its conduct of foreign relations. Little if anything in the way of archives devoted to foreign affairs or personnel specialising in this field seems to have existed during the first three centuries AD, which has lent support to the conclusion that the imperial government of that period was not greatly interested in acquiring information about foreign peoples.[93] To what extent did this situation persist during late antiquity?

Records

The administrative arrangements of the first three centuries AD have been characterised as 'government without bureaucracy',[94] reflecting the disparity between the enormous geographical size of the empire and the comparatively

---

91 *Ibid.*, 672 (reign of Anastasius; 627, 630 for similar procedures in the fourth century).
92 For further instances from the northern frontier, see Amm. Marc. xiv.10.6–8; xviii.2.7–8; xxvii.5.2; 10.7; Th. Sim. vi.6.2–14; vii.7.3; viii.1.11–2.4; and for further general discussion of this subject, see Lee, 'Campaign preparations' (with examples from the eastern frontier – to which add Amm. Marc. xxi.6.6; Lib. *Or.* xi.177–8).
93 Millar, 'Emperors, frontiers and foreign relations', especially 5–6 (personnel), 18 (archives).
94 P. Garnsey and R. Saller, *The Roman Empire: Economy, Society, Culture* (London, 1987), Chapter 2.

tiny number of imperial administrators. Consistent with this is an emphasis on the limited nature of governmental archives available to emperors during this period,[95] including the absence of any formal archives relating to the empire's external affairs.[96] However, the reforms of Diocletian and Constantine in the late third and early fourth century witnessed a substantial increase in the size of the imperial bureaucracy, even if the overall number of administrative staff remained modest (by modern standards) as a proportion of the empire's population.[97]

One might reasonably have inferred that such an expansion in the number of bureaucrats (especially shorthand writers) would have generated more paper-work, thereby creating conditions conducive to more extensive government archives, but the causal link 'more bureaucracy – more paperwork' has recently been challenged apropos of late antiquity by William Harris.[98] His argument, however, by no means takes account of all the relevant evidence. This is partly because, for Professor Harris, 'late antiquity' by and large means the period from 250 to the early fifth century. It will no doubt seem gratuitous to carp about this restricted chronological definition when his study, beginning in archaic Greece, has already covered an enormous time-span, but this limitation is nevertheless significant.[99] For his specific argument about volume of paperwork, Harris relies primarily on the papyrological data from Egypt indicating a steady decline in the number of papyrus documents from the mid-fourth to the late fifth century, though he acknowledges that Egypt may not have been typical, and that from the 470s onwards there is once again a steady increase lasting through the sixth century. What is surprising is his neglect of the legal evidence. The Theodosian Code, for example, contains many fifth-century laws which would have generated considerable quantities of paperwork,[100] while the law-making process itself involved the promulgation of imperial edicts throughout the

---

[95] F. Millar, *The Emperor and the Roman World (31 BC–AD 337)* (London, 1977), 259–68.

[96] Millar, 'Emperors, frontiers and foreign relations', 18. Note, however, the more optimistic view of A. R. Birley, 'Roman frontier policy under Marcus Aurelius' in S. Applebaum (ed.), *Roman Frontier Studies 1967* (Tel Aviv, 1971), 7–13, at 7.

[97] R. MacMullen, 'Imperial bureaucrats in the Roman provinces', *Harvard Studies in Classical Philology* 68 (1964), 305–16, at 311–12.

[98] W. V. Harris, *Ancient Literacy* (Cambridge, Mass., 1989), 289–94, especially 290 (he acknowledges that there was an increase under Diocletian and Constantine, but sees this as only a temporary reversal of the underlying trend).

[99] It means that among other things he does not refer to the north African *Tablettes Albertini* (ed. C. Courtois, L. Leschi, C. Perrat and C. Saumagne; Paris, 1952), or the documentary papyri from fifth- and sixth-century Ravenna (ed. J.-O. Tjäder; Lund and Stockholm, 1955–82). Note also the intriguing references which imply a significant level of literacy in the city of Edessa in the late fifth and early sixth century (J. Styl. 29 – a complaints box set up by a beneficent governor soon fills up; 96 – citizens write down their grievances about the misbehaviour of Roman troops and post them around the city).

[100] E.g., vii.4.24 (398); 16.3 (420); xi.5.3 (436); 26.2 (400); 28.13 (422). Cf. *CJ* xii.37 for the paper-work involved in army supplies.

provinces. This is apparent not in the codes themselves, where the preambles and epilogues of the laws have been excised,[101] but in the collections of imperial novels ('new' laws), which retain these features.[102] The epilogues of the novels frequently include instructions for copies of the law to be distributed throughout the empire, such as the following: 'make it known by the usual edicts throughout all the communities of the provinces' (Valentinian III Novel vi.1.4 (440)); 'by displaying edicts according to established practice throughout all the cities subject to our authority' (Theodosius II Novel xvii.2.7 (444)); 'it shall be sent throughout the land to all the peoples . . . When the officials of the major cities receive it, . . . they shall transmit it to every city' (Justinian Novel i, epilog. 1 (535)). The fact that the preambles often contain justifications of imperial policy implies that the laws were seen as a vehicle for communicating with the public,[103] which in turn makes it unlikely that the instructions in the epilogues concerning distribution were simply empty rhetoric.[104]

Much of the paperwork generated by late Roman bureaucracy was concerned with fiscal and judicial matters, but it would not be surprising if, in combination with the necessarily greater importance of foreign relations during late antiquity, there was some 'spin-off' effect on documentation relevant to foreign affairs. We may begin by considering the evidence for more formal types of diplomatic document – treaties and official letters. There can be little doubt about the existence of an archive containing the texts of treaties and related items in sixth-century Constantinople. The most detailed and best attested indicator is that of the documents arising from the settlement reached with Persia in 561/2. Menander Protector reproduces a literal Greek translation of the Persian text of Khusro's letter of ratification, and then the treaty clauses themselves (fr. 6,1/175–202, 314–93); his apology for reproducing non-literary Greek (fr. 6,2/3–11) confirms his use of official documents and hence their availability at least twenty years after the negotiation of the agreement.[105]

Also of considerable interest in this context is a letter from Pope Gregory the Great to the Visigothic king Reccared in 599, from which it emerges that

---

[101] Though note CTh xi.28.9 (414) where an epilogue similar to those in the novels remains.

[102] Jones, Later Roman Empire, 170, 475, 267.

[103] R. Scott, 'Malalas and Justinian's codification' in E. and M. Jeffreys & A. Moffatt (eds.), Byzantine Papers (Canberra, 1981), 12–31, at 17–20, 28 n. 30; idem, 'Malalas, The Secret History, and Justinian's propaganda', DOP 39 (1985), 99–109.

[104] These instructions are similar to the order that copies of Diocletian's taxation edict be sent to every village in Egypt, whose implementation Harris seems ready to accept (Literacy, 291 n. 19). Harris' scepticism about the amount of paperwork in the fourth-century army (294) also seems unwarranted in the light of measures such as CTh vii.4.24 (398) (annual army returns indicating levels of provisioning) and the incident involving the traitor Antoninus who deserted to the Persians in 359 after studying army records (ratiocinia) about unit strengths, dispositions and future plans (Amm. Marc. xviii.5.1–3).

[105] O. Veh, Beiträge zu Menander Protektor (Fürth, 1955), 10; B. Baldwin, 'Menander Protector', DOP 32 (1978), 101–25, at 104, 109; Blockley, Menander, 260 n. 84.

Reccared had asked Gregory to write to the emperor Maurice on his behalf and request from the imperial archive (*cartofilacium*) a copy of a treaty (*pacta*) concluded between Constantinople and the Visigoths during the reign of Justinian. Gregory replies that there is no point in his doing this, since a fire during Justinian's reign had destroyed the relevant archive and the terms of the treaty were disadvantageous to the Visigoths anyway.[106] The fact that he had spent a period as papal legate in Constantinople during the late 570s and early 580s creates a strong presumption in favour of Gregory knowing of the existence of an archive for treaties there and its destruction at one point in the recent past.

These two cases derive from the sixth century. Explicit evidence of this kind for the preservation of treaties in archives is not forthcoming from the earlier centuries of the late Roman period, but when the terms of a settlement such as the Roman–Persian peace settlement in 363 are known to have been committed to writing,[107] it is difficult to believe that such documents were not kept by the Roman government – especially when there does seem to have been a tradition of depositing copies of treaties on the Capitol in Rome during earlier centuries back into the Republican period.[108] This is not to say, of course, that all agreements will necessarily have involved the formulation of a written instrument between the two parties. Although the drawing-up of written treaties did not preclude their confirmation with oaths,[109] Ammianus refers on a number of occasions to northern peoples making agreements with the Romans by swearing oaths according to their own customs in a way which suggests that no written document was involved.[110] This would be consistent with the general lack of literacy among northern peoples, as a result of which

---

[106] *Registrum Epistolarum* ix.229 (CCSL cxl A, pp. 810–11). The essential background to this is that during the 550s, Constantinople had seized (and continued to hold) an enclave of territory in south-eastern Spain. For discussion of possible dates for this treaty, see E. A. Thompson, *The Goths in Spain* (Oxford, 1969), 331–2. For the frequent occurrence of fires in Constantinople during late antiquity, see M. Whitby and M. Whitby, *Chronicon Paschale, 284–628 AD* (Liverpool, 1989), 236 (s.v. fires).

[107] Zos. iii.31.2; Mal. p. 336; Faustus of Buzand iv.21. Peter the Patrician's account of the terms of the Roman–Persian settlement of 298/9 (fr. 14, *FHG* iv.180) is problematic: although as *magister officiorum* he will undoubtedly have had access to any relevant files, his description of the provisions is far less detailed than the treaty clauses preserved by Menander, suggesting resort to a source other than a treaty text (and although it is highly likely that this treaty involved a written document, there is no explicit statement to that effect in any source). The peace with the Persians in 505 involved written documents (J. Styl. 98: *ktaba*), as did the 'Eternal Peace' of 532 (Zach. *HE* ix.8, vol. 2, p. 100/12: *ktaba*).

[108] F. Millar, 'Government and diplomacy in the Roman empire during the first three centuries', *International History Review* 10 (1988), 345–77, at 350.

[109] See, e.g., Amm. Marc. xxv.7.14 on the settlement with Persia in 363; cf. Proc. *Wars* vi.25.21 (ὅρκους ἐν γράμμασι – 'oaths in writing').

[110] xvii.1.13; 10.7; 12.21; xxx.3.5; cf. xiv.10.16; Dio lxxi.3.2; Malchus fr. 2/22. An agreement with the Blemmyes and Nobades of southern Egypt in 453 was, however, made in writing (Priscus fr. 27,1/21).

sacred oaths presumably carried more weight with them than pieces of paper.[111]

Official letters between rulers are another category of formal diplomatic document which features in the sources. Indeed, a number of writers from late antiquity claim to preserve the text of particular letters (or in some cases the gist of the letter). Eusebius does so with respect to a letter from Constantine to Shapur II (*Life of Constantine* iv.8–13), while Ammianus includes an exchange of letters between Constantius II and Shapur, though with the important qualification that he does not claim to reproduce the precise wording (xvii.5).[112] From the sixth century, Procopius presents (among others) the texts of letters from Kavad to Justin I, and from Justinian to Khusro (*Wars* i.11.7–9; ii.4.17–25), Malalas has what purports to be a letter from Kavad to Justinian (pp. 449–50), Agathias claims to reproduce the sense of a letter from Justinian to the Utigur Hun leader Sandlich (v.24.3–7), Menander gives the gist of a letter from Tiberius II to Khusro I, and quotes one from Khusro (fr. 23,8/14–21, 28–41), and Theophylact gives the text of a letter from Khusro II to Maurice (iv.11.1–11). From the early seventh century, the *Paschale Chronicle* includes the text of a letter from the senate in Constantinople to Khusro II (pp. 707–9).

Scholarly opinion about these individual instances varies: although another document quoted by Eusebius in his *Life of Constantine* has been proven authentic,[113] some scholars have understandably been reluctant automatically to give credence to all other documents reproduced in the *Life* on this basis, and so doubts remain about Constantine's letter to Shapur;[114] on the other hand, it has been acknowledged that Theophylact's example 'could have been found in Roman archives'.[115] It is certainly not a plausible objection that letters sent *by* the Romans could not by definition have been sighted subsequently by a Roman writer, since it had long been standard Roman administrative practice for the daybooks (*commentarii*) of officials to have recorded in them incoming and outgoing correspondence.[116] A more substantial obstacle to accepting the texts of many of these letters as genuine is the way in which the conventions of historical writing in late antiquity permitted historians to compose letters in the same way as they did speeches.[117] However, the instance from the *Paschale*

---

[111] This does not rule out the possibility that the Roman government may have kept its own written record of such agreements, though there is no explicit evidence to this effect.

[112] This does not necessarily mean that he had not seen copies of these letters, for on another occasion when he claims only to present the import of a letter (in this case, one from Julian to Constantius: xx.8.4), it is clear that he had nevertheless been able to read the actual document (8.18).

[113] A. H. M. Jones and T. C. Skeat, 'Notes on the genuineness of the Constantinian documents in Eusebius' "Life of Constantine"', *JEH* 5 (1954), 194–200.

[114] See, e.g., Millar, 'Emperors, frontiers and foreign relations', 2.

[115] Whitby, *Maurice*, 235.

[116] E. Posner, *Archives in the Ancient World* (Cambridge, Mass., 1972), 213.

[117] See, e.g., Cameron, *Procopius*, 148–9.

Chronicle cannot be dismissed on this basis; it is much more plausible, on grounds of language and of proximity in time and place, that the author actually had access to a copy of the letter.[118] Moreover, the actual exchange of letters was undoubtedly a genuine phenomenon.[119] Given this, the question to be asked is not why such documents should have been kept, but rather why they should have been thrown away; it was the latter action which required a conscious decision. So although uncertainty will continue to surround the texts of most of the particular letters referred to in the previous paragraph, the argument from administrative inertia favours the general idea that diplomatic letters were kept.

When it came to making decisions affecting foreign relations, however, these sorts of formal documents would have been of limited use. Of greater value would be *aides-mémoires* by Roman envoys concerning negotiations with and conditions among neighbouring peoples. The question is, of course, whether records of this sort were made and kept. There are a number of statements to the effect that envoys reported back to the emperor, at least in the later centuries of the late Roman period. The Roman envoys Anatolius and Nomus, who had engaged in negotiations with Attila in 449, reported (διεξῆλθον) all that had passed between them to the emperor on their arrival back in the capital (Priscus fr. 15,4/14–16); in 479 Adamantius wrote to the emperor about his discussions with Theoderic the Amal near Dyrrhachium (Malchus fr. 20/257–8); Alexander, Demetrius and Hypatius reported (ἤγγειλαν) to Justinian on their discussions with Gothic leaders in 533 (Proc. *Wars* v.3.29); on his return from his embassy to the Turks in 571, Zemarchus told the emperor everything (ἔφρασε τὸ πᾶν: Men. fr. 10,5/23); and George 'reported in detail (διεξοδικῶς διηγήσατο) to the emperor all that had occurred' on his embassy to Khusro II in the 590s (Th. Sim. viii.1.7). There is nothing in any of these cases to suggest that this procedure of reporting back was out of the ordinary, and indeed it would be odd if envoys had not done so. However, in only one of the five cases – that of Adamantius – is there explicit reference to the use of writing, and this example cannot be used as a basis for generalisation. Adamantius' case is less usual in that he did not return immediately to Constantinople, but remained near Theoderic's position to await further imperial instructions; it was these circumstances which necessitated his providing a written version of his negotiations. The envoys in the other cases all reported personally to the emperor, so that it cannot be assumed automatically that their reporting back involved anything more than presenting a verbal

---

[118] Whitby and Whitby, *Chronicon Paschale*, xx, 162 n. 444.
[119] E.g., Amm. Marc. xvii.14.1; Pet. Pat. fr. 17, *FHG* iv.190; Priscus fr. 11,2/176; *De Caer.* i.89, p. 406/12–13; for further examples, see R. Helm, 'Untersuchungen über den auswärtigen diplomatischen Verkehr des römischen Reiches im Zeitalter der Spätantike', *Archiv für Urkundenforschung* 12 (1932), 375–436, at 405 n. 3.

account. There is, nevertheless, reason to think that written records were made and preserved.

Menander's detailed account of Zemarchus' journey (frs. 10,2–5) obviously derives from a written record of some sort, as does that of John of Ephesus concerning the same embassy, who says that his is an abbreviated version of events 'as the envoys described [them]' (*HE* vi.23, p. 324/12–13). Similarly, Malalas has clearly resorted to an account of the embassy of Julianus to the Axumites in 530/1 written by the envoy himself: at one point he uses the phrase 'as the envoy himself related (ἐξηγήσατο)' (p. 457/12–13); the polished style of this section stands in contrast to Malalas' own lacklustre idiom,[120] and at another point Malalas has carelessly failed to transpose the first person of the original account into the third person (p. 458/7). The difficulty with the written accounts of Zemarchus and Julianus used by Menander, John of Ephesus and Malalas is, of course, that these were not necessarily reports found in the government archives; they might well have been privately published memoirs or histories comparable to Priscus' account of his participation on an embassy to Attila, or that of Nonnosus concerning his mission to the Arabs, Himyarites and Axumites early in the reign of Justinian (Photius *Bibl.* cod.3).

This uncertainty cannot be resolved, but even if Julianus and Zemarchus did subsequently publish their own accounts, there is still reason to think that reports about embassies were preserved in government archives during the fifth and sixth centuries. Menander's comments on his account of the negotiations with Persia in 561/2 imply the use of an official record of more than just the treaty text and other documents, for his apology for the non-literary character of the Greek extends to 'what was said' (fr. 6,2/8), and his subsequent verdict on the accuracy of Peter the Patrician's own account of the negotiations (/22ff.) presupposes Menander's access to an official version of proceedings.[121] Further evidence is provided by the fragments of the history of Malchus of Philadelphia which deal with Roman relations with the Goths during the course of the 470s. It has been persuasively argued that the sheer detail Malchus provides about the proposals and counter-proposals offered by each side on a number of occasions can only be explained by recourse to written accounts of those negotiations held in a government archive.[122]

Such accounts might have been written up for the archives by the envoy himself after his audience with the emperor, but the most convenient method would have been for a verbatim record of the audience itself to have been taken down on the spot by imperial shorthand writers who were undoubtedly

---

[120] M. Jeffreys in E. Jeffreys, B. Croke and R. Scott (eds.), *Studies in John Malalas* (Sydney, 1990), 274.

[121] Cf. Blockley, *Menander*, 19–20, 260 n. 84.

[122] This is the argument of Dr Peter Heather in an as yet unpublished seminar paper (with particular reference to Malchus frs. 2, 18 and 20); cf. his *Goths and Romans*, 236.

available for comparable tasks.[123] This last possibility directs attention to a final category of document worth considering, namely the minutes of the imperial consistory, the emperor's advisory council (*acta consistorii*: *CTh* i.22.4), which are known to have been kept by imperial shorthand writers.[124] Since questions of foreign policy were undoubtedly discussed by the consistory (e.g., Amm. Marc. xvi.10.21; Eunap. fr. 42/11–14), these minutes will have contained material of possible value on subsequent occasions – and why was a written record of consistory meetings taken down if not for subsequent consultation? This will have been the case, however, primarily only for the fourth century, since the consistory declined as a forum for discussion during the fifth century.[125]

The pattern that emerges from the rather unsatisfactory material discussed in this section is that most of the evidence for government records bearing on foreign relations derives from the fifth and especially the sixth centuries. This may in part be a mere quirk of source survival, but there is some reason to see it as reflecting the changing circumstances of the late Roman period. For example, the building up and use of archives bearing on foreign relations by the central government during the fifth century will have been facilitated by emperors relinquishing personal command of the armed forces after the death of Theodosius I (395): prior to this, the need to be mobile would have acted as a strong incentive for emperors to limit the quantity of paperwork that accompanied them. But it may also reflect a shift in attitudes under the impact of serious crises along the northern frontiers during the late fourth and early fifth century, a growing awareness on the part of emperors and/or officials of the need to give closer attention to foreign relations and of the value of written records in their conduct. This possibility can be explored further by considering the question of personnel.

Personnel

It has been observed that during the first three centuries AD there were no imperial officials specifically concerned with foreign affairs, a situation which the lists of bureaucratic titles in the *Notitia Dignitatum* of the early fifth century indicate remained unchanged during the fourth century, at least in any explicitly organisational sense.[126] Strictly speaking, this observation continues to hold force for the remainder of the late Roman period, through to the early seventh century, insofar as there was never an official whose sole or primary responsibility related to the conduct of foreign relations.

---

123 Cf. the notaries on hand to record Justin II's abdication statement in 574: John Eph. *HE* iii.5, p. 95/13–16.
124 J. A. Crook, *Consilium Principis* (Cambridge, 1955), 102.
125 Jones, *Later Roman Empire*, 337–9.
126 Millar, 'Emperors, frontiers and foreign relations', 5–6.

But to leave matters here would be to overlook the role of the 'Master of the Offices' (*magister officiorum*). This important office, created in the early fourth century, always encompassed a number of other significant spheres of authority, so that foreign relations can never be described as the *magister's* primary area of competence. But during the fifth and sixth centuries diplomacy was undoubtedly one of his special concerns, to such an extent that he has been described as 'a sort of minister for foreign affairs'.[127] This is evident in the direct involvement of *magistri* of the fifth and sixth centuries in diplomatic missions[128] and the reception of foreign envoys in Constantinople (*De Caer.* i.87–90), and in various indications from fifth-century sources that the emperor took advice from the *magister* on foreign relations – as when Euphemius made a recommendation to the emperor Marcian concerning affairs in the Caucasus during the mid-450s (Priscus fr. 33,2), and Theodosius II consulted Martialis concerning relations with Attila in 449 (fr. 11,1/59–66). These were not isolated incidents, for in this latter case Priscus says that '[the emperor] of necessity confides in this official, for the *magister* is privy to all the emperor's plans, since he is responsible for the messengers, interpreters and soldiers of the imperial guard'.

The origins of the office in the early fourth century are obscure,[129] but its title suggests it was initially conceived as having oversight of the bureaux in the palace administration. Further responsibilities, such as charge of the imperial arms factories and the *limitanei*, were undoubtedly added at later dates,[130] and diplomatic duties may also have been acquired in an analogous, if more piecemeal, fashion over the course of time. Certainly there is little evidence for the involvement of the *magister* in foreign relations during the fourth century. The only incident from this period when a *magister* can be seen acting in this connection is Ursacius' dispensing of gifts to Alamannic envoys in 364 (Amm. Marc. xxvi.5.7). This does suggest that by the mid-fourth century the *magister* had a role in the reception of foreign envoys, but it is hardly a sufficient basis for concluding that the fourth-century *magister* was already as involved in foreign relations as his successors were to be in subsequent centuries; Ursacius' ability to exasperate the envoys suggests that diplomatic skills were not then considered an important criterion in selection for the office. Interpreters are found under the *magister's* jurisdiction in the *Notitia* (*Or.* xi.52, *Occ.* ix.35), that is, by the early fifth century, but there is no way of telling whether this was a longstanding arrangement or a recent addition.

Explicit evidence for major involvement by the *magister* in diplomacy and

---

[127] Jones, *Later Roman Empire*, 369.
[128] See *PLRE* vol. 2, Helion 1, Celer 2 (possibly also Hilarianus 2); vol. 3, Hermogenes 1, Petrus 6.
[129] For an overview, see M. Clauss, *Der magister officiorum in der Spätantike* (Munich, 1980), 7–14.
[130] *Ibid.*, 51–4.

foreign affairs is therefore only available from the fifth century onwards, and this, combined with the Ursacius incident, suggests the gradual acquisition of this responsibility as the office evolved, rather than its being part of his original remit. The late fourth/early fifth century would appear to mark an important stage in this development, and it is tempting to see this as also relating in some degree to the shift from mobile emperors to emperors resident in Constantinople. While they remained personally active on the frontiers, emperors retained much more direct involvement in negotiations with foreign peoples,[131] whereas by relinquishing this role and remaining in the capital emperors of the fifth and sixth centuries created greater scope for officials to play a mediating role in diplomacy.

It would be interesting to be able to assess whether this trend was reflected in changes in the criteria used in the appointment of *magistri*: was experience relevant to the conduct of foreign relations given greater weight? At first sight, the evidence suggests a negative conclusion. Only two *magistri* from the fifth and sixth centuries are definitely known to have had prior experience in the role which one might have thought would be the most obvious recommendation for the office, namely that of ambassador: Anthemius in the fifth century, and Peter the Patrician in the sixth (in this latter case his promotion to the mastership was consequent on the successful completion of one such embassy: Proc. *Wars* vi.22.24); Eusebius, who was *magister* in the 490s, may be a third case,[132] and Strategius, deputy *magister* in 532, had recently been an envoy.[133] All this seems like very slim pickings. Moreover there are cases from the fifth century where individuals are reported to have been promoted to the office through the influence of kinship and friendship with members of the imperial family (Paulinus and Valerius, *Chr. Pasch.* pp. 578–9).

These details, however, need to be placed in perspective – namely, the very patchy nature of the evidence concerning the backgrounds and careers of *magistri*. Although the names of more than ninety *magistri* are known, the majority are little more than that – most often, merely the addressee of a law preserved in one of the codes. In only twenty-three of these ninety odd cases is something known about their earlier career or experience, and that something is itself usually very incomplete.

The sole hint of a pattern which does emerge from the material is that a number of *magistri* had previously occupied the post of 'Count of the Sacred Largesses' (*comes sacrarum largitionum*), who supervised the imperial treasury.[134] It is more than likely that the *comes* oversaw the depositing in and provision from

[131] Cf. Millar, 'Emperors, frontiers and foreign relations', 6.
[132] See *PLRE* vol. 2, Eusebius 19 and 28.
[133] Clauss, *Der magister*, 191.
[134] *PLRE* vol. 1, Palladius 12, Macedonius 3, Hadrianus 2, Hosius; vol. 2, Anthemius 1, Gaiso, Ioannes 12, Valerius 6.

the treasury of diplomatic gifts and subsidies,[135] and since both officials were ex-officio members of the imperial consistory, the *comes* would have had the opportunity to observe the *magister* dealing with some aspects of his work. Nevertheless, these remain somewhat tenuous grounds for seeing this financial post as a preparation for the responsibilities of the *magister*. In fact, for many of the individuals in question, the office of *magister* was only one more stepping-stone *en route* to a praetorian or city prefectship, so there need not have been any logical relationship between the offices of *comes* and *magister* beyond the simple one of individuals acquiring experience and useful connections in a range of positions with a view to attaining the most highly prized ones.[136] More significantly from our point of view, this pattern of progression is concentrated in the late fourth and early fifth century – in other words, prior to and at the beginning of the period when the *magister* can be seen becoming more closely concerned with foreign relations.[137] In short, therefore, the minimal amount of available data means that an investigation of the backgrounds of the *magistri* yields very little of substance one way or the other.

Another angle of approach which might shed light on this subject is the length of service of individuals in the office. A pattern of increasing numbers of years in office over the course of late antiquity might lend support to the idea that the value of specialisation in a particular role was coming to be recognised. A preliminary glance at the evidence suggests that there could be something in this idea: three men were *magister* for significantly longer periods than the rest, one of them – Helion (13 years) – in the fifth century, the other two – Celer (15), Peter the Patrician (26) – in the sixth century. However, the detailed evidence is not adequate to endorse this unequivocally. Just as nothing is known about the backgrounds of the majority of office-holders, so too the length of service of the majority is an unknown. The problems involved may be illustrated by the case of Valerius, known from two laws to have been *magister* on 29 January and 12 March 435 (*CTh* vi.28.8; vii.8.16). When did his period in office begin and end? The most recent known incumbent prior to him, John, is last attested in office on 22 February 433 (*CTh* vii.8.15, as amended by Seeck), while the next known incumbent after Valerius is Phlegetius, known only from one law dated to 17 April 441 (Theodosius II *Novel* xxi). Valerius could potentially have been in office for anything between 43 days and eight years. Cases such as his clearly have to be excluded from consideration.

---

[135] R. Delmaire, *Largesses sacrées et 'res privata'* (Rome, 1989), 539–46 (note especially *De Caer.* i.88, p. 397/12).

[136] Cf. *ibid.*, 114.

[137] It is also worth noting that the office of *comes sacrarum largitionum* declined in importance from the 430s onwards (*ibid.*, 707–8).

Table 1. Magistri officiorum *whose full period in office is known*

Name	Period as *magister*	No. of years
Anatolius 5	360–3	3
Leo 1	371–5	4
Rufinus 18	388–92	4
Olympius 2	408–9	1
Illus 1	477–81	4
Longinus 3	484–91	7
Tribonianus 1	533–5	2
Basilides	536–9	3
Petrus 6	539–65	26
Domentziolus 1	603–10	7

There are only eleven instances where the full period in office is known with reasonable certainty (Table 1).[138] There are a further twenty-two cases where the first and last known dates for an individual as *magister* may or may not represent the full length of time in office, *and* the known period in office is at least twelve months (Table 2). If the data in these two tables are combined, and then analysed by centuries, the average length of service during the fourth century is 2.3 years, rising to 4.1 years in the fifth century, and rising again to 9.5 years in the sixth. This last figure is obviously distorted by the inclusion of Peter the Patrician's unusual tenure in office of 26 years, but even if he is excluded, the revised average for the sixth century, 6.2 years, still represents an increase.

This finding is certainly consistent with the initial observation concerning the three longest-serving *magistri*, but it cannot be used to prove that the value of specialisation was increasingly recognised. There are too many other potential factors affecting length of service – the mortality of incumbents and emperors, the further ambitions of incumbents, the unpredictability of imperial favour – and the available body of data, representing not much more than one-third of known *magistri*, is not sufficiently comprehensive to minimise the impact of these other imponderables on the results. At best, the results do not disprove the specialisation hypothesis.

This brief enquiry into those who held the office of *magister officiorum* has failed to produce anything very conclusive. However, more definite results are forthcoming when attention is turned to a related question – experience as a criterion in the selection of imperial ambassadors. During earlier centuries, no

---

[138] This and the following table have been compiled from the fasti in *PLRE*, and the number after each name refers to the entry in the relevant volume. I am most grateful to John Martindale for providing me with the relevant information from *PLRE* vol. 3 in advance of its publication. It should be remembered that during the fourth and fifth centuries there were sometimes two or more *magistri* at the same time, depending on the number of emperors.

Table 2. Magistri officiorum *known to have served for at least twelve months*

Name	Known period as *magister*	No. of years
Pentadius 2	358–60	2
Florentius 3	359–61	2
Musonius 1	357–8	1
Ursacius 3	364–5	1
Remigius	367–71	4
Sophronius 3	369–74	5
Florus 1	380–1	1
Palladius 12	382–4	2
Caesarius 6	386–7	1
Theodotus 2	393–4	1
Marcellus 7	394–5	1
Hadrianus 2	397–9	2
Hosius	395–8	3
Helion 1	414–27	13
Ioannes 12	431–3	2
Nomus 1	443–6	3
Opilio 1	449 50	1
Vincomalus	451–2	1
Hilarianus 2	470–4	4
Eusebius 28	492–7	5
Celer 2	503–18	15
Hermogenes 1	529–33	4

corps of specialist diplomats existed,[139] and this situation did not change in any formal sense during the late Roman period or indeed throughout Byzantine history.[140] There was never a body of men whose sole or primary function was to act as imperial envoys – an unlikely development, anyway, so long as the idea of establishing permanent foreign legations was not contemplated.[141] Occasionally, one finds reference to individuals in late antiquity being chosen as envoys on account of their training and skill in speaking,[142] but throughout the period ambassadors continued to be chosen from a variety of backgrounds – civil

---

[139] Millar, 'Government and diplomacy', 367.

[140] D. Lee and J. Shepard, 'A double life: placing the *Peri presbeon*', BS 52 (1991), 15–39, at 37–8.

[141] For the absence of the necessary preconditions for such a development in antiquity, see Matthews, 'Hostages, philosophers, pilgrims', 35.

[142] Eustathius, philosopher and envoy to Persia in 358, 'a master of the art of persuasion' (Amm. Marc. xvii.5.15); Sporacius, rhetor and envoy to Persia in 384 (John Lydus *De mag.* iii.53); Epigenes, proposed as an envoy to Attila because he had 'a great reputation for wisdom' (Priscus fr. 2/19); Peter the Patrician, chosen for his first mission to the Goths in 534 because he was a rhetor 'amply endowed by nature with powers of persuasion' (Proc. *Wars* v.3.30); Constantianus and Sergius, envoys to Persia twice on account of being rhetors and 'particularly clever' (Proc. *Wars* ii.24.3; 28.2); Zacharias of Sura, physician-sophist who was four times an envoy to the Persians (R. C. Blockley, 'Doctors as diplomats in the sixth century AD', *Florilegium* 2 (1980), 89–100, at 93–4), and who on one occasion is one of a group of envoys described as being 'good at resolving disagreements' (Men. fr. 20,1/17–18).

officials of both high and more modest status, high-ranking military officers and members of the imperial bodyguard, clergy and physicians.[143] It is, nevertheless, possible to discern a growing recognition of the value of experience in one important respect − the way in which individuals were increasingly employed as envoys on more than one occasion, particularly where they were sent again to the same destination. The number of such individuals rises significantly over the course of the late Roman period.

From the fourth century I have been able to find only one case, the *magister equitum* ('Master of the Cavalry') Victor who undertook two missions to the Goths for Valens in the 360s, and an embassy to Persia in 377.[144] The number of examples increases during the fifth century. From Constantinople, there is bishop Marutha of Martyropolis, twice an imperial envoy to Persia during the early years of Theodosius II's reign (Soc. *HE* vii.8); Anatolius, three times an envoy to Attila; Phylarchus, sent in 462/3 to Marcellinus, then the effective ruler of Dalmatia, and in 467 to the Vandal king Geiseric; and possibly Pelagius, who may have been sent to Theoderic Strabo twice in the 470s; in the west, there is Censorius, twice envoy to the Suebi in the 430s, and Trygetius, who participated in embassies to the Vandals and the Huns.[145] In the sixth century, the number increases again, and in a rather striking manner:[146] multiple missions to Persia were undertaken by Rufinus (seven embassies), Hermogenes (three), Zacharias of Sura (four), Constantianus and Sergius (two together);[147] Peter the Patrician was an ambassador three times to both the Goths and the Persians;[148] Abraham conducted two embassies to Arab tribes for Justin I and Justinian (Nonnosus, in Photius *Bibl.* cod. 3); Valentinus undertook two missions to the Turks, and may also have gone once to the Avars (Men. frs. 19/13–14; 5,2/6); Elpidius served as envoy to the Avars in 583 and 584 (Th. Sim. i.4.6; 6.4); Strategius was an envoy to Persia in 531 (Mal. p. 467) and to the Arab Mundhir in 539 (Proc. *Wars* ii.1.9); Julian was sent to the Himyarites and Axumites early in Justinian's reign, and to the Persians in 540 (Proc. *Wars* i.20.9; ii.7.15); and George, praetorian prefect in the 590s, may have conducted several embassies to Persia during that decade.[149]

The advantages of sending an individual as envoy to the same destination again (assuming of course that he has not proved incompetent on the first occasion) involved more than just the obvious ones of familiarity with

---

[143] Lee and Shepard, 'Placing the *Peri presbeon*', 37.

[144] *PLRE* vol. 1, Victor 4.

[145] *Ibid.*, vol. 2, Anatolius 10; Phylarchus; Pelagius 2 with Telogius; Censorius; Trygetius 1.

[146] I significantly underestimated their number in *BS* 52 (1991), 37 n. 122.

[147] *PLRE*, vol. 2, Rufinus 13; vol. 3, Hermogenes 1; Zacharias: Blockley, 'Doctors as diplomats'; Constantianus and Sergius: Proc. *Wars* ii.24.3, 28.2.

[148] *PLRE* vol. 3, Petrus 6.

[149] Whitby, *Maurice*, 234–5.

conditions and people, and greater preparedness for what he might encounter. There was also the opportunity to develop further and exploit contacts at the relevant court, as illustrated by the example of Rufinus and his dealings with Khusro in 532:

> Since this Rufinus was well-known there [viz. the court in Ctesiphon], as one who had been sent many times to Kavad and was his friend, and had bestowed many gifts on the leading men of his kingdom, and the queen, Khusro's mother, was well-disposed towards him, because he advised Kavad to make her son king . . . , she earnestly pressed Khusro her son, and . . . he made peace. (Zach. *HE* ix.7, vol.2, p. 100/2–11).

The case of Rufinus also reveals a further variation on the theme of expertise and specialisation in the sixth century – that of successive generations of a particular family engaging in diplomatic service. Rufinus' father Silvanus is reported to have known Kavad's father Peroz (Proc. *Wars* i.11.24), presumably as a result of serving as an envoy, while Rufinus' son John was sent as an envoy to Khusro in 540 (ii.7.15). Similarly, three generations of the family of Nonnosus undertook embassies to Arabia and its environs,[150] while Peter the Patrician's son Theodore was both *magister officiorum* and an envoy to Persia at different stages of his life (Men. fr. 20,1/19-20). One might also note in passing the analogous phenomenon of brothers as envoys: Julian, mentioned above as an envoy to Himyarites, Axumites and Persians, had a brother Summus who undertook an embassy to the Arabs in 539 (Proc. *Wars* ii.1.10), while Athanasius, whose brother Alexander had been an envoy to the Goths in 533 (and possibly also to the Persians in 532), was himself an envoy to the Goths in 536 (Proc. *Wars* i.22.1; v.3.13, 6.22). One's instinctive reaction is perhaps to label this phenomenon as a case of pride in a family tradition, or, less charitably, as nepotism, but behind it there clearly lies much good sense. The son of a former envoy who had cultivated a favourable reputation at a foreign court (as Rufinus clearly had at Ctesiphon) could very reasonably hope to capitalise on goodwill towards the family name there, and so begin his mission with a significant advantage compared to someone who arrived as an unknown.

This general trend towards increasing use of individuals with previous experience as envoys coincides with the pattern noted earlier of the *magister officiorum* becoming more closely involved in foreign relations during the fifth and sixth centuries. Formal organisational structures may not have changed, but adaptation was undoubtedly taking place within existing frameworks, reflecting an increasing recognition of the need for greater attention to the conduct of foreign relations and of the value of some degree of specialisation in

---

[150] I. Kawar (Shahid), 'Byzantium and Kinda', *BZ* 53 (1960), 57–73.

personnel.[151] And these trends regarding personnel are in turn consistent with the pattern observed concerning the preservation and use of written records relating to diplomatic affairs. Taken together, these developments are indicative of late Roman government gradually adopting a more organised approach to the empire's relations with neighbouring peoples and endeavouring to make better use of available resources and skills. This was largely a response to the force of changing circumstances, but the change is no less significant for that.

---

[151] Although interpreters must always have been available for use in diplomacy in earlier centuries, the appearance by the early fifth century of specially designated bodies of interpreters in the *Notitia Dignitatum* (*Or.* xi.52, *Occ.* ix.35) is surely a further indication of the government taking a more systematic attitude towards the conduct of foreign relations.

2

AT THE INTERFACE: THE
FRONTIER REGIONS

NO treatment of late Roman foreign relations would be complete without some consideration of the frontier regions within which those relations were played out. In the case of this study, however, an investigation of the relevant frontier regions is especially vital because their character exercised an important influence on the availability of information. The Roman empire as a whole encompassed considerable diversity, both environmentally and culturally, and this is particularly apparent in the contrasts between the frontier region shared with Persia in the east, and that (or rather those) along the northern bounds of the empire. These differences form the focus of this chapter; their full significance will become apparent at a later stage (see Chapter 5).

THE EAST

The formal political boundary between the Roman and Persian empires was subject to some variation during the course of late antiquity, but apart from a brief period in the early seventh century, the southern half of its course always lay within the open region of northern Mesopotamia.[1] The northern half of the boundary proceeded across the mountainous territory which lay between the Taurus range and the Black Sea, though the existence of the kingdom of Armenia during parts of the first century and a half of Roman–Persian relations meant that the two empires did not always have a common boundary in this area.[2] But even when a common boundary did exist here, the difficult nature of the terrain meant that the geographical focus of relations between the two

---

[1] 'Mesopotamia' refers in this expression not to the Roman province of Mesopotamia, but to the broad geographical region defined by the middle Euphrates and Tigris rivers.

[2] For the period until the early fourth century, see M.-L. Chaumont, *Recherches sur l'histoire d'Arménie de l'avènement des Sassanides à la conversion du royaume* (Paris, 1969); for the final division of Armenia in the late fourth century, see R. C. Blockley, 'The division of Armenia between the Romans and the Persians', *Historia* 36 (1987), 222–34.

empires, whether in war or peace, was usually in the southern half, across the north Mesopotamian plain, and so it will be on this latter region that the following remarks will concentrate. Nevertheless, the fundamental point which emerges from this discussion – that the political boundary never corresponded to any obvious cultural division – clearly applies with equal force to the situation in Armenia, where the majority of the inhabitants possessed a common language (Armenian) and (from the fourth century) a common religion (Christianity) irrespective of whether a particular district fell under Roman or Persian rule.[3]

The north Mesopotamian plain was part of a larger region characterised by greater cultural diversity than the Armenian highlands, but it was a diversity present on both sides of the boundary. This larger region, the so-called Fertile Crescent, was unified most obviously by the widespread use of dialects of the Semitic language Aramaic, one of which – Syriac – functioned as the *lingua franca* in this part of the world during late antiquity.[4] Aramaic had become the dominant language of the region during the first millennium BC, thanks in no small part to its adoption by the Achaemenid Persians as the administrative language for this part of their empire. The conquests of Alexander had resulted in the introduction of Greek language and culture into the region, though it tended to be an urban phenomenon[5] and its influence in the eastern half of the Crescent was waning by the advent of the Sasanians.[6] Greek was one of the languages used in the trilingual triumphal inscription of Shapur I in the mid-third century, but there is nothing comparable to this from subsequent

---

[3] For the most northerly reaches of the boundary, in the Caucasus, see Isaac, *Limits of Empire*, 229–35.

[4] For a succinct survey of the Aramaic dialects, see K. Beyer, *The Aramaic Language: its Distribution and Subdivisions*, tr. J. F. Healey (Göttingen, 1986). For the linguistic situation in the east as a whole, see R. Schmitt, 'Die Ostgrenze von Armenien über Mesopotamia, Syrien bis Arabien' in G. Neumann and J. Untermann (eds.), *Die Sprachen im römischen Reich der Kaiserzeit* (Cologne, 1980), 188–214. For Syriac as a *lingua franca*, see J. B. Segal, 'The Jews of northern Mesopotamia before the rise of Islam' in J. M. Grintz and J. Liver (eds.), *Studies in the Bible presented to M. H. Segal* (Jerusalem, 1964), 32–63, at 33; P. Brown, 'The diffusion of Manichaeism in the Roman empire', *JRS* 59 (1969), 92–103, at 96–7; F. Millar, 'Paul of Samosata, Zenobia and Aurelian: the church, local culture and political allegiance in third-century Syria', *JRS* 61 (1971), 1–17, at 1–8.

[5] For a recent assessment which emphasises the limited impact of Hellenisation, see F. Millar, 'The problem of Hellenistic Syria' in A. Kuhrt and S. Sherwin-White (eds.), *Hellenism in the East* (London, 1987), 110–33. It is of interest that the dossier of Greek and Syriac texts from third century Mesopotamia recently brought to light (D. Feissel and J. Gascou, 'Documents d'archives romains inédits du Moyen Euphrate (IIIe siècle après J.-C.)', *CRAI* (1989), 535–61) includes two private letters in Greek between individuals whose names clearly are neither Greek nor Roman (Item 16: 'Ourodes to his son Nisraios'; Item 17: 'Roumas to Roumas' – which might be ambiguous, were it not that one of them has a daughter Bithilaa and a brother Sadallathos).

[6] This is not to deny the subsequent interest of individual Sasanian monarchs such as Khusro I in Greek philosophy and medicine.

centuries. There are a number of references from the sixth century to Persian interpreters competent in Greek,[7] though these are likely to have been drawn, not from indigenous inhabitants of Persia, but from Roman prisoners resettled there – of whom there were large numbers in the third, fourth and sixth centuries,[8] and whom one can readily imagine subsequently acquiring some fluency in Persian.

The ubiquity of Aramaic dialects in the region ought not, however, to be equated with ethnic homogeneity.[9] In addition to the autochthonous Aramaean population, Aramaic dialects were used by the Jewish communities which were found all the way along the Fertile Crescent from Palestine to Babylonia,[10] and by those Arabs who forsook nomadic pastoralism in the Syrian desert for a sedentary form of life, creating the kingdoms of Palmyra, Osrhoene, Hatra and the Nabataeans.[11] Nor does consideration of linguistic and ethnic patterns exhaust the cultural dimensions of the picture; there is also the religious aspect. The extensive Jewish presence within both empires has just been noted, and mention might also be made of the existence of Zoroastrian communities in the eastern parts of the Roman empire, though their size and significance by late antiquity should not be exaggerated.[12] On the other hand, the presence on both sides of the boundary of substantial Christian communities is a

---

[7] Paulus, whom Procopius says was of Roman origin (*Wars* ii.6.22-3); Braducias (*Wars* ii.28.41); an interpreter used by the Persian commander at Nisibis in the 530s (Elias *Life of John*, p. 71/23); unnamed official interpreters involved in the peace settlement of 561/2 (Men. fr. 6,1/415-16), and from whom John of Ephesus derived information about events in 576 (*HE* vi.9, p. 301/7; tr. p. 228/13). For inhabitants of the Roman empire with a knowledge of Persian, note the imperial interpreters available in Constantinople for diplomatic dealings with Persia (*De Caer.* i.89, p. 404/16,18), of whom Sergius (Agath. iv.30.2-4) was presumably one.

[8] For deportations in the third and fourth centuries, see S. N. C. Lieu, 'Captives, refugees and exiles: a study of cross-frontier civilian movements and contacts between Rome and Persia from Valerian to Jovian' in Freeman and Kennedy, *Defence*, 475-505; for the sixth and seventh centuries, see Morony, *Iraq*, 266-7. A number of fifth-century synods of the church in Persia attest the practice of several towns having both a Greek-speaking and a Syriac-speaking bishop, but the Greek-speakers probably ministered to communities comprising Roman captives (S. Brock, 'Christians in the Sasanian empire', *Studies in Church History* 18 (1982), 1-19, at 3).

[9] For judicious reflections on the complexities of this situation, see F. Millar, 'Empire, community and culture in the Roman Near East: Greeks, Syrians, Jews and Arabs', *Journal of Jewish Studies* 38 (1987), 143-64.

[10] For the Jewish communities of Babylonia and the eastern half of the Fertile Crescent, see J. Neusner, *A History of the Jews in Babylonia* (Leiden, 1965-70) and Oppenheimer, *Babylonia Judaica*; for Jewish communities further west along the Crescent, see Segal, 'The Jews of northern Mesopotamia'.

[11] For the Nabataeans, see G. W. Bowersock, *Roman Arabia* (Cambridge, Mass., 1983) Chapters 2-5; for the remainder, see J. B. Segal, *Edessa, 'The Blessed City'* (Oxford, 1970), H. J. W. Drijvers, 'Hatra, Palmyra und Edessa', *ANRW* ii.8 (1977), 799-906; J. Matthews, 'The tax law of Palmyra', *JRS* 74 (1984), 157-80.

[12] See M. Boyce and F. Grenet, *A History of Zoroastrianism* vol. 3, *Zoroastrianism under Macedonian and Roman Rule* (Leiden, 1991).

feature whose importance can hardly be overemphasised (about which more below).[13]

These, then, were the most important elements in the complex cultural mosaic on which the Roman and Persian governmental presences were imposed. Even before the advent of the Sasanian dynasty, the growing importance of the region in Roman thinking is apparent in the significant redistribution of Roman forces towards the east by the end of the second century AD.[14] The political configuration of the region also underwent major changes before the demise of the Parthians. The Nabataean kingdom became the province of Arabia during the reign of Trajan, while Osrhoene gradually lost its independence to the Romans from the 160s onwards until the last vestiges of that kingdom disappeared in the early third century. Hatra succumbed to the first Sasanian monarch, Ardashir, leaving Palmyra to play a crucial but short-lived role during the first half-century of Roman–Persian relations. Far from signalling the demise of Arab influence, however, the dissolution of Osrhoene and Palmyra created the opportunity for other Arabs to play what proved in many ways an even more important role during late antiquity. During the late third century, a new confederation of tribes, the Tanukh, arrived from the Arabian peninsula in the northern reaches of the Syrian desert. The Persian kings established enduring ties with one element of this confederation, the family of the Lakhmids who, from their base at Hira on the desert fringes near Ctesiphon, organised and co-ordinated various Arab tribes in the service of Persia against the Roman empire.[15] The ability of Arabs to move with ease and speed through the environmentally hostile desert regions to the south of northern Mesopotamia made them a potent weapon in the warfare of this period, albeit one best suited to destructive raiding, and the only feasible strategy by which the Romans could effectively counteract this threat was to build up their own Arab clientele. As a result the Romans developed links during the fourth century with other groups in the Tanukh confederation,

[13] There is no need to document Christianity as a feature of the Roman east, though it is worth noting the need for caution concerning the extent of Christianisation: W. Liebeschuetz, 'Problems arising from the conversion of Syria', *Studies in Church History* 16 (1979), 17–24; H. Drijvers, 'The persistence of pagan cults and practices in Christian Syria' in N. Garsoïan, T. Mathews and R. Thomson (eds.), *East of Byzantium: Syria and Armenia in the Formative Period* (Washington D.C., 1982), 35–43; A. D. Lee, 'Close-kin marriage in late antique Mesopotamia', *GRBS* 29 (1988), 403–13. For the growth of Christianity in the Persian empire (for which the deportations from the Roman empire in the third century were important, but by no means solely responsible), see Brock, 'Christians in the Sasanian empire', and M.-L. Chaumont, *La Christianisation de l'empire iranien des origines aux grandes persécutions du IVe siècle* (Louvain, 1988).

[14] Millar, 'Empire, community and culture', 146–7.

[15] C. E. Bosworth, 'Iran and the Arabs before Islam', *CHI* vol. 3, 593–612.

though the latter were subsequently displaced from this role by the Salih (fifth century) and then the Ghassanids (sixth century).[16]

Arab allies thus came to constitute a vital complement to the imperial army, which was the most obvious manifestation of the Roman presence in northern Mesopotamia. Detailed evidence for the distribution of Roman troops in the region during late antiquity comes from the relevant chapters of the *Notitia Dignitatum*, which essentially presents the position in the east in the early fifth century. On the north Mesopotamian plain itself, legions were stationed at Sura (*Or.* xxxiii.28) and Circesium (xxxv.24) on the Euphrates, at Constantina, and at Cepha on the Tigris (xxxvi.29–30); to the south-west, along the fringes of the Syrian desert, stretched the chain of fortified positions linked by the *strata Diocletiana*,[17] while to the north, legions were based to the west of the upper Euphrates at Melitene and Satala, and at Trabzon on the Black Sea (xxxviii.13–15); Edessa possessed an arms factory (xi.23). Smaller units were present in many other centres in the region, though from the frequency with which the term *indigenae* features in the names of these units it would seem that many of them had been recruited locally.[18] Supporting all these units of *limitanei*[19] was a regional field army (*ND Or.* vii), based around Antioch.[20] This distribution of troops across the landscape had, of course, varied during the preceding century: for example, a regional field army for the east was a development of the mid-fourth century; *legio II Parthica* at Cepha had probably been stationed at Bezabde prior to its loss to the Persians in 360 (Amm. Marc. xx.7.1);[21] Amida had had a legion in 359 (Amm. Marc. xviii.9.3); and it seems likely that *I Parthica Nisibena*, at Constantina in the *Notitia*, had been at Nisibis prior to the surrender of that city to the Persians in 363.[22] Likewise, changes are evident by the sixth century, most obviously in the establishment of fortresses very close to the border at Dara and Armenian Theodosiopolis, the transfer of the major commands to cities nearer the frontier, multiplication of the number

---

16 For detailed treatment of Roman relations with its Arab allies during late antiquity, see the sequence of volumes by I. Shahid, *Byzantium and the Arabs in the Fourth Century* (Washington D.C., 1984), *Byzantium and the Arabs in the Fifth Century* (1989), and *Byzantium and the Arabs in the Sixth Century* (forthcoming), though note also the criticisms of certain important details in the first volume by G. W. Bowersock in *Classical Review* 36 (1986), 111–17. See also M. Sartre, *Trois études sur l'Arabie romaine et byzantine* (Brussels, 1982) and J. S. Trimingham, *Christianity among the Arabs in pre-Islamic Times* (London, 1979).

17 For its role in the protection of travellers against raids by nomadic Arabs, see Isaac, *Limits of Empire*, Chapter 4, especially 213ff.

18 Cf. Jones, *Later Roman Empire*, 57.

19 On the meaning of this term, see B. Isaac, 'The meaning of the terms *limes* and *limitanei*', *JRS* 78 (1988), 125–47.

20 J. C. Mann, '*Duces* and *comites* in the fourth century' in D. E. Johnston (ed.), *The Saxon Shore* (CBA Research Report 18, 1977), 11–15, at 13.

21 Isaac, *Limits of Empire*, 168 n. 25, expresses caution on this point.

22 C. S. Lightfoot, 'Facts and fiction – the third siege of Nisibis (AD 350)', *Historia* 37 (1988), 108–9.

of *duces*, and the creation by Justinian of a new *magister* with responsibility for Armenia.[23]

Whatever rearrangements there were over the centuries, however, it is clear that the defence of northern Mesopotamia in late antiquity never relied on a continuous line of fortifications along the border, such as was proposed by Antoine Poidebard during the interwar years.[24] 'Neither Mesopotamia nor Osrhoene show the classic structure of the frontier supported by a paved road, itself served by routes coming from the interior. This region retained the character of a zone of transit . . . Its defence [was] based not on continuity of lines, but on concentration of resources in certain well-situated cities.'[25] Similarly, although the Persians are known to have constructed continuous lines of fortifications at other points on the extremities of their empire,[26] there is nothing to suggest that they erected such structures in northern Mesopotamia.[27] On neither side of the boundary in northern Mesopotamia, therefore, did there exist a continuous line of frontier installations such as was in evidence further south along the *strata Diocletiana* where Arab raiders posed a qualitatively different threat to inhabitants and travellers.

This in turn has important implications for the degree to which the Roman and Persian authorities were able to monitor and control the movements of individuals between the two empires. There is no doubt that late Roman emperors were concerned to regulate contact between Romans and non-Romans across certain frontiers,[28] and there are some incidents from the north Mesopotamian context which might suggest difficulties in crossing between the two empires at will. A hermit from Nisibis, Malchus, told Jerome that, earlier

---

[23] For these changes, see W. Liebeschuetz, 'The defences of Syria in the sixth century' in *Studien zu den Militärgrenzen Roms II* (Cologne, 1977), 487–99; M. Whitby, 'Procopius and the development of Roman defences in upper Mesopotamia' in Freeman and Kennedy, *Defence*, 717–35; Jones, *Later Roman Empire*, 655–6.

[24] A. Poidebard, *La Trace de Rome dans le désert de Syrie* (Paris, 1934). For criticism of Poidebard's failure to use sufficiently rigorous criteria in dating the structures which his aerial surveys revealed, see (among others) L. Dillemann, *Haute Mésopotamie orientale et les pays adjacents* (Paris, 1969), 198–201, 216; D. Oates, *Studies in the Ancient History of Northern Iraq* (London, 1968), 67 n. 1.

[25] E. Frézouls, 'Les fluctuations de la frontière orientale de l'empire romain' in T. Fahd (ed.), *La Géographie administrative et politique d'Alexandre à Mahomet* (TCRPGA 6, 1979), 177–225, at 209. Cf. Dillemann, *Haute Mésopotamie*, 212, 224, who speaks of a network (*un réseau*) of fortified positions.

[26] Frye, 'The Sasanian system of walls', 7–15; note the reservations expressed by P. Gignoux (L'organisation administrative', 14 n. 58) concerning Frye's interpretation of a critical word in one of the relevant texts.

[27] There were of course individual fortified towns and forts with garrisons in the vicinity of the border, such as Nisibis (after 363), Sisauron (Proc. *Wars* ii.19.2–3) and Thebothon (Th. Sim. iii.10.5).

[28] See, e.g., Anastasius' constitution of 501, concerning the frontier in the south of Cyrenaica (*Supplementum Epigraphicum Graecum* ix.356, cited by Liebeschuetz, 'Defences of Syria', 490 n. 38).

in the fourth century, 'I was unable to go to the east on account of Persia's proximity and the Roman soldiers on guard, so I turned my feet towards the west' (Jerome *Life of Malchus* 3, *PL* xxiii.54). Similarly, the pilgrim Egeria in the 380s was told that she could not travel further east from Carrhae to visit Ur of the Chaldees where Abraham had first lived: 'that place...is ten staging-posts (*mansiones*) from here, inside Persia . . . , but there is now no access to it for Romans, for it is entirely in Persian hands' (*Itinerarium Egeriae* xx.12, CCSL clxxv.64). Finally, John of Ephesus reports that some time during the 530s 'the borders of Persia . . . were closed by war' (*Lives* 24, *PO* xviii.522).[29] In this last instance the fact that the closure of the frontier is attributed to a state of war implies that during peacetime the frontier was usually 'open'. Indeed one commentator has remarked that John's observation 'can scarcely mean more than that the border garrisons were put on the alert, and would detect the passage of large companies of men. It was never impossible or even difficult for the individual to cross the frontier.'[30] Echoing this remark, another commentator has stressed the uniqueness of Malchus' statement, and noted that 'what we call the "Eastern frontier" of the Roman empire . . . dictated the positioning of some soldiers and customs officials, but hardly affected the attitudes or the movements of the people on either side'.[31] As for the explanation given to Egeria, it runs counter to the very substantial body of evidence, to be discussed shortly, which indicates the free movement of Christians between the two empires during the fourth century and subsequently. As a pilgrim from the distant west, she might easily have gained a misleading impression of the difficulties of the journey, or even been deliberately given false information by a reluctant guide. In order to gain a more accurate idea of the volume of cross-frontier traffic, the following pages will examine in a systematic manner the various categories of individuals who traversed the border and their reasons for doing so.[32]

29 If this refers to conflict which actually broke out, as opposed to fear of war, then it must refer to the fighting in 530 and 531.

30 J. B. Segal, 'Mesopotamian communities from Julian to the rise of Islam', *Proceedings of the British Academy* 41 (1955),109–39, at 127.

31 Millar, 'Paul of Samosata', 1. I have not included here the encounter of the ascetic Alexander Acoemitis with a Roman frontier garrison and *castella* (*Life of Alexander* 33, *PO* vi.683), since this incident occurred in relation to the installations of the *strata Diocletiana* rather than the north Mesopotamian plain (cf. *PO* vi.648: 'dans la région du *limes* qui s'étend entre l'Euphrate et Palmyre').

32 For other discussions of this subject, see Segal, 'Mesopotamian communities'; Garsoïan, 'Byzantium and the Sasanians'; Lieu, 'Captives, refugees and exiles', especially 491–5. It has been claimed on the basis of *CTh* vii.16.2 (410) that Roman law prohibited cross-frontier interchange with foreign peoples and that Roman soldiers had the task of enforcing this prohibition (K. Güterbock, *Byzanz und Persien* (Berlin, 1906), 71; R. Andreotti, 'Su alcuni problemi del rapporto fra politica di sicurezza e controllo del commercio nell'impero romano', *RIDA* 16 (1969), 215–57, at 247 and n. 51; E. Winter, 'Handel und Wirtschaft in sasanidisch-(ost-)

The presence within both empires of religious communities, notably Christians and Jews, was responsible for generating a great deal of interaction. For Christians there was a host of motivations. One of the most potent lures for Persian Christians was the existence in Roman territory of sites of great significance in the church's history. The most obvious attractions were Jerusalem and places in Palestine associated with the life of Christ, but Egypt also constituted an important goal, 'a second Holy Land',[33] on account of both its Old Testament significance and its role as the seed-bed of monasticism. Although it is now generally accepted that monastic practice in fourth-century Persia had indigenous origins,[34] it is also accepted that during the first half of the fourth century, a Persian bishop, Miles, travelled first to Jerusalem, then to Alexandria, from where he visited the surrounding monasteries.[35] The sixth century undoubtedly saw cross-fertilisation from Egypt to Persia, most notably in the person of Abraham of Kaskar, who journeyed from Persia to Egypt, where he lived for a period in the monastic communities of the Skete valley, before retracing his steps northwards via Sinai and Jerusalem.[36] During the same century, a number of other individuals who subsequently became prominent in the Persian church made similar journeys – Abraham of Nethpar (*Chr. Seert* ii.31, *PO* xiii.172), Rabban Haia (ii.49, *PO* xiii.453) and Mar Makika (Jesusdenah *Le Livre de la chasteté* 95). John of Ephesus also tells of a young woman called Susan who lived in Persian Arzanene in the first half of the sixth century:[37]

> This virtuous girl decided that she should go and worship in the holy places where the salvation of our lives took place, and she implored her parents. But they laughed at her . . . Then the child . . . placed her soul in the hands of God and ran away. After crossing three or four miles, she chanced upon a caravan of women

römischen Verträgen und Abkommen', *MBAH* 6/2 (1987), 46–74, at 62 and n. 78), but the context of this law has been overlooked, viz. Alaric's proclamation of the usurper Attalus in Italy in 410. The law, issued in Constantinople, aimed to prevent the infiltration of agents favourable to Alaric and Attalus from the western half of the empire into the eastern (cf. W. E. Kaegi, *Byzantium and the Decline of Rome* (Princeton, 1968), 18), and as such was a temporary measure concerned with internal security rather than the external boundaries of the empire. Laws which were no longer valid were still incorporated in the Theodosian Code (*CTh* i.1.5), and this one is not repeated in Justinian's Code, in contrast to the law immediately following on contraband (*CTh* vii.16.3 = *CJ* xii.44.1).

[33] D. Gorce, *Les Voyages, l'hospitalité et le port des lettres dans le monde chrétien des IVe à Ve siècles* (Paris, 1925), 11–12.

[34] J. Labourt, *Le Christianisme dans l'empire perse sous la dynastie sassanide (224–632)* (Paris, 1904), 302–15; A. Vööbus, *History of Asceticism in the Syrian Orient* vol. 1 (Louvain, 1958), 138–46; J. M. Fiey, *Jalons pour une histoire de l'église en Iraq* (Louvain, 1970), 100–12.

[35] J.M. Fiey, 'L'Elam la première des métropoles ecclésiastiques syriennes orientales', *Parole de l'Orient* 1 (1970), 141–2.

[36] Labourt, *Le Christianisme*, 316–17.

[37] *Lives* 27, *PO* xviii.543–4; tr. S. P. Brock and S. A. Harvey in *Holy Women of the Syrian Orient* (Berkeley and Los Angeles, 1987), 134–5.

and men travelling toward Jerusalem . . . Thus she reached Jerusalem joyously. But when she had worshipped there, her companions wished to return and begged her to go back with them to her own country . . . So she parted from them . . . and searched around to find a convent where she could live.

The interest of this episode lies not so much in the adventures of Susan herself as in the incidental reference to the large party of Persian pilgrims whom she accompanied and who then returned home. Although most of these examples are from the sixth century, they suggest that Jerome's remark in the late fourth century, that Jerusalem was thronged with pilgrims from Persia (among other more distant places), may not have been the case of extravagant language suggested by one commentator.[38]

Famous ascetics also attracted pilgrims. Theodoret comments on the great numbers, including Persians, who came to observe Simeon the Stylite in Syria during the first half of the fifth century (HR xxiv.11,13,20). At a more localised level, news of the activities of a holy man in the Roman frontier city of Martyropolis in the early sixth century reached inhabitants of the neighbouring Persian territory, who then brought friends in need of healing (John Eph. Lives 1, PO xvii.11–12). The shrines of Edessa, which boasted an impressive array of saintly relics, were 'the goal of pilgrims from Mesopotamia, from Persia and Syria and Asia Minor, even from the Far East and Europe'.[39] In the early sixth century, Procopius of Gaza commented on the presence of Indians and Persians, among other foreigners, at Hierapolis (Panegyric on Anastasius 18, PG lxxxvii.2817). Although it is possible that this is a reference to merchants,[40] there is no explicit allusion to commercial activity in the text. These individuals are more likely to have been pilgrims: Procopius precedes his comment with a remark about the city's reputation for piety, and though paganism had strong roots in Hierapolis, the city had also become sufficiently associated with an array of saints by the sixth century for it to have been a justifiable object of pilgrimage.[41]

---

[38] Ep. 107.2.3, with E. D. Hunt, Holy Land Pilgrimage in the Later Roman Empire AD 312–460 (Oxford, 1982), 54.

[39] Segal, Edessa, 173.

[40] Suggested by J. H. W. G. Liebeschuetz, Antioch. City and Imperial Administration in the Later Roman Empire (Oxford, 1972), 77.

[41] G. Goossens, Hierapolis de Syrie (Louvain, 1943), 175. This is perhaps an appropriate context in which to mention the interesting Middle Persian inscription found on a sarcophagus at Constantinople, commemorating a Persian Christian who had passed a year in the Roman capital where he unexpectedly died; it has been suggested that he may have been a pilgrim or perhaps a merchant: see P. Gignoux and D. Feissel, 'Encore un mot sur l'inscription pehlevie de Constantinople', StIr 15 (1986), 119–22, with full citation of previous discussions. The traditional dating of the inscription to the early fifth century has, however, recently been challenged by F. de Blois, 'The middle Persian inscription from Constantinople: Sasanian or post-Sasanian?', StIr 19 (1990), 209–18, who argues for a provenance in the ninth or tenth century.

Another powerful attraction which drew Persian Christians to the Roman empire was the desire for learning. When the peace of 363 required the population of Nisibis to vacate the city and move to Roman territory, many of the former inhabitants settled in Edessa and this city became the location of the celebrated School of the Persians. The quality of the teaching there and the incidence of persecution in Persia during the fourth and fifth centuries induced many Persian Christians to go and study in Edessa.[42] The drain was such that at the end of the fourth century a school was established near Anbar so that students 'would have no need to go to Edessa' (Chr. Seert i.60, PO v.308, tr. Scher). But the flow westwards continued: 'after the conclusion of peace between Yazdgerd and Theodosius [in 441], some Persians went to Edessa with the aim of acquiring knowledge' (Chr. Seert ii.3, PO vii.104, tr. Scher).

In the later fifth century, however, the growth of Nestorian influence in the Edessan school brought it into increasing conflict with Chalcedonian orthodoxy and in 489 the emperor Zeno finally closed the school. The scholars moved back to Nisibis, where the school continued to function effectively. Statutes governing the conduct of students were laid down in 496, and included the following provision: 'The fourth canon: Those brothers who are in the school are not allowed to go over to the country of the Romans without precept and order of the brothers and that of the rabbaita of the school, neither for the cause of instruction nor because of a pretence of prayer, nor in order to buy or sell.'[43] The canon proceeds to elaborate at length on the consequences for those who disregarded this general principle. It seems unlikely that this regulation should have been laid down, and in far greater detail than any of the other canons, if frontier controls had been such as to make crossing difficult. The inclusion of this regulation suggests the contrary, and the fact that the canon proceeds to make concessions (albeit of a limited nature) in the punishment of those who disregarded it further implies that the directors of the school regarded it as unrealistic to expect students to restrain their Wanderlust completely.[44]

Although the re-establishment of the school at Nisibis must have significantly reduced the flow of would-be students into Roman territory, the desire for learning still drew people across the frontier throughout the sixth century. The

---

[42] E.R. Hayes, L'Ecole d'Edesse (Paris, 1930), 144ff.

[43] The Statutes of the School of Nisibis, ed. and tr. A. Vööbus (Stockholm, 1961), 75–6. As noted by Vööbus in his commentary (n. 12), these restrictions were inspired by the fear that the presence of students in Roman territory might expose them to doctrines which Nestorian Christianity regarded as heterodox.

[44] Cf. the reference to a certain Izdegherd, son of the Persian governor of Arzanene, 'who, as a neighbour, was familiar with the district of Attakhaye [around Roman Amida]' (Zach. HE ix.5, p. 96/17–18). Izdegherd's knowledge of the region around Amida means he must have crossed into Roman territory with some frequency; and since his knowledge was the result of being 'a neighbour', others who lived in similar proximity may be presumed to have possessed comparable knowledge – which would imply that Izdegherd was not alone in having crossed the border with some regularity.

most notable example was Mar Aba who later became head (*catholicos*) of the church in Persia (540–52). After conversion from Zoroastrianism and a period of study in Nisibis, he travelled in the Roman empire for a number of years, learning Greek, and visiting Egypt, Greece and Constantinople.[45] Two other *catholicoi* of the sixth century – Elisha (521–36) and Joseph (552–67) – had also studied in the Roman empire, both to become physicians (*Chr. Seert* ii.25 and 32, *PO* vii.148, 176). Medical schools were certainly available within the Persian empire by the sixth century – the school at Gundeshapur near Ctesiphon had a good reputation in the field[46] – but it seems that Roman medical education was still regarded as superior; Khusro I certainly showed a preference for physicians trained in the Roman empire.[47]

Some individuals were motivated to move from one empire to the other by the desire not to learn but to teach. The most notable case of this emanating from Persia was the spread of Manichaeism in the third and fourth centuries,[48] while in the other direction there was the assiduous work of Monophysite missionaries. The Monophysite bishop Simeon made many visits from Roman territory to Hira and Ctesiphon in Persia at the end of the fifth century (John Eph. *Lives* 10, *PO* xvii.140ff.), while in the early sixth century John of Tella and James Baradeus were active in consecrating Monophysite bishops throughout the east, including candidates who travelled from Persian territory (John Eph. *Lives* 24, *PO* xviii.519; 'Life of James', *PO* xix.238ff.). Nor can the reality of these contacts be doubted, for although Monophysitism never became a serious rival to the Nestorian church in Persia in terms of numbers of adherents, Monophysites gained positions of considerable influence at the Sasanian court towards the end of the sixth century.[49] Of particular interest is the encounter of John of Tella with the local Persian commander at Nisibis, following his apprehension by Persian soldiers on the Jebel Sinjar in the 530s. Significantly, the Persian authorities were only alerted to John's presence within their jurisdiction by a message from the Roman authorities who had themselves been trying to catch John, and when the Persian commander expressed surprise that John should have dared to enter Persian territory, John replied that this was the third occasion on which he had done so (Elias *Life of John*, p. 72/2).

Finally, mention should also be made of the exchange of letters and other

[45] *Life of Mar Aba* 6–10; text in P. Bedjan (ed.), *Histoire de Mar-Jabalaha, de trois autres patriarches, d'un prêtre et deux laïques, nestoriens* (Leipzig, 1895), 206–74, at 217–23; tr. O. Braun, *Ausgewählte Akten persischer Märtyrer* (Kempten and Munich, 1915), 188–220, at 192–4; with discussion by P. Peeters, 'Observations sur la vie syriaque de Mar Aba', *Miscellanea Giovanni Mercati* vol. 5 (Rome, 1946) (= *Studi e Testi* 125), 69 112, at 76–84.

[46] Christensen, *Les Sassanides*, 422–3.

[47] Blockley, 'Doctors as diplomats', 95–6.

[48] Brown, 'Diffusion of Manichaeism'; S. N. C. Lieu, *Manichaeism in the Later Roman Empire and Medieval China* (Manchester, 1985), 63–5.

[49] Labourt, *Le Christianisme*, 217ff.

documents between the Christian leaders in each empire, which presupposes the movement of clergy or other individuals as letter-carriers. For example, the bishop of Edessa in the 320s sent an account of the council of Nicaea to Persian Christians,[50] Theodoret communicated by letter with bishops in Persarmenia during the fifth century (*Epp.* 77–8), and in 445 a Persian bishop wrote to the patriarch of Antioch requesting prayer for himself and those under his care during a time of persecution by the Persian authorities.[51] Indeed, the knowledge of persecutions in Persia shown by Roman writers such as Sozomen (*HE* ii.6–14) also points to regularity of contact. At an official level, bishops were used with some frequency as envoys by the governments of both empires.[52] Indicative of the way in which travelling clerics had become a common sight both within the Roman empire and between it and the Persian empire is the fact that when the Gothic king Vittigis sent a secret embassy from Italy to Ctesiphon in the late 530s, the envoys adopted the guise of a bishop and his retinue, and in this way reached Persia without any questions being asked (Proc. *Wars* ii.2.1–3).

Travelling rabbis may well have been almost as common a sight as bishops and other clergy, for the existence of substantial Jewish communities in both empires also generated regular intercourse, and for similar reasons. Many leading Jewish scholars in Persia had been students in Palestine during their youth, and as the intellectual prestige of the Jewish academies in Babylonia increased during the third and fourth centuries, there developed a steady movement of rabbis back and forth between the academies in each empire.[53] The Jews in Persia often consulted Jewish leaders in Palestine on matters of importance,[54] and until its abolition in 429 the Jewish patriarchate in Palestine regularly sent out legates to inspect all the widely scattered Jewish communities,[55] even during periods of hostilities between the Romans and Persians.[56] Moreover, despite the destruction of the Temple in AD 70, Jerusalem remained a goal for Jewish

---

[50] I. Ortiz de Urbina, *Patrologia Syriaca*, 2nd edn (Rome, 1965), 84 – though a Persian bishop also seems to have been present at Nicaea: Eusebius *Life of Constantine*, iii.7.1; Soc. *HE* i.8; J.-D. Mansi, *Sacrorum conciliorum nova et amplissima collectio* (Florence and Venice, 1759–98), vol. 2, 694 (Johannes Persidis). Eusebius also says that many Persian bishops were present at the Council of Tyre in 335 (*Life* iv.43.3).

[51] *History of the Martyrs of Karka de Beth Selok* 10; text in P. Bedjan (ed.), *Acta Martyrum et Sanctorum* vol. 2 (Leipzig, 1891), 520; tr. Braun, *Ausgewählte Akten*, 180.

[52] N. G. Garsoïan, 'Le role de l'hiérarchie chrétienne dans les rapports diplomatiques entre Byzance et les Sassanides', *Revue des études arméniennes* 10 (1973–4), 119–38; L. Sako, *Le Role de l'hiérarchie syriaque orientale dans les rapports diplomatiques entre la Perse et Byzance aux Ve-VIIe siècles* (Paris, 1986).

[53] Neusner, *The Jews in Babylonia*, vol. 2, 126–9, 144–5; vol. 3, 218; vol. 4, 288–9.

[54] Segal, 'The Jews of northern Mesopotamia', 37; S. Safrai, 'The era of the Mishnah and the Talmud' in H. H. Ben-Sasson (ed.), *A History of the Jewish People* (London, 1976), 374.

[55] G. Alon, *The Jews in their Land in the Talmudic Age*, tr. G. Levi (Jerusalem, 1980), 234–5.

[56] S. Lieberman, 'Palestine in the third and fourth centuries', *Jewish Quarterly Review* 36 (1945–6), 329–70, at 332.

pilgrims,[57] while the desire of many Persian Jews to have their remains buried in Palestine[58] required others to transport them there and then return home. For all these reasons, therefore, interchange between the Jewish communities of the two empires must have been frequent.

There were of course motivations for crossing the border other than those arising from religious identity. Another obvious one is the search for profits. The merchant was a figure noted in late antiquity for his wide travelling (which is not of course to say that all merchants engaged in long-distance trade). Augustine was conscious of the freedom of movement enjoyed by many merchants when he evoked the sentiments of one in the following manner (*Enarrationes in Psalmos* cxxxvi.3, *PL* xxxvii.1762):

> To traverse the seas and to trade is a great thing; to be familiar with many lands, to make profits from every quarter, never to be under obligation to any powerful man in your city, always to be on the move, feeding your mind with the various customs of the nations you visit and returning enriched with the increase of your gains.

Jerome likewise remarked that Syrian merchants 'have an innate fervour for trading, seeing that they hurry over the entire earth' (*Commentary on Ezechiel* 8 on xxvii.15f., *PL* xxv.255). The Antoninus who appears in the pages of Ammianus might well have been one such individual. Before becoming a government official, he had been a successful merchant which, Ammianus says, had made him widely known throughout the east; significantly, this seems to have included contact with Persian officials (xviii.5.3). Merchants engaging in long-distance trade also existed within the Persian empire. The construction of caravanserai and port facilities testifies to the interest of the Sasanian monarchs in encouraging commerce,[59] while Sasanian law books describe arrangements for making 'loans at risk' to merchants against a range of potential disasters likely to be encountered in long-distance trade.[60] The existence of a vigorous Persian trade in both the Indian Ocean and Russia is well documented.[61]

Some of these ventures were also directed westwards to the Roman empire. The trade in silk from China and in spices from India was particularly

[57] M. Avi-Yonah, *The Jews of Palestine: a Political Hisory from the Bar Kokhba War to the Arab Conquest* (Oxford, 1976), 79–81.

[58] Safrai, 'Mishnah and Talmud', 374.

[59] M. G. Raschke, 'New studies in Roman commerce with the east', *ANRW* II.9.2 (1978), 604–1361, at 821 n.726; D. Whitehouse and A. Williamson, 'Sasanian maritime trade', *Iran* 11 (1973), 29–49.

[60] *CHI* vol. 3, 627–80, at 674–5 (A. Perikhanian).

[61] Whitehouse and Williamson, 'Sasanian maritime trade'; B. E. Colless, 'Persian merchants and missionaries in medieval Malaya', *Journal of the Malaysian Branch of the Royal Asiatic Society* 42 (1969), 10–47; R. N. Frye, 'Byzantine and Sasanian trade relations with northeastern Russia', *DOP* 26 (1972), 265–9.

lucrative.[62] Some of this trade was seaborne and reached the Roman empire via the Red Sea, but the various routes which ran north-west from Ctesiphon through northern Mesopotamia were also used,[63] so that at least some of this commercial interchange took place across the Roman–Persian border in northern Mesopotamia. It has been suggested that the Roman empire's eastern trade suffered a downturn during the third and fourth centuries,[64] and no doubt the destruction of Palmyra in 273 had a deleterious effect on the prosperity of overland commerce. But there are a number of indications that this was only a temporary setback. A contemporary document from the mid-fourth century comments on the wealth of the merchants of Nisibis and Edessa who engaged in trade with Persia (*Expos.* 22),[65] while in a much-cited passage, Ammianus describes an annual fair at the town of Batnae in Roman Mesopotomia in 354 at which goods from China and India were regularly available in quantity (xiv.3.3), and also refers to Callinicum, on the Euphrates, as a city noted (in 363) for 'the richness of its trade' (xxiii.3.7).[66]

The existence of a substantial trade across the north Mesopotamian plain is further presupposed by various attempts during late antiquity to regulate this trade – though of course it is also important to assess the extent to which these controls served to inhibit commerce. The first was instituted by Diocletian as part of the peace imposed on the Persians in 298/9. Among the terms was one to the effect that 'the place of exchange (τόπον τῶν συναλλαγμάτων) is to be the city of Nisibis' (Pet. Pat. fr. 14, *FHG* iv.189). A more detailed law of 408/9 (apparently confirming a previous agreement) specifies Nisibis, Callinicum and Artaxata as the only three places in which Roman and Persian merchants are permitted to trade with one another (*CJ* iv.63.4). Finally, the peace of 561/2 reaffirmed that merchants from both empires were to restrict their trading with one another to 'the specified customs posts' – though no locations are

---

[62] Raschke, 'Roman commerce', 606–50; J. I. Miller, *The Spice Trade of the Roman Empire* (Oxford, 1969), with the comments of Raschke, 650ff. Hides and leather goods from Persia also appear to have been highly valued: *Digest* xxxix.4.16.7; Diocletian *Prices Edict*, ed. S. Lauffer, 8.1, 9.23, 10.8a.

[63] Miller, *Spice Trade*, 120–1; Liebeschuetz, *Antioch*, 76–7; N. Pigulevskaja, *Byzanz auf den Wegen nach Indien* (Berlin and Amsterdam, 1969), 81.

[64] Raschke, 'Roman commerce', 678, where further literature is cited. A downturn after the 330s has been suggested by E. Frézouls, 'Les fonctions du Moyen-Euphrate a l'époque romaine' in J. C. Margueron (ed.), *Le Moyen Euphrate: zone de contacts et d'échanges* (TCRPGA 5, 1977), 355–86, at 384.

[65] It has been argued by some scholars that 'Edessa' here should read 'Amida': see J. Rougé in the edition in SC 124, pp. 20–1.

[66] Available information about late Roman coinage from the region of the Fertile Crescent is unfortunately 'negligible' (E. J. Prawdzic-Golemberski and D. M. Metcalf, 'The circulation of Byzantine coins on the south-eastern frontiers of the empire', *Numismatic Chronicle* 7th series, 3 (1963), 83), which means that one important category of evidence of potential relevance to commercial activity is essentially lacking for the east (in contrast to the north).

mentioned (Men. fr.6,1/323-6).[67] Only one of these restrictions – that of 408/9 – is accompanied by an explicit statement of purpose: to prevent trade being used as a pretext for spying (*ne alieni regni . . . scrutentur arcana*). This concern has been seen as in part underlying all these restrictions,[68] but other motivations are also apparent. Facilitation of the collection of customs duties is an obvious one,[69] while another is prevention of the export from the Roman empire of prohibited items. Increasing concern in late antiquity about this latter problem prompted the creation of the *comites commerciorum*, officials with responsibility for supervising trading points (*commercia*) along specified sectors of the frontier.[70] A *comes commerciorum per Orientem et Aegyptum* is attested (*ND Or.* xiii.6–7), and Persia is known to have been particularly interested in acquiring an important category of prohibited items, namely iron and iron weapons (Lib. *Or.* lix.67; cf. *Expos.* 22).

There are, however, a number of difficulties in taking at face value the provisions for the restriction of trade to specified locations. There is ambiguity as to whether some of these measures were intended to restrict trade to specific sites, and in the case of those that were, there is reason to doubt their effective enforcement. There are various considerations which cast doubt on the assumption that the clause of 298/9 was intended to restrict the transaction of all trade between the two empires to Nisibis. In the passage from the mid-fourth century *Expositio Totius Mundi et Gentium* (22) noted earlier, reference is made to merchants enriched by trade with Persia not only in Nisibis but also in Edessa,[71] while Antoninus' contact with Persian officials in his merchant days implies movement on his part within Persian territory. Moreover if trade in the fourth century was limited to Nisibis alone, it is curious that the measure of 408/9 should give as its aim the inhibiting of spying under the pretext of trade and yet increase the number of locations for trade threefold. Peter the Patrician's expression τόπον τῶν συναλλαγμάτων has been taken by some scholars to mean that commercial traffic had to *pass through* Nisibis.[72] If the main concerns were to maximise customs revenue and prevent the export of contraband, these aims could have been achieved as effectively by requiring merchants to travel

---

67 It is generally assumed that the locations were those specified in 408/9: Güterbock, *Byzanz und Persien*, 78; Blockley's commentary on Menander, *ad loc.*

68 Andreotti, 'Su alcuni problemi', especially 243–5.

69 E. Stein, *Histoire du Bas-Empire*, ed. and tr. J.-R. Palanque (Paris, 1949–59), vol. 1, 80; Frézouls, 'Les fluctuations', 214–15; I. Kawar [Shahid], 'The Arabs in the peace treaty of AD 561', *Arabica* 3 (1956), 181–213, at 193.

70 Delmaire, *Largesses sacrées*, 283–5, with K. Stock, 'Comes commerciorum. Ein Beitrag zur spätrömischen Verwaltungsgeschichte', *Francia* 6 (1978), 599–609. The office is first attested in a law (*CJ* iv.40.2) dated to 383/392 by O. Seeck (*Regesten der Kaiser und Päpste für die Jahre 311 bis 476 n. Chr.* (Stuttgart, 1919), 124), in turn referring to an earlier measure.

71 Or perhaps Amida (cf. n. 65).

72 Stein, *Histoire*, vol. 1, 80; cf. Frézouls, 'Les fluctuations', 214 ('canalisant les échanges vers un seul passage').

via Nisibis. But if the intention was to restrict all transactions to Nisibis itself, then the evidence noted above suggests that it was difficult to enforce.

There is no ambiguity about the law of 408/9. The wording is more detailed and explicit, and is confirmed by a subsequent law (of 422/3) under the same title in the code which reiterates that Roman merchants are neither to proceed beyond 'the cities specified by name in earlier laws', nor deal in them with foreign traders without the presence of a *comes commerciorum* (*CJ* iv.63.6). Nevertheless, there is again evidence which suggests that the authorities had difficulty or were lax in enforcing the restrictions. John of Ephesus describes two brothers from Amida who, in the early sixth century, 'worked for merchants and travelled with them . . . to the lands of the Persians' (*Lives* 31, *PO* xviii.576), while another Syriac source includes the following account of the early life of a Persian saint: 'Mar Job . . . was a Persian, from the city of Riwardashir. His parents owned slaves and servants, and his father was a merchant in pearls and precious stones. His father sent him to the land of the Romans, carrying pearls for the capital' (Jesusdenah *Le Livre de la chasteté* 44).[73] Socrates Scholasticus also says that one of the factors contributing to the outbreak of war between the two empires in 421 was the plundering of Roman merchants by the Persians (*HE* vii.18.4).[74]

The most significant item, however, is the canon from the statutes of the school of Nisibis referred to earlier: the need to forbid students from going from Nisibis into Roman territory to buy and sell indicates very clearly the difficulties entailed in enforcing the regulations of 408/9. Confirmation of this may be found in the fact that the law of 408/9 claims to be reiterating an earlier agreement,[75] and the law of 422/3 (*CJ* iv.63.6) noted above would appear to be a reiteration of the provisions of 408/9. It is worth noting, too, that this latter text specifically allows merchants travelling with official embassies to conduct business beyond the usual frontier locations (*CJ* iv.63.4.3), an exception repeated in the peace settlement of 561/2 (Men. fr.6,1/331–2).

Finally, it ought not to be forgotten that the specified locations themselves constituted important centres of interaction between inhabitants of both empires. Consider Procopius' description of the town of Dwin, which replaced Artaxata as the administrative capital of Armenia during the fifth century, and so

---

[73] According to Labourt (*Le Christianisme*, 318), Job was a contemporary of Abraham of Kaskar (491/2–586); this incident occurred during Job's youth and so can be placed in the first half of the sixth century.

[74] Though this incident could conceivably have occurred in Nisibis or Artaxata. Cf. also the fragment from Part II of John of Ephesus' *Ecclesiastical History* concerning the foundation legend of Dara, which features an Antiochene merchant of the fifth century who travelled regularly to Persia via the site where Dara later stood (in E. A. W. Budge, *The Chronography of Gregory Abu'l Faraj* (Oxford, 1932), vol. 2, xxii).

[75] 363 and 387 have both been proposed: for the references, see Andreotti, 'Politica di sicurezza', 249 n. 54.

presumably also as the official market in that region:[76] 'Many densely inhabited villages are situated close to one another there and many merchants undertake their business in them. For they gather there with one another, bringing their goods from India, neighbouring Iberia, from nearly all the peoples of Persia, and some from the Roman empire' (*Wars* ii.25.2–3).[77]

Travel motivated by religion or commerce accounts for the largest numbers of individuals traversing the boundary between the two empires, many of whom will have had occasion to cross and recross a number of times. There are those, however, who crossed the frontier once, never to return. This would appear to include Persians serving in the Roman army. A number of Persian names appear in positions of command during the fourth and early fifth century[78] – presumably fugitives like the Persian prince Hormizd – and in the sixth century, Persians who deserted or were captured were allowed to serve in the army, though in a part of the empire removed from the east (e.g., Proc. *Wars* i.12.22; ii.19.24–5; viii.26.13).[79] On the other hand, the *Notitia*, from the early fifth century, refers to cavalry units of *clibanarii Parthi* and *Persae* (*Or.* v.40; vi.32,40; vii.32), one of which was based in the east,[80] as well as an *ala* of 'Cardueni' and a cohort of 'Zabdeni' stationed in the province of Mesopotamia itself (*Or.* xxxvi.34, 36) – presumably comprising recruits from the regions of Corduene and Zabdicene beyond the Tigris.[81] Desertion from one empire to the other appears to have been a fairly common phenomenon. An embassy from Ctesiphon actually complained to the emperor Leo in the 460s about the numbers of Persians fleeing to Roman territory (Priscus fr. 41,1/3–5), the peace settlement of 561/2 included a clause stipulating the forcible return of deserters by each empire to the other (Men. fr. 6,1/345–7), and deserters from both sides appear with some frequency in Ammianus' account of events during the 350s

---

76 Güterbock, *Byzanz und Persien*, 76–7.

77 The role of Dwin as a trade centre is supported by the discovery of significant numbers of sixth-century Roman and Sasanian coins there (Raschke, 'Roman commerce', 734 n. 362, 735 n. 365), and of storerooms containing many clay seals from all over Persia whose purpose seems to have been to identify the origin of wares (V. G. Lukonin, *Persia II: from the Seleucids to the Sasanians*, tr. J. Hogarth (London, 1967), 106–7). Cf. also Procopius' description of the region of Chorzane, in the sector to the north of the upper Tigris: 'The inhabitants here, Roman and Persian subjects, have no fear of one another and do not suspect each other of treachery at all. On the contrary, they intermarry, have a common market for their necessities, and work together in their farming' (*Bld.* iii.3.10).

78 See *PLRE* vol. 1, s.v. Barzimeres (?), Pusaeus (surrendered during Julian's Persian campaign), Sapores, and *PLRE* vol. 2, s.v. Arsacius 3, Varanes 1, with D. Hoffmann, 'Wadomar, Bacurius und Hariulf: zur Laufbahn adliger und fürstlicher Barbaren in spätrömischen Heere des 4. Jahrhunderts', *Museum Helveticum* 35 (1978), 307–18, at 310–11.

79 Cf. for the early empire D.L. Kennedy, 'Parthian regiments in the Roman army' in J. Fitz (ed.), *Limes: Akten des XI. internationalen Limeskongresses* (Budapest, 1977), 521–31.

80 But perhaps the name of these units is a reference not to the origin of the recruits, but of the type of cavalry?

81 Cf. also the unit of mounted archers from Corduene serving in the west (*Occ.* vi.40, 83; cf. vii.209).

(xiv.3; xviii.6.8,16; xix.9.2,3ff.; xx.4.1) – most famously in the person of Antoninus, who defected to the Persians in 359 and took with him valuable information concerning Roman troop dispositions and future moves (xviii.5.1–3).

The overriding impression of the frontier in northern Mesopotamia is therefore of considerable permeability and the existence of a high degree of interaction between the inhabitants of the two empires. This impression is strengthened when one turns to consider the same questions for the empire's northern boundary.

THE NORTH

The northern boundary of the empire was subject to greater variation than the boundary with Persia during the late Roman period. During the course of the third century, control was lost of the province of Dacia, lying to the north of the lower Danube, and of the wedge of territory between the upper Rhine and upper Danube (the *agri decumates*), so that the boundary essentially coincided with the courses of the Rhine and the Danube during the fourth century (control of the Rhine was temporarily lost during the early 350s). For the western half of that boundary the late Roman period came to an early end during the fifth century, while in the east, the inroads of Huns, Ostrogoths and Avars meant that Constantinople's control of the lower Danube was tenuous or non-existent for some parts of the fifth and late sixth/early seventh centuries. Sirmium, for example, was only ever in Roman hands again for brief periods after its capture by the Huns in 441.[82]

In so far as the Rhine-Danube line represented the empire's boundary for the greater part of the late Roman period, it cannot be regarded as having cut through an homogeneous cultural zone (or zones) in the same way that the boundary between the Roman and Persian empires did. Consider the linguistic dimension. Undoubtedly there were individuals with competence in both Greek and/or Latin and a northern language. Epigraphic evidence from the period of the early empire attests the presence of interpreters of various northern languages on the staff of provincial governors[83] and in units of the Roman army,[84] which suggests that the position was a necessary adjunct along

---

[82] For a brief survey of the lower Danube down to 582, see Whitby, *Maurice*, 66–80, 86–9, with detailed treatment of the late sixth and early seventh centuries in Chapters 5–6. On Sirmium, see M. Mirkovic, 'Sirmium – its history from the I century AD to 582 AD' in D. Boskovic (ed.), *Sirmium* vol. I (Belgrade, 1971), 5–90, at 41ff.

[83] *CIL* iii.10505 (*interpres Germanorum*, Aquincum), 14349 (*interprex Sarmatorum*, Pest); *AE* 1947.35 (*interprex Dacorum*, Brigetio).

[84] *CIL* iii.14507 and 8773 (*interpretes* without a specified language, Viminacium and Germania Inferior).

all sectors of the northern frontier, while a fourth-century reference to the presence of *interpretes Sarmatorum* in the army (Amm. Marc. xix.11.5) points to continuity of the office into the late empire. The bureaux of the *magistri officiorum* included interpreters – *interpretes omnium gentium* ('of all peoples') in the west (*Occ.* ix.35), and the more realistically entitled *interpretes diversarum gentium* ('of different peoples') in the east (*Or.* xi.52). Possible examples of these are Vigilas, fluent in Hunnic and employed on an embassy to Attila (Priscus fr. 11,2/5ff.), and Vitalian, who spoke Avar and features in negotiations in the 560s (Men. frs. 12,4/2; 12,6/1–8). When someone competent in both Greek and Gepid was needed at Maurice's court (Th. Sim. vi.10.6), there was apparently no difficulty in finding an individual with the requisite skills, nor were various northern rulers at a loss to find individuals who could interpret Greek or Latin for them.[85] Elsewhere interpreters are mentioned without it being entirely clear who provided them.[86] One can speculate intelligently as to the ways in which such linguistic competence was acquired – while residing in the empire or in barbaricum[87] as prisoner or hostage, from service in the Roman army (cf. Amm. Marc. xviii.2.2), or from being settled permanently within the empire, as happened to many from northern lands.[88] An interesting inscription is also suggestive of the way in which involvement in cross-frontier trade demanded (and developed) basic competence in a foreign language: found near Carnuntum on the middle Danube, it commemorates Q. Atilius Primus, who apparently spent a period in the army as an interpreter before returning to civilian life as a merchant.[89]

However, in spite of the evidence showing a degree of linguistic interchange across the empire's northern boundary, there are no grounds for assuming that any Germanic language came to hold a position comparable to Syriac in the east. The settlement of barbarian groups within the empire during late antiquity may have had the potential to create analogous situations along parts of the empire's northern boundary, but it is unlikely that this in fact happened to any significant

---

[85] The Utigur Hun Sandilch (Agath. v.25.1); the Avar khagan Baian (Th. Sim. vi.5.16).

[86] Aurelian negotiating with the Juthungi in 270 (Dexippus fr. 24, *FHG* iii.682); Julian negotiating with the Chamavi in the late 350s (Eunap. fr. 18,6/5); Avar envoys addressing Justin II (Men. fr. 8/11); negotiations between a Roman commander and the Avar khagan in the early 580s (Men. fr. 27,2/10).

[87] For the use of the term 'barbaricum' for the lands to the north of the Danube and Rhine during late antiquity, see I. Weiler, 'Orbis romanus und Barbaricum', *Carnuntum Jahrbuch* (1963/4), 34–9.

[88] See the exhaustive listing of such settlements in G. E. M. de Ste Croix, *The Class Struggle in the Ancient Greek World* (London, 1981), Appendix 3.

[89] T. Kolnik, 'Q. Atilius Primus – *interprex, centurio* und *negotiator*', *Acta Archaeologica Academiae Scientiae Hungaricae* 30 (1978), 61–75. It is noteworthy that many of the Latin words which established themselves in Gothic and early Germanic were commercial in character, while the few Germanic words which found their way into Latin referred to items which were traded (Thompson, *Visigoths*, 39; J. P. Wild, 'Loanwords and Roman expansion in north-west Europe', *World Archaeology* 8 (1976), 57–64, at 60–1).

degree. The specific locations of such settlements are often uncertain, but those whose locations are known tend to be at sites well within the empire, rather than adjacent to the frontier.[90] The *Notitia* contains a partial listing of the barbarian reservations known as *terrae laeticae* (*Occ.* xlii), all of which fall either within Italy or at sites in Gaul well removed from the frontier;[91] moreover, such enclaves were probably resistant to integration with the surrounding provincial population.[92] The clearest case of the same people straddling the border is that of the Franks who were settled in or perhaps simply occupied Toxandria on the lower Rhine in the late third century; but what this effectively meant was that the political boundary in this region had shifted south and no longer coincided with the Rhine.

If no Germanic language functioned on the same scale as Syriac, however, there remains another possibility to consider – namely, Celtic. Archaeological and onomastic evidence has shown that, at the time of the Roman conquest of Gaul in the first century BC, Celtic tribes were not confined to the regions lying west of the Rhine but also occupied areas extending some distance to the east of the river.[93] Writing at the end of the first century AD, Tacitus remarked on the presence of *Galli* in the *agri decumates* (*Ger.* 29.4), which is generally taken to mean that a Celtic people was still living in the wedge of territory between the upper Rhine and Danube. It seems likely therefore that Celtic was spoken on both sides of the Rhine during the early empire. Did this situation remain unchanged during the late Roman period?

It is apparent from literary and epigraphic evidence that even by the fourth century Latin had by no means completely displaced Celtic in Roman Gaul; indeed there are some indications in later authors such as Sidonius, Venantius Fortunatus and Gregory of Tours that some knowledge of Celtic lingered on into the fifth and sixth centuries.[94] The impact of Romanisation was strongest in cities and towns, while Celtic would seem to have remained in substantial use in rural areas.[95] West of the Rhine, therefore, Celtic was still in use in the fourth century, though its concentration in rural areas means its speakers will have tended to be located away from the network of communication and interchange represented by cities, towns and roads.

---

[90] Cf. the details in de Ste Croix's catalogue.
[91] See the map (Fig. 30) in R. Günther and H. Köpstein (eds.), *Die Römer an Rhein und Donau* (Berlin, 1975), 345. The site closest to the frontier (Tungri) is still about 100 km from the Rhine.
[92] R. MacMullen, 'Barbarian enclaves in the northern Roman empire', *Antiquité classique* 32 (1963), 552–61, at 555.
[93] For a summary of the literature, see Todd, *Northern Barbarians*, 29–35.
[94] References in L. Fleuriot, *Les Origines de la Bretagne* (Paris, 1980), 55–9 ('Quand le Gaulois disparut-il?').
[95] R. MacMullen, 'Provincial languages in the Roman empire', *American Journal of Philology* 87 (1966), 1–17, at 14–15; J. Whatmough, *The Dialects of Ancient Gaul* (Cambridge, Mass., 1970), Prolegomena, 68–76.

What was the fate of Celtic to the east of the Rhine in its encounter with Germanic speakers? The outcome is difficult to determine because we are dealing with the interaction of preliterate languages. The only scholar who seems to have considered the limited evidence for the persistence of Celtic in the Rhineland and southern Germany after the early empire has concluded that the 'survivals are clearly of isolated items, possibly even of a small isolated community of speakers here and there in remote districts, not of speech-habits that could be called a "dialect"'.[96] Such a conclusion finds support in the hypothesis that 'the Roman administration of Gallienus, the Gallic emperors, or Aurelian . . . evacuated, at least partially the Black Forest area . . . and resettled the remnants of its mixed Romanised Celtic population in the Decem Pagi, a much reduced area in the Vosges and the River Saar valley, east of Metz'.[97] As for Celtic speakers who remained to experience Alamannic rule in the *agri decumates* (or Frankish rule further north), it is worth considering an analogous but more fully investigated situation where a Germanic-speaking people conquered a Celtic population – the Anglo-Saxon occupation of Britain. What was the fate of Celtic here?

> The Britons learned the language of their conquerors, and they acquired its sound system and vocabulary very completely, their own phonetics having no discernible effect on the new language and their own vocabulary very little. There must have been at least some degree of close relationship and intermarriage, through which British personal names were taken into Anglo-Saxon. All this suggests a bilingual stage, where the Britons knew both Anglo-Saxon and British, though it is not likely to have been a long one, especially in the East, and it is not probable that the conquerors learned much of the language of the conquered.[98]

A plausible explanation has been offered for this rather comprehensive displacement of the language of the defeated:

> Neither the Roman occupation of the first century AD, which brought a Latin-speaking administrative class to Britain, nor the Norman Conquest of 1066, which brought a new French-speaking aristocracy, caused a major replacement of the pre-existing place-names by new place-names in the language of the conquerors. It seems likely that a replacement of the kind which happened after the end of the Roman period...occurs only when the newcomers are farmers rather than, or as well as, overlords.[99]

The Franks and Alamanni were as much farmers as the Angles and Saxons, so it would seem reasonable to assume that a similar process occurred with respect to

---

[96] *Ibid.*, 1158.
[97] J. G. F. Hind, 'Whatever happened to the *agri decumates*?', *Britannia* 15 (1984), 187–92, at 192.
[98] K. Jackson, *Language and History in Early Britain* (Edinburgh, 1953), 245.
[99] M. Gelling, *The Place-Names of Berkshire* Part 3 (Cambridge, 1976), 811, quoted in P. H. Sawyer, *From Roman Britain to Norman England* (London, 1978), 89–90.

whatever Celtic population remained east of the Rhine after the mid-third century. Such a process of displacement can only have taken place over a number of generations, but any possibility of Celtic as a common language on both sides of the Rhine will have dwindled as the fourth century progressed.

Celtic speakers also inhabited both banks of the middle Danube during the first century BC,[100] but this situation did not persist either:

> The Osi, Cotini and Eravisci belonged to one and the same Celtic group of peoples in the northern Carpathian region. It was not until the end of the first century AD that fate intervened to separate them; the Cotini and Osi outside the empire came under the control of the Quadi and Sarmatians and were gradually Dacianised . . . whereas the Eravisci were able to maintain their Celtic language and culture under Roman rule.[101]

The implication is that those Celts who remained beyond the Danube were unable to maintain their language. By the criterion of language, therefore, the northern frontier undoubtedly cut through areas of cultural homogeneity during the first three centuries AD, but this was increasingly less the case during the late Roman period.

Although it greatly facilitates the process, cultural homogeneity is not, however, an essential prerequisite for a high degree of interregional interaction, so it is worth examining the evidence for ease of access between the empire and barbaricum, as a first step towards trying to gauge levels of interaction. The ability of the imperial authorities to control movements into and out of the empire was largely dependent on the army. Diocletian is known to have been responsible for increasing the number of soldiers along the Rhine and Danube, and for distributing units evenly along the rivers.[102] Constantine's creation of the field army would have meant some reduction in the size of these forces, but it is clear above all from archaeological evidence for military installations that the army maintained a strong presence along the rivers throughout the fourth century.[103] The positioning of many of these installations at potential crossing points is indicative, at least in part, of an interest in controlling transfluvial

---

[100] A. Mócsy, *Pannonia and Upper Moesia* (London, 1974), 57f.

[101] *Ibid.*, 60.

[102] D. van Berchem, *L'Armée de Diocletian et la réforme constantinienne* (Paris, 1952), 90–7.

[103] For overviews (covering the Rhine and upper and middle Danube), see H. von Petrikovits, 'Fortifications in the north-western Roman empire from the third to the fifth centuries AD', *JRS* 61 (1971), 178–218; S. Johnson, *Late Roman Fortifications* (London, 1983), Chapters 6, 7 and 11. For more detailed treatments of individual sectors, see J. J. Wilkes, 'The frontier of Noricum', *JRA* 2 (1989), 347–52 (not exclusively concerned with the late empire); Mócsy, *Pannonia*, Chapter 8; S. Soproni, *Der spätrömische Limes zwischen Esztergom und Szentendre* (Budapest, 1978), and *Die letzten Jahrzehnte des pannonischen Limes* (Munich, 1985) (though note the cautionary remarks on Soproni's dating criteria by V. A. Maxfield, 'The frontiers of Roman empire: some recent work', *JRA* 2 (1989), 334–46, at 338–9); C. Scorpan, *Limes Scythiae* (BAR s88, 1980).

movement,[104] but of course the uppermost concern was with invading forces rather than individuals, and the number of possible crossing points for individuals was very much greater than those suitable for large bodies of men.[105] Although there were times when the Roman government did try to impose restrictions on the access of northern peoples to the empire on an individual basis,[106] the imposition of these very restrictions presupposes previous times of free access, and it must have been impossible to monitor without lapse the movements of individuals across a boundary the length of the Rhine–Danube line. Indeed the behaviour of the Alamannic king Vadomarius suggests a much more relaxed state of affairs in practice. Ammianus (xxi.4.3) has him crossing the Rhine into Roman territory, chatting with a Roman officer at the crossing point, and accepting a dinner invitation from the local Roman commander! Significantly, Ammianus glosses the reference to conversation with the officer with the phrase 'as usual' (ex more). This, together with other evidence for northern leaders dining with Roman officers (e.g., xxix.6.5) and Ammianus' remark at another point (xviii.2.17) that Vadomarius was 'familiar with our affairs, since he lived near the frontier', presupposes the regularity of such behaviour.

One of the most obvious motives for traversing the northern boundaries of the empire was, as in the east, the pursuit of commerce. Evidence bearing on the nature of trade between the empire and barbaricum comes from a variety of sources. Literary texts refer to individuals who engaged at one time or another in trade across the Danube, such as the future emperor Maximinus Thrax, who traded with the Goths in the early third century (HA Maxim. 4.4), or the Roman encountered by Priscus in the camp of Attila who had once operated as a prosperous merchant from the frontier city of Viminacium on the lower Danube (fr. 11,2/423–4). Literary sources also indicate some of the goods which Roman merchants obtained. Slaves were clearly a major component in fourth-century trade with the Goths,[107] while the slaves for which the province of Pannonia had a reputation as a source of supply in the mid-fourth century (Expos. 57) presumably derived ultimately from the Sarmatians.[108] In the early 370s Roman soldiers operating in Alamannia encountered traders conducting slaves for sale (Amm. Marc. xxix.4.4), while in 394 the senator Symmachus wrote to a friend in a position of authority on the upper Danube with a request

---

104 See, e.g., Mócsy, Pannonia, 269–71 for late Roman fortified landing-places at seven points along the Danube bend.

105 For further discussion of crossing points, see pp. 96–9.

106 From the early empire: Tac. Ger. 41.2 (all beyond Rhine except Hermunduri), Dio lxxi.11.3 (Iazyges and Marcomanni); late empire: Themistius Or. x.135cd (Goths limited by Valens to two trading points), Priscus fr. 46/4–5 (Hun request for a market on the Danube).

107 Thompson, Visigoths, 40–2.

108 A. Piganiol, L'Empire chrétien (325–395), 2nd edn (Paris, 1972), 13 n. 2.

for twenty young men, 'since slaves can easily be found along the frontier and the price is usually reasonable' (*Ep.* ii.78.2). This evidence certainly accords with the arguments against the long-accepted view that slave numbers declined significantly from the second century AD.[109]

While literary sources indicate that trade with northern peoples existed during late antiquity, these sources generally cannot provide a guide to the intensity of commercial interchange.[110] This is the sort of question where one would have thought archaeological evidence might be of more assistance, for there has been considerable research into Roman goods found in northern Europe. The situation is not straightforward, however, for goods can circulate through mechanisms other than trade: 'A variety of different mechanisms of circulation have been defined. Among those concerned with more-or-less voluntary circulation are barter . . . , gift-giving, administered trade, and market trade. Others include payment of tribute, ransoms, taxes, and tolls. Goods also circulate through violent means such as plunder in wars and during raids.'[111] Thus the value of Eggers' important collation of archaeological evidence on Roman imports into 'free Germany'[112] is limited by the difficulties in determining which goods had their origin in trade and which goods were 'imported' as a result of raiding, subsidies or diplomatic gifts.[113] Items which are both intrinsically more valuable and more portable, such as gold and silver coinage and fine metalwork, could have reached barbaricum by any of these mechanisms, and so are of less help in trying to gauge the level of trade. However, not all items of Roman origin are so valuable and/or easy to

[109] M. I. Finley, *Ancient Slavery and Modern Ideology* (Harmondsworth, 1980), 123–30, with C. R. Whittaker, 'Labour supply in the late Roman empire', *Opus* 1 (1982), 171–9.

[110] Ammianus' comment that Valens was able to force the Goths to sue for peace in 369 by imposing an economic blockade on them (xxvii.5.7) has sometimes been taken as indicative of the extent of Gothic dependence on trade with the empire, but as noted by Heather and Matthews, Goths, 93 n. 74, 'the Goths' distress followed three years [*sic*] of Roman campaigns, during which they could not have planted a harvest. The interruption to trade must be seen against this background: as a reinforcement of distress, but not its only cause.'

[111] P.S. Wells, *Culture Contact and Culture Exchange: Early Iron Age Europe and the Mediterranean World* (Cambridge, 1980), 8. The classic exposition of how mechanisms other than trade have been neglected in accounting for circulation of goods in a pre-industrial context is P. Grierson, 'Commerce in the Dark Ages', *Transactions of the Royal Historical Society* 5th series, 9 (1959), 123–40.

[112] H. J. Eggers, *Der römische Import im freien Germanien* (Hamburg, 1951), now updated for certain categories of find for the period before late antiquity by J. Kunow, *Der römische Import in der Germania libera bis zu den Markomannenkriegen. Studien zu Bronze- und Glasgefässen* (Neumünster, 1983). The relative scarcity of Roman metalwork in the 200 km 'buffer zone' adjacent to the imperial boundary, as compared with areas deeper in barbaricum (noted by L. Hedeager, 'A quantitative analysis of Roman imports in Europe north of the Limes (0–400 AD), and the question of Roman–Germanic exchange', *Studies in Scandinavian Prehistory and Early History* 1 (1978), 191–216), does not mean that such items were not originally present there on a significant scale during Roman times (see Fulford, 'Roman material in barbarian society', 100–2).

[113] Eggers himself (72–3) recognised the variety of mechanisms by which goods could circulate.

transport, notably pottery. Pottery is improbable as an acceptable form of subsidy or gift. Moreover, 'it is impossible to regard merely as loot the considerable
quantities of other material [besides coinage], especially pottery and glass.
Amphorae in particular must surely represent trade.'[114] Roman pottery has certainly been found in quantity in regions of barbaricum adjacent to the empire.[115]
Nevertheless, one can only agree with Malcolm Todd's lament that insufficient
attention has been directed to the study of the more mundane items of trade.[116]

As already noted, gold and silver coinage in barbaricum can be accounted for
most readily in terms of subsidies, gifts, booty and ransoms. After 374/5 it was
illegal to export gold from the empire for commercial purposes (CJ iv.63.2), and
although this will not have prevented smuggling, it makes it more likely that
gold coin of dates later than this will have found its way out of the empire by
one of the non-commercial mechanisms.[117] On the other hand, low value
coinage, of bronze or copper, will not have been attractive either as booty or as
subsidies/gifts, and so, although some was no doubt carried off by raiders in too
much of a hurry to separate out the baser metals from the more precious, the
greater part of it is more likely to testify to trading activity. Much of this type of
coinage has been found in regions of barbaricum adjacent to the empire.[118]

Apart from slaves, goods sold by northern peoples to the Romans are more
difficult to trace, since they probably comprised perishable items like hides and
clothing materials.[119] The persistence into the fourth century of the trade in

---

114 J. C. Mann, 'The northern frontier after AD 369', Glasgow Archaeological Journal 3 (1974), 34–42,
    at 35 (with specific reference to the northern frontier in Britain, but having more general
    application).
115 Germany (first to fourth centuries): Eggers, Import, Map 62; south Germany (fourth century):
    R. Christlein, Die Alamannen (Stuttgart, 1978), 96–8; middle Danube (first to fourth centuries):
    U.-B. Dittrich, 'Die Wirtschaftsstruktur der Quaden, Markomannen und Sarmaten im mittleren
    Donauraum und ihre Handelsbeziehungen mit Rom', MBAH 6/1 (1987), 9–30, at 22; L. F.
    Pitts, 'Relations between Rome and the German "kings" on the middle Danube in the first to
    fourth centuries AD', JRS 79 (1989), 45–58, at 55; Wallachia (fourth century): B. Mitrea and
    C. Preda, 'Quelques problèmes ayant trait aux nécropoles de type Sîntana-Tcherniakov
    découvertes en Valachie', Dacia 8 (1964), 211–37, at 216–17; Heather and Matthews, Goths, 71;
    Wallachia (sixth century): M. Comsa, 'Socio-economic organisation of the Daco-Roman and
    Slav populations on the lower Danube during the 6th–8th centuries' in Constantinescu et al.,
    Populations in Romania, 171–200, at 194; Moldavia (fifth to seventh centuries): D. G. Teodor,
    The East Carpathian Region of Romania in the V–IX Centuries AD (BAR s81, 1980), 18–19.
116 Northern Barbarians, 25.
117 For discussion of this law and examples of subsidy and ransom payments, see M. Γ. Hendy,
    Studies in the Byzantine Monetary Economy, c. 300–1450 (Cambridge, 1985), 257–63.
118 Germany (first to fourth centuries): S. Bolin (in Swedish) cited by Hedeager, 'Quantitative
    analysis', 209; south Germany (fourth century): K. Christ, Antike Münzfunde Südwestdeutschlands
    (Heidelberg, 1960), vol. 2, Maps xx–xxii and Fig. 14; Hungarian lowlands (fourth century):
    Mócsy, Pannonia, 322; Wallachia (fourth century): Heather and Matthews, Goths, 92, Table 14;
    Wallachia/Moldavia (sixth to seventh centuries): C. Preda 'The Byzantine coins – an expression
    of the relations between the empire and the populations north of the Danube in the 6th–13th
    centuries' in Constantinescu et al., Populations of Romania, 219–33, at 222 (Fig. 1). Teodor,
    Carpathian Region, 13–14.
119 Cf. Wild, 'Loanwords', 61.

amber, which in earlier centuries at least had been carried into the Roman empire by Germanic traders (Pliny *Natural History* xxxvii.43) is confirmed by archaeological discoveries on the Danube.[120] Salt, resin and tar were also obtained from Germanic tribes on the Rhine.[121] Other evidence is ambiguous. The discovery of a wooden cask at Roman Aquincum using wood from a particular type of fir tree now found only in the Carpathian mountains, north of the Danube, led one historian to deduce the existence of a logging trade on the middle Danube.[122] Yet as the archaeologist who carried out the original investigations himself stressed, the absence of this particular species of fir tree from modern Hungary, south of the Danube, could well be the result of deforestation by the Romans themselves![123]

In contrast with Persia, therefore, northern peoples do not seem to have been able to supply the Romans with any particularly valuable commodities (except perhaps slaves). The evident imbalance in trade will have been rectified to some extent through barbarian possession of Roman gold and silver gained as subsidies.[124] Nevertheless, although some scholars have emphasised the degree of economic dependency across the northern frontier,[125] others have remained sceptical about the volume of Roman goods found beyond the Rhine and Danube, and the intensity of trade across the northern boundary of the empire, particularly when compared with the empire's eastern trade.[126]

The other major source of interchange in the east – movement motivated by religion – is even less evident in the north. First, it seems that virtually none of the northern peoples with whom the empire had dealings in the third to fifth centuries became predominantly Christian until after they settled in Roman territory.[127] This meant that there were comparatively few peoples beyond the

---

[120] Mócsy, *Pannonia*, 322.
[121] R. E. H. Mellor, *The Rhine* (Aberdeen, 1983), 67–8.
[122] J. Kolendo, 'Les influences de Rome sur les peuples de l'Europe centrale habitant loin des frontières de l'empire', *Klio* 63 (1981), 453–72, at 454 n. 3.
[123] J. Stieber, 'Xylotomic examination of the Roman cask unearthed at Aquincum in 1975', *Budapest Regisegei* 24 (1976), 211–12 (Hungarian with English summary).
[124] C. D. Gordon, 'Subsidies in Roman imperial defence', *Phoenix* 3 (1949), 60–9, at 68.
[125] Notably C. R. Whittaker, 'Trade and frontiers of the Roman empire' in P. Garnsey and C. R. Whittaker (eds.), *Trade and Famine in Classical Antiquity* (Cambridge, 1983), 110–27; *idem*, 'Supplying the system: frontiers and beyond' in J. C. Barrett, A. P. Fitzpatrick and L. Macinnes (eds.), *Barbarians and Romans in North-west Europe* (BAR s471, 1989), 64–80; *idem*, *Les Frontières*, Chapter 2.
[126] Notably M. G. Fulford, 'Roman and barbarian: the economy of Roman frontier systems' in Barrett *et al.*, *Barbarians and Romans*, 81–95 (comparison with the east at 90). Cf. Fulford, 'Roman material', 91 ('the relatively low volume of artefacts discovered'); B. H. Warmington, 'Frontier studies and the history of the Roman empire – some desiderata' in D. M. Pippidi (ed.), *Actes du IXe congrès international d'études sur les frontières romaines* (Bucharest, 1974), 291–6, at 293 ('instead of being surprised at its quantity, we should rather be surprised at how little there was over the centuries').
[127] E. A. Thompson, 'Christianity and the northern barbarians' in A. Momigliano (ed.), *The Conflict between Paganism and Christianity in the Fourth Century* (Oxford, 1963), 56–78, at 69–77.

Danube or Rhine interested in entering the empire for purposes of pilgrimage or religious study. Indeed given that such Christians as existed were predominantly Roman prisoners captured in incursions,[128] they will hardly have been at liberty to make such journeys. Nor does the fourth-century church appear to have shown much interest in exploiting the mission-field which lay to the north of the empire.[129]

This is not to say that there was no contact whatsoever between Christians in the empire and Christians in barbaricum during the fourth century. The *Passion of St Saba*[130] recounts the life of a Gothic Christian who underwent persecution during the early 370s until finally martyred in 372. The text explains how Saba's drowned body was recovered by fellow-Christians and hidden until 'Junius Soranus, *vir clarissimus, dux Scythiae*, who honoured the Lord, sent trustworthy men who carried [the body] from barbaricum to Romania' (8, p. 221/10ff.). Implicit in this account is the existence of contacts between a Roman official on the lower Danube and Christians living in Gothia. Furthermore, individuals from the empire apparently had no difficulty in gaining access to Gothia and removing the body. Nor was this a unique instance, for earlier in the *Passion* it is recorded that, when the persecution began, a Gothic (Christian) priest named Sansalas 'fled and stayed in Romania' (4, p. 218/23–4), as indeed did many others at this time.[131] To these cases may be added that of an unnamed Christian in the 390s who travelled for an unstated purpose[132] from Italy to the land of the 'Marcomanni', and through whom their queen Fritigil was converted and established contact with Ambrose of Milan (Paulinus *Life of Ambrose* 36, *PL* xiv.39).

Some individual initiatives to convert the Huns during the fifth century are recorded, but these efforts do not appear to have achieved anything, and no missions are known to have been undertaken to the Avars during the sixth century.[133] The subject populations over whom the Avars ruled did, however,

---

The one exception would appear to have been the Rugi, living north of Noricum in the fifth century. (Thompson's assumption that the Goths were converted some years after entry to the empire requires revision in the light of P. J. Heather, 'The crossing of the Danube and the Gothic conversion', *GRBS* 27 (1986), 289–318, who argues for formal acceptance of Christianity as a condition of entry in 376.)

128 Thompson, 'Christianity', 57–8.

129 *Ibid.*, 64. Cf. W. H. C. Frend, 'The missions of the early church 180–700 AD', *Miscellanea Historiae Christianae* 3 (1970), 3–23. Note, however, the astute remarks on the subject by P. Brown, *Religion and Society in the Age of Saint Augustine* (London, 1972), 148.

130 Ed. H. Delahaye, *AB* 31 (1912), 216–21.

131 Thompson, *Visigoths*, 98 n. 3. At the time of an earlier persecution, in the late 340s, Gothic Christians had sought refuge in the empire and had been settled by Constantius II near Nicopolis in Moesia (*ibid.*, 96–7). One might reasonably expect them to have maintained links with Christians who remained in Gothia, which would account for knowledge in the empire of Saba's martyrdom.

132 Thompson, 'Christianity', 60, has suggested that he was a merchant.

133 Thompson, *Attila*, 37–9; Maenchen-Helfen, *Huns*, Chapter 6; Pohl, *Awaren*, 199–205.

include substantial Christian elements, and archaeological finds suggest the possibility that some of these individuals undertook a pilgrimage to the Holy Land around the end of the sixth century.[134] Some northern peoples are found requesting instruction in the Christian faith from Constantinople during the sixth century, and Hunnic peoples dwelling in the Caucasus were successfully evangelised, though this was a result of those responsible living outside the empire for years on end rather than making regular crossings of the frontier.[135] Contacts arising from religious interests did therefore exist between the empire and northern peoples, but were clearly much more circumscribed than those in the east.

This limitation in the north was to some extent compensated for, at least during the fourth century, by another form of cross-frontier exchange which was much less prominent in the east — namely, the service of individuals from outside the empire in the Roman army. The increasing use of northern peoples in the Roman army during the fourth century has long been recognised, as indicated by Gibbon's lament concerning the 'barbarisation' of the armed forces. Indeed concern of this sort was perhaps current in late antiquity itself, when Vegetius advised that it would be cheaper for the government to recruit from within the empire than to pay foreigners (i.28). The best-documented cases concern individuals who held high rank. One study provides the names of twenty individuals of Germanic origin who reached the highest rank open to any officer, that of *magister*, during the fourth century.[136] Moreover, 'the fact that German officers often Latinized their names means that we are more likely to underestimate than to exaggerate their numbers'.[137] Barbarian names are found down through the ranks[138] to the level of ordinary soldier, such as the one who describes himself on an inscription from Aquincum as both a Frankish subject and a Roman soldier (*ILS* 2814).[139] As Dietrich Hoffmann has observed, those Germans who reached high office in the Roman army during the fourth century can only have been a fraction of the total number who served; the

---

134 *Ibid.*, 204.
135 E. A. Thompson, *Romans and Barbarians: the Decline of the Western Roman Empire* (Madison, Wis., 1982), 240–5.
136 M. Waas, *Germanen im römischen Dienst im 4. Jh. n. Chr.* (Bonn, 1965), 16. Waas' list includes neither Fravitta nor Stilicho (the latter perhaps excluded because a second-generation German), though Frigeridus and Vitalianus, whom he does include, are *comites* rather than *magistri* in PLRE. Cf. also R. MacMullen, *Corruption and the Decline of Rome* (New Haven and London, 1988), Appendix A.
137 Liebeschuetz, *Barbarians and Bishops*, 8.
138 Waas, *Germanen*, 16; MacMullen, *Corruption*, Appendix A. A further example of a barbarian *protector domesticus* is provided by an inscription from Trier commemorating Hariulfus, *filius Hanhavaldi regalis gentis Burgundiorum* (*ILS* 2813). For the dating of this inscription to the last quarter of the fourth century, see Hoffmann, 'Wadomar, Bacurius und Hariulf', 317.
139 For discussion of Frankish involvement in the Roman army, see Zöllner, *Geschichte der Franken*, 164–7; for the Alamanni, see K. F. Stroheker, 'Alamannen im römischen Dienst' in his *Germanentum und Spätantike* (Zurich and Stuttgart, 1965), 30–53.

number who did reach high office was considerable, so the total number in all ranks must have been very great indeed.[140] Indicative of the importance of barbarian volunteers in the ordinary ranks is Julian's reaction to Constantius' request for the transfer of units from Gaul to the east in 360: he feared that this source of recruits would dry up if they thought that they would be posted to regions distant from the Rhine, and he regarded this as the most detrimental consequence if Constantius' request were met (Amm. Marc. xx.4.4).

A proportion of Germans serving in the army will of course have been recruited from within the empire, from amongst the barbarian groups settled permanently on Roman territory, but significant numbers also came from outside the empire (e.g., Zos. ii.15.1; iii.8.1; iv.12.1). If, as seems likely, most of these recruits were attracted to the Roman army by the prospect of a regular supply of food, clothing and weapons,[141] rather than being fugitives from their homeland, then presumably many will have wanted to maintain ties with their kin if they were not stationed too far away – and it is apparent that the Roman authorities were not usually concerned to ensure that Germanic troops were deployed in provinces well removed from their homelands.[142] Furthermore, Ammianus reports the case of an Alamannic *scutarius*, a member of the imperial guard, who returned home temporarily while on leave in 377/8, and says nothing to suggest that such behaviour was out of the ordinary (xxxi.10.3). (Zos. iv.31.1, on the other hand, clearly described an exceptional and unusual situation.) Others seem to have returned home permanently on retirement, for it has been suggested that fourth-century graves in north-west Germany containing belt parts from Roman military workshops on the Rhine and Danube should 'be interpreted as those of Germanic officers who had served in the regular Roman army before returning to Germania with at least some of their equipment'.[143] But they are unlikely to have retired beyond the frontier unless they had maintained links with their homeland during their period of service within the empire. The case of the Frankish *magister* Silvanus who was advised in 355 that it would be dangerous for him to return to his homeland (Amm. Marc. xv.5.15–16) is probably the exception rather than the rule, for against it can be placed that of Mallobaudes who held rank in the Roman army (*comes domesticorum*) while also a 'King of the Franks' during the reign of Gratian (xxxi.10.6).

---

[140] *Das spätrömische Bewegungsheer und die Notitia Dignitatum* (Düsseldorf, 1969–70), vol. 1, 145.

[141] Jones, *Later Roman Empire*, 619.

[142] Theodosius I's concern to transfer Gothic recruits to Egypt in the early 380s (Zos. iv.30) is explicable in terms of specific circumstances – the depletion of Roman recruits arising from Adrianople, and understandable suspicions about Gothic loyalties in the light of recent events.

[143] M. Todd, 'Germanic burials in the Roman Iron Age' in R. Reece (ed.), *Burial in the Roman World* (London, 1977), 39–41, at 40–1. For other discussions of this evidence, see the references cited in Liebeschuetz, *Barbarians and Bishops*, 39 n. 75.

It is important to note, however, that this mode of interchange between the Roman empire and barbaricum was predominantly a phenomenon of the fourth century. Instances of Huns in Roman service are rare, and the best documented show them employed away from the Danube frontier.[144] Although it has been argued that crises such as the great plague of the mid-sixth century forced the empire to draw more heavily on barbarian manpower,[145] A. H. M. Jones concluded that in the sixth century 'Romans greatly predominated not only in the army as a whole, but in the expeditionary forces, where alone barbarians . . . were used on any considerable scale.'[146] Moreover, many of these barbarians were recruited from groups already settled within the empire.[147] In the final decades of the sixth century, 'the government relied increasingly on recruits from warlike peoples *within* the empire'.[148] During the sixth century, therefore, the level of cross-frontier interchange generated by barbarian service in the imperial army must have been significantly lower than in the fourth century.

Although it is clearly impossible to compare interaction across the eastern and northern frontiers in strictly quantitative terms, the overall impression derived from the available evidence is that interchange in the east was more intense than in the north. The economies of northern peoples were not sufficiently developed to generate trade with the Roman empire on a scale comparable to that in the east, and the powerful impetus to cross-frontier movement provided by religious motivations in the east was much less evident in the north. Even the factor where the north surpassed the east – foreign service in the Roman army – was subject to chronological limits which reduced its importance over late antiquity as a whole. The significance of these differences will become apparent at a later point in this study (see Chapter 5).

---

[144] Thompson, *Attila*, 31–5; Maenchen-Helfen, *Huns*, 255–8. Cf. the way in which defeated Bulgars in the sixth century were employed in army units in Armenia and Lazica, well away from the Danube (Theoph. p. 219/14–16).

[145] J. L. Teall, 'The barbarians in Justinian's armies', *Speculum* 40 (1965), 294–322.

[146] *Later Roman Empire*, 667.

[147] E.g., the Heruls, who feature in the African and Italian expeditions, derived from groups settled by Anastasius in the early sixth century (Proc. *Wars* vi.14.33, vii.33.13). The Huns who also appear on these expeditions could have been recruited from those settled by Marcian in the mid-fifth century (references in de Ste Croix, *Class Struggle*, 516, no.26).

[148] J. F. Haldon, *Recruitment and Conscription in the Byzantine Army c. 550–950* (Vienna, 1979), 25 (my emphasis).

PART II

INFORMATION AND UNCERTAINTY

3

BACKGROUND KNOWLEDGE
AND ASSUMPTIONS

IN his inaugural lecture at the London School of Economics in 1967, entitled '1914: the unspoken assumptions', the distinguished historian of modern Europe, James Joll, drew attention to the need for those investigating the origins of the First World War to explore the underlying presuppositions which influenced decision-makers in the years and months leading up to August 1914 – 'to reconstruct, so to speak, their ideological furniture'.[1] Among other things, this would involve giving attention to the values and beliefs inculcated in the upper classes by the educational systems of the Great Powers, and to intellectual currents, such as Social Darwinism, exercising influence at a popular level. Clearly, a concern with 'unspoken assumptions' is a desideratum in the study of foreign relations in any period. As Joll readily acknowledged, however, it is no easy task to make connections between these sorts of areas and the conduct of foreign policy. If that is the case for the modern historian, with a mountain of letters, diaries and memoirs at his or her disposal, how much more difficult, if not impossible, for the historian of antiquity, for far more elementary matters such as what late Roman government knew of the geography and socio-political organisation of neighbouring peoples. Nevertheless, questions of this sort clearly need to be considered and some attempt made to answer them, even if rendered far from satisfactory by the nature of the available sources.[2]

GEOGRAPHICAL KNOWLEDGE[3]

It has recently been observed that in most modern discussions of ancient geographical knowledge 'scholars have taken for granted the thought-world of

[1] Reprinted in H. W. Koch (ed.), *The Origins of the First World War* (London, 1972), 307–28.
[2] Cf. Millar, 'Emperors, frontiers and foreign relations', 15–20.
[3] Useful surveys of the *Realien* of late Roman geographical writings and cartography include W. Wolska-Conus, 'Geographie', *RAC* 10 (1978), 155–222; H. Hunger, *Die hochsprachliche profane Literatur der Byzantiner* vol. 1 (Munich, 1978), Chapter 5; A. L. F. Rivet and C. Smith,

easy, habitual map-literacy'.[4] There is undoubtedly a danger of unconsciously importing unrealistic expectations from the modern world into this subject, for it does not take long to discover what, by modern standards, are major deficiencies in late Roman geographical knowledge, and if expectations have not been adjusted appropriately, it becomes all too easy to adopt a dismissive attitude when one is discussing the subject.[5] This sort of attitude can be unhelpful, in so far as it can lead to exaggeration. For example, one catalogue of errors includes the fact that 'Ammianus, a professional soldier and an intelligent officer, places the river Durance on the wrong side of the Alps, although he had probably seen it himself'.[6] Such an elementary misconception would be a very serious indictment indeed, if valid, but in fact it carries the critique too far. Its inclusion overlooks the necessary distinction between narrative and digression in Ammianus' writing. Even where he had personal experience relevant to the subject-matter of his digressions, Ammianus still generally allowed their content to be dictated by the written authorities he consulted, with the result that, in contrast to the circumstantial detail of his narrative, the digressions are charac-terised by 'artificial formality' and 'bookishness', and should not therefore be taken as indicative of his personal knowledge or views of a subject.[7] His misplacement of the Durance occurs in one such formal digression concerning Gaul (and more specifically Hannibal's crossing of the Alps), at the beginning of which Ammianus explicitly acknowledges his close adherence to Timagenes of Alexandria for the information which follows (xv.9.2).[8]

However, even if their ignorance did not extend as far as not knowing on which side of feature *A* point *B* lay, it must nevertheless be acknowledged that

---

The Place-Names of Roman Britain (London, 1979); O. A. W. Dilke, Greek and Roman Maps (London, 1985); J. B. Harley and D. Woodward (eds.), The History of Cartography vol.1 (Chicago and London, 1987), Chapters 12–16 (by O. A. W. Dilke). There have been important reviews of Dilke's work by P. Janni (Gnomon 59 (1987), 230–3), R. J. A. Talbert (JRS 77 (1987), 210–12; AHR 94 (1989), 407–8) and D. Wood (Cartographica 22/4 (1985), 97–101; 24/4 (1987), 69–78).

[4] N. Purcell, 'The creation of provincial landscape' in T. Blagg and M. Millett (eds.), The Early Roman Empire in the West (Oxford, 1990), 6–29, at 8.

[5] E.g., R. MacMullen, Roman Government's Response to Crisis (New Haven, 1976), 52–4. For reservations about these pages and the chapter in which they occur, see J. F. Gilliam, Yale Review (1978), 284–5, and P. Brown, Representations 2 (1983), 2 and 22 n. 10.

[6] MacMullen, Response, 53, citing Amm. Marc. xv.10.11.

[7] Matthews, Ammianus, 390 (contrasting Ammianus' treatment of Nicomedia in narrative and digression) and 545 n. 10.

[8] The digression as a whole, however, seems to have drawn on a variety of writers in addition to Timagenes, who may not therefore have been the source for Ammianus' statement about the Durance: for a summary of the scholarly debate, see P. de Jonge, Philological and Historical Commentary on Ammianus Marcellinus XV.6–13 (Groningen, 1953), 47–8. MacMullen (Response, 53, 237 n. 18) also comments on the 'mythologising picture of the East' and the 'Herodotean fantasies' contained in the first part of the fourth-century Expositio Totius Mundi et Gentium (1–21); but for a different perspective which interprets this part as a coherent quasi-anthropo-logical description of the evolution of human society, see G. Dagron, '"Ceux d'en face". Les peuples étrangers dans les traités militaires byzantins', TM 10 (1987), 207–32, at 212.

the available evidence concerning late Roman geographical knowledge at levels more sophisticated than this does not inspire confidence. From the middle of the sixth century, for example, there survives the *Christian Topography* of the Alexandrian merchant Cosmas Indicopleustes. This work was written to combat the Aristotelian view of a spherical world then being taught in Alexandria by the Christian philosopher John Philoponus, a view which Cosmas believed to be unbiblical. Influenced by Nestorian teachings, Cosmas took the tabernacle of Moses as his model and presented the world in the shape of a rectangular box with rounded lid, the base of which was the surface of the earth. Within this framework, he elaborated the workings of the heavens and the geography of the earth as he understood them from scripture.[9] The peculiar nature of Cosmas' conceptions can readily incline one to dismiss them as idiosyncratic; but in fact 'there can be little doubt that the Antiochene conception of the universe, as exemplified by Cosmas, reflected the views of the average [sixth-century] Byzantine on this subject'.[10] It is nevertheless of interest that, in spite of his misconceptions, he does seem to have been able to travel successfully, in his capacity as a merchant, to the Persian Gulf and the Horn of Africa,[11] which suggests that he possessed useful practical knowledge uncontaminated by the flaws of his theorising. Nor should this occasion surprise, for as has been noted, albeit in a rather different context, it is 'extremely easy for academics to over-emphasise the degree to which the majority of ordinary people are either aware of, or bothered by, different categories of belief'.[12]

But if Cosmas' views do reflect those of the 'average' inhabitant of the Roman empire in the mid-sixth century, what about the educated elite from whom high government officials were likely to be drawn? As Joll suggested apropos of 1914, it is their underlying assumptions which are important and it is their education which may provide some clues to those assumptions. What part therefore did geographical study play in late Roman education? Geography certainly was not recognised as a subject in its own right; it may have impinged on the study of geometry and astronomy, but its main role was as an auxiliary to the understanding of literary texts.[13] This is evident from the various geographical handbooks which seem to have been in use as school texts during late antiquity, such as Dionysius' *Periegesis*, and its various Latin translations, the *Cosmographia* of Julius Honorius, the handbook of Vibius Sequester, and the

9 W. Wolska, *La Topographie chrétienne de Cosmas Indicopleustès. Théologie et science au VIe siècle* (Paris, 1962). Cosmas' work was accompanied by numerous illustrations, including one showing his box-like view of the world (Plate 1).

10 C. Mango, *Byzantium. The Empire of New Rome* (London, 1980), 176.

11 In spite of the epithet 'Indicopleustes', and his references to India and Taprobane (Sri Lanka), it is probable that he had not travelled to these parts himself (Wolska, *Cosmas*, 9).

12 M. Spufford, *Small Books and Pleasant Histories. Popular Fiction and its Readership in Seventeenth-Century England* (London, 1981), 155.

13 Wolska-Conus, 'Geographie', 205.

geographical gazetteer of Stephanus Byzantinus.[14] It has been observed with regard to this last work that 'the emphasis throughout is linguistic . . . It was . . . more useful to the teacher than to officials of the foreign office [sic] or provincial administration.'[15] In the preface to his short alphabetical listing of rivers, springs, lakes, woods, mountains and peoples, Vibius Sequester indicates that he compiled the work to facilitate his son's reading of literature, while the didactic purpose of Julius Honorius' *Cosmographia* is likewise evident in both its preface and conclusion. This literary orientation of geographical learning was bound to be a handicap for anyone having to deal with the empire's neighbours as a matter of practical politics, as was the primary concern of these works with places within the Roman empire, and their content is usually so generalised or brief as to be of little practical use, if it is not positively misleading. These latter features can be illustrated from Julius Honorius' work. 'The River Jordan rises under Mount Lebanon, passing around which it proceeds into Lake Tiberias. It leaves this and flows along its course to Scythopolis, the middle of which it cuts through. Leaving this, it pours into the Dead Sea' (12, *GLM* 31). The Jordan flows near, rather than through, Scythopolis, but otherwise this is broadly accurate as a description; yet its generalised nature renders it of little practical value to the would-be traveller. Far more typical, however, is the following: 'The River Chrysorrhoas originates in the plains of Syria, extending its course by Syria, Antioch, Palaestina and the other cities of Syria. It empties itself into the Aegean Sea, in which lies the island of Cyprus' (11, *GLM* 30-1).

These works all take the form of topographical lists or written descriptions, but Julius Honorius' work at least also appears to have been intended for use in conjunction with a map; at any rate, it contains a parting admonition not to separate the written text from an accompanying globe (*sphaera*). Whatever this particular item may have been, there is no doubt that maps are a crucial issue for the general subject under consideration here in so far as they bear on the ability of the Romans or otherwise to conceptualise the regions adjacent to the empire. A number of comments suggest that maps were recognised as having some role in education during late antiquity. In his speech of 298, the Gallic orator Eumenius referred to his intention that the schools which he planned to build at Autun should contain in their porticos for the benefit of the students depictions of all lands and seas, showing the positions of places and distances between, and the courses of rivers and coastlines (*Pan.Lat.* v(9).20.2–3). In the

[14] Dionysius and translations: *GGM* vol. 2, 104–99; Julius Honorius: *GLM*, 24–55; Vibius Sequester, ed. R. Gelsomino (Leipzig, 1967); Stephanus Byzantinus *Ethnika*, ed. A. Meinecke (Berlin, 1849; repr. Graz, 1958). On this genre, note the astute discussion by C. Jacob, 'L'œil et la mémoire sur la *Périégèse de la terre habitée* de Denys' in C. Jacob and F. Lestringant (eds.), *Arts et légendes d'espaces: Figures du voyage et rhétoriques du monde* (Paris, 1981), 21–97, especially 43 and 57.
[15] N. G. Wilson, *Scholars of Byzantium* (London, 1983), 56.

early fifth century, Theodosius II ordered the preparation of a map of the world for public display (perhaps an updated version of the map of Agrippa) – an event which has been associated with his inauguration of the university at Constantinople.[16]

Neither of these maps has survived, and in fact there are extant only two examples of late Roman cartography covering large areas:[17] the so-called Peutinger Table whose representation of the Mediterranean world strikes the modern eye as a gross distortion of reality, with its stretching out of landforms along the east–west axis, and compression of them on the north–south axis;[18] and the shield-cover from Dura-Europos on which is preserved part of a very approximate representation of the Black Sea coastline.[19] Both items present information about distances between points along routes and have been regarded by scholars as examples of the illustrated itineraries (itineraria picta) used by the Roman army, of which Vegetius gives a description (iii.6, p. 75/11ff.). In fact, strictly speaking, neither conforms in detail to this description:[20] Vegetius' itineraria picta covered smaller areas than the Mediterranean-wide Peutinger Table, and provided much more detailed information about the nature of routes than either the Peutinger Table or the Dura shield contains.

Nevertheless, both are clearly schematic representations of itineraries of some sort. The more important issue is what deductions may legitimately be made from these cartographic representations as to how Romans conceived the geography of their world. On the one hand, there are those who claim that 'the Romans did not have a sufficiently clear or accurate notion of topographical realities to allow them to conceive of the overall military situation in global strategic terms'.[21] On the other hand, there are those who maintain that 'it

---

[16] W. Wolska-Conus, 'La "carte de Théodose II": sa destination?', TM 5 (1973), 274–9. Note, however, that the comes formarum (ND Occ. iv.5) was not head of a late Roman department of maps and plans (as suggested by Dilke in Harley and Woodward, History of Cartography vol. 1, 244, 252), but an official responsible for the maintenance of Rome's aqueducts (Seeck, RE iv.654).

[17] I exclude from consideration here the famous Madaba mosaic.

[18] The best edition of the map is E. Weber, Tabula Peutingeriana: Codex Vindobonensis 324 (Graz, 1976), 2 vols. Some sense of the distortion involved can be gained from its dimensions: measuring 675 cm × 34 cm, its width is about twenty times its height.

[19] The fullest recent discussion is R. Rebuffat, 'Le bouclier de Doura', Syria 63 (1986), 85–105, though he fails to address the argument of K. Uhden ('Bemerkungen zu dem römischen Karten-fragment von Dura Europos', Hermes 67 (1932), 117–25) that 'Trapezus' refers not to Trabzon, but to the mountainous area of the Crimean peninsula. This point is taken up by Dilke (Greek and Roman Maps, 121), who adds the suggestion that 'Arta' does not refer to Artaxata in Armenia, but is a transliteration into Greek of the Latin word arta, meaning 'straits', and on this basis argues that the Dura shield covers a significantly smaller portion of the Black Sea coast than has normally been assumed. Dilke's suggested interpretation of 'Arta' is certainly consistent with the other evidence for a Latin archetype (on which see Rebuffat, 'Le bouclier', 90).

[20] As observed by Rebuffat, 'Le bouclier', 91 and n. 19; cf. Dillemann, Haute Mésopotamie, 134.

[21] Isaac, Limits of Empire, 401–2, summarising and endorsing Millar, 'Emperors, frontiers and foreign relations', 15–18.

should not be thought that the Peutinger Table was typical of Roman maps, or that Romans were incapable of drawing a map to scale'.[22] The essential argument underlying the former, conservative position is that although these schematic itineraries may not have purported to be maps, they are nevertheless the only surviving evidence of cartographic representation of large areas, and in the absence of other evidence to the contrary, there is no choice but to take them as indicators of how erroneous Roman geographical conceptions could be. The alternative viewpoint stresses that there are possible explanations for the distortion in the Peutinger Table, such as the likelihood that its elongation is due to the original having been inscribed on a papyrus roll, or the probability that Agrippa's world map (on which it may have been based) was elongated in the same way simply so as to fit the portico in which it was placed. Moreover, it is argued, the undoubted ability of the Roman surveyors (*agrimensores*) to survey extensive tracts of provincial territory shows that they were able to conceptualise large-scale geographical space accurately.[23]

A way of circumventing this apparent impasse is provided by the recent work of Pietro Janni which has sought to apply insights from the cognitive sciences concerning the conceptualisation of space to the problems of ancient cartography.[24] Janni does not doubt that the Peutinger Table was never intended to present a true cartographic representation,[25] but neither does he accept that the Romans were capable of producing a genuine map of an area the size of the Mediterranean world: it was, quite simply, conceptually beyond them. Closely related to their ability in road construction, the Roman conception of space, which he terms *spazio odologico* (as distinct from *spazio cartografico*), was defined primarily in terms of the line. The itinerary, with all its attendant limitations, was the natural reflection of this mode of thought, which Janni describes as being 'one-dimensional'.[26] As others on whose work Janni draws have observed, the distinction between the itinerary and the map 'nicely parallels the stages of the development in human consciousness from purely topological space notions (and the restrictions they impose) to an all-points-of-view, projective Euclidean space'.[27] On this basis, he argues persuasively that there is an enormous conceptual leap from the sort of activity in which the Roman surveyors were engaged to the ability to draw accurate maps of whole

---

[22] Dilke, *Greek and Roman Maps*, 120.

[23] O. A. W. and M. S. Dilke, 'Perception of the Roman world', *PrG* 9 (1976), 39–72.

[24] P. Janni, *La mappa e il periplo. Cartografia antica e spazio odologico* (Rome, 1984). For an appreciation and development of some of Janni's insights, see Purcell, 'Creation of provincial landscape' and 'Maps, lists, money, order and power', *JRS* 80 (1990), 178–82.

[25] Janni, *La mappa*, 61 and n. 112.

[26] *Ibid.*, 58–65, 79–90, 147–58. The fundamental limitation is that the itinerary does not provide the necessary information for the traveller to move with ease from one route to another in mid-course.

[27] A. H. Robinson and B. B. Petchenik, *The Nature of Maps* (Chicago and London, 1976), 13.

continents.[28] Janni's analysis derives much of its power from the fact that he tries to avoid 'taking for granted the thought-world of easy, habitual map-literacy'.

In the light of this, it is apparent that the Romans cannot have been able to conceive accurately the geography of the Mediterranean world in a global sense.[29] If we move down a level to their knowledge of particular regions outside the empire during late antiquity, matters are not as clear-cut. Although the evidence is sketchy, there are indications that while knowledge of the geography of lands to the north of the Rhine and the Danube was inadequate, that of the western regions of the Persian empire was rather less so. On a number of occasions, for example, Ammianus is explicit about the need for Roman forces operating beyond the Rhine to make use of native guides (ductores) in order to locate Alamannic settlements (xvii.10.2, 5; xxvii.10.7; xxix.4.5), while troops who ventured across the Rhine against the Franks in the early fifth century soon became lost in the forests (Greg. Tur. HF ii.9). It is also clear from Priscus' account of the embassy to Attila in 449 that the Roman participants had little sense of where they were being led once they were north of the Danube (fr.11,2), and there is a reference to the use of guides (ποδηγοί) by the army when it was operating north of the lower Danube in the late sixth century. It is unclear whether these were local inhabitants press-ganged into the job for that particular campaign, or individuals holding a regular post in the army, but even if it was the latter, their knowledge was clearly deficient, for they successfully managed to get the army lost (Th. Sim. vii.5.6).

The situation in the east was rather different, as shown by Julian's Persian expedition in 363. It has been claimed that a major factor in the failure of Julian's expedition was the inadequacy of his understanding of the geography of the regions he was invading.[30] However, the arguments for this claim are unconvincing, while more persuasive explanations for the débâcle may be found in the failure of the forces under Procopius to fulfil their part of the plan and Julian's 'failure to anticipate the readiness of the Persians to damage their own land in order to resist him' through destruction of irrigation canals and dykes.[31] Julian had a sufficiently clear idea of the relative positions of routes to Ctesiphon down

---

[28] Janni, La mappa, 62–4 (cf. E. Rawson, Intellectual Life in the Late Roman Republic (London, 1985), 259). Dilke, who 'appears too quick to attribute modern attitudes to Romans and modern functions to their maps' (Talbert, AHR 94 (1989), 408), has yet to offer a detailed critique of Janni's views. His only comments to date appear in his paper 'Rome's contribution to cartography' in M. Sordi (ed.), Geografia e storiografia nel mondo classico (Milan, 1988), 194–201, at 195, and these fail to engage with Janni's fundamental thesis.

[29] With the attendant consequences for theories of 'grand strategy' which have been ably set out by Isaac, Limits of Empire.

[30] S. N. C. Lieu, The Emperor Julian: Panegyric and Polemic (Liverpool, 1986), 93–5.

[31] For these explanations, see Ridley, 'Julian's Persian expedition', 317–30 (surprisingly, absent from Lieu's bibliography), and Matthews, Ammianus, 139, 159–60 (the quotation).

the Euphrates and across the north Mesopotamian plain to be able to formulate a strategy of deception whereby he managed to convince the Persians that he was aiming to advance by the latter route,[32] and it has been suggested that Severus Alexander may have had a similar plan in mind in 232.[33] The idea that Julian relied on the fugitive Persian prince, Hormizd, for guidance as to the topography of Persia finds little corroboration in the sources; the one reference which might have lent support to this is in fact ambiguous.[34] The route down the Euphrates must, after all, have been well known, for it had been used repeatedly by invading Roman emperors since Trajan, as well as being described in the first part of Isidore of Charax's *Parthian Stations* (dating from the Augustan period: *GGM* vol. 1, 244–54).[35]

When it came to withdrawing from Ctesiphon, there was also a clear understanding of the alternatives: either to return back up the Euphrates – this must be what Ammianus means when he refers to the option of returning 'through Assyria'[36] – or to proceed northwards along the foot of the Zagros mountains (Amm. Marc. xxiv.8.4). This latter route, following the course of the ancient Persian 'Royal Road', would likewise have been familiar to Roman officials, since this is the route by which Roman envoys seem usually to have been conducted to Ctesiphon.[37] The claim found in Theodoret (*HE* iii.25.4),

---

[32] Dillemann, *Haute Mésopotamie*, 302; Ridley, 'Julian's Persian expedition', 319 n. 8.

[33] Potter, *Prophecy and History*, 22.

[34] Both Ammianus (xxiv.2.4) and Zosimus (iii.15.4) mention an occasion during the advance down the Euphrates when Hormizd was sent ahead to reconnoitre, but this in itself proves nothing. Zosimus, however, adds the comment that he was selected because of his accurate knowledge of τὰ Περσῶν. R. T. Ridley, in his 1982 translation of Zosimus, renders this as 'since he had a very accurate and detailed knowledge of the country', but τὰ Περσῶν is an annoyingly vague expression which F. Paschoud, in the Budé edition, translates with equal justification as 'les usages des Perses'. As for Julian's taking on of Persian deserters as guides, this occurred only after he had reached Ctesiphon and was apparently contemplating marching deeper into the Persian empire, i.e. into parts much less familiar to Romans; in any case Ammianus' account at this point (xxiv.7.3, 5) is most unsatisfactory due to a lacuna, and the whole story of the Persian guides has even been queried by some (e.g., Ridley, 'Julian's Persian expedition', 322).

[35] 'When emperors embarked on invasions of Mesopotamia it did not prove an arduous task of planning and transport to conduct the legions as far as Ctesiphon' (R. Syme, 'Military geography at Rome', *California Studies in Classical Antiquity* 7 (1988), 227–51, at 235). M. Gawlikowski, 'La route de l'Euphrate d'Isidore à Julien' in P.-L. Gatier, B. Helly and J.-P. Rey-Coquais (eds.), *Géographie historique au Proche-orient* (Paris, 1990), 76–98, argues that Julian's progress corresponded in detail to the route described by Isidore.

[36] Matthews, *Ammianus*, 159.

[37] This at any rate is the pattern from the better-documented sixth century, when Roman envoys are received on Persian territory at Nisibis (Men. fr. 9,1/27; for Nisibis' location on the ancient Royal Road, see Dillemann, *Haute Mésopotamie*, 147–55) and are found returning from Ctesiphon via Karka de Beth Selok (Kirkuk) (*Acta S. Shirin* 17 in *AB* 64 (1946), 124). The fact that the army actually ended up following the course of the Tigris does not mean it got lost; the arrival of the Persian army after the choice of route had been made obviously forced Julian to rethink his options, and the Tigris route offered advantages in these circumstances – protection of the army's left flank, more broken terrain (Oates, *Studies*, 6) to hinder the enemy cavalry, and access to water (cf. J. Fontaine in the Budé edition of Ammianus, vol. 4(2), p. 195 n. 470).

and echoed by other Christian sources, that the withdrawing Roman army was 'without guides and wandering aimlessly in the desert' can be dismissed as part of a patent polemic against the apostate emperor.

There are a number of possible explanations as to why the Romans should have had a better understanding of the geography of the Fertile Crescent than of northern barbaricum. One very obvious point is that the former comprised a much smaller area than the latter. A second factor must have been the higher level of human interaction between the Roman and Persian empires compared with that between the Roman empire and any of its northern neighbours (cf. Chapter 2 above), and a third the fact that the Euphrates and Tigris rivers were known to lead to the vicinity of Ctesiphon, so providing extremely useful points (or rather lines) of orientation.

But perhaps most significant is a consideration suggested by combining Janni's argument concerning the primacy of the line in the Roman conception of space with the urban-oriented mentality of the Roman elite. This latter feature is evident, for example, in the prominence given to the binary opposition of 'urban/non-urban' in the delineation of other cultures by Roman writers: Tacitus notes the absence of cities among the Germanic tribes (*Ger.* 16.1), as does Pomponius Mela among the Sarmatians (iii.33), and Ammianus, referring to the Alamannic occupation of northern Gaul in the early 350s, comments on how they avoided living in cities as if they were tombs (xvi.2.12). Particularly striking is the recurrent reference to the relative density of cities in each of the regions he describes throughout his wide-ranging and lengthy description of the Persian empire (xxiii.6.11, 22, 23, 26, 31, 39 etc.). For educated Romans, of course, cities were synonymous with the refinements of civilised life,[38] but I would also suggest that the presence of cities – and roads (to resume Janni's point) - in a region must have greatly facilitated the 'imageability' of that region in the Roman mind.[39] The landscape of the western parts of the Persian empire presented precisely this sort of familiar configuration of cities and towns linked by well-defined roads.

On the other hand, it must have been very difficult for Romans to gain any kind of conceptual purchase on regions to the north of the Danube and Rhine, where there was no well-established infrastructure of towns and roads. This is certainly the implication of Tacitus' image of Germany as 'a land bristling with forests and unhealthy marshes' (*terra . . . silvis horrida aut paludibus foeda: Ger.* 5.1), and the allusion in a fourth-century oration to the 'trackless wastes' (*solitudines*

---

[38] Cf. Matthews, *Ammianus*, 392ff.; cf. also 345–6 (on Proc. *Wars* ii.1.1–11).

[39] The term 'imageability' derives from the work of Kevin Lynch, whose studies have had a major impact on research into environmental perception; for a discussion of his contribution, see R. M. Downs, 'Geographic space perception. Past approaches and future prospects', *PrG* 2 (1970), 65–108, at 70–5.

avias) of Alamannia (*Pan.Lat.* xii(2).5.2).[40] It is surely significant in this context that the Peutinger Table incorporates routes well into Persian territory but, apart from roads of Roman construction lying within the former province of Dacia and the *agri decumates*, confines its information about topography north of the empire to features such as the 'Marcian forest' (*silva Marciana*), the 'Bastarnic mountains' (*alpes Bastarnicae*), the 'Sarmatian wastelands' (*solitudines Sarmatarum*), and 'the deserted region' (*sors desertus*).[41]

THE ROLE OF ENVIRONMENTAL PARAMETERS

The focus thus far has been on the extent of formal Roman knowledge of the geography of regions beyond the empire, to the east and the north. This was of particular relevance when the empire was engaging in offensive operations, but of course much time in late antiquity was spent in trying to ward off attacks directed at the empire. The ability of the empire to do this successfully or otherwise was influenced by many factors. One which has received less attention is the impact of environmental parameters, namely the climate and topography which characterised the relevant frontier regions. In northern Mesopotamia, the climatic regime exercised an important influence on the times of year when warfare was normally feasible, while the topography of the region affected the direction from which attacks could be mounted. In other words, these environmental conditions tended to define limits within which military action was possible. As such, they constituted a set of underlying assumptions arising from experience over the centuries, a form of practical knowledge, and are a good illustration of information as the reduction of uncertainty, the narrowing of possibilities. Again, however, the east stands in contrast to the north, where comparable environmental constraints were

---

[40] Although Ammianus' language echoes that of Tacitus (xv.4.3: *horrore silvarum squalentium inaccessum*; xvii.1.8: *silvam . . . squalore tenebrarum horrendam*; cf. Caesar *Gallic War* vi.25; Pliny *Natural History* xvi.5; Mela iii.29; Greg. Tur. *HF* ii.9; cf. also Th. Sim. vi.8.10), and there is perhaps some element of exaggeration, the image was probably broadly accurate with respect to the extent of forest and woodland (see Todd, *Northern Barbarians*, 4, with further references in n. 1).

[41] If this seems all too self-evident, a sense of perspective can be restored by the realisation that there are other, non-urbanised cultures which *are* able to describe unurbanised environments with enormous precision. For example, the language of the Southern Paiute, who early this century lived among the desert plateaux of the south-western United States, included single words for features which require whole phrases in English, such as 'spot of level ground in mountains surrounded by ridges', 'slope of mountain or canyon wall receiving sunlight', and 'rolling country intersected by several small hill-ridges' (E. Sapir, 'Language and environment', *AA* 14 (1912), 226–42, at 228–9) – one illustration of the general observation that 'different cultures have large taxonomies of those elements of the environment that are finely discriminated, important and used' (A. Rapaport, 'Environmental cognition in cross-cultural perspective' in G. T. Moore and R. G. Golledge (eds.), *Environmental Knowing* (Stroudsberg, Penn., 1976), 220–34, at 223).

significantly less in evidence. The scope for uncertainty was correspondingly wider and the empire at a greater disadvantage.

Eastern Syria and northern Iraq – the modern areas which cover ancient northern Mesopotamia – do not enjoy the Mediterranean climate typical of western Syria. The mountain chain which runs parallel with the Syrian and Lebanese coast effectively deprives eastern Syria and the land beyond it of any moderating maritime influence. This fact, together with its proximity to the Arabian desert, accounts in large part for the markedly polarised annual cycle which characterises the region in question: hot rainless summers, followed by cold wet winters, with barely an autumn or spring to mark the transition. It is the winter which is of particular relevance, for the conditions of that season, which extends from November to March, are such as to render most activities of the summer months impracticable. Communications relying on unpaved roads become much more difficult when the effects of the heavy rainfall start to make themselves felt and temperatures can be low enough to make outdoor work impossible. Temperatures at Mosul on the upper Tigris, for example, have been known to remain below freezing point for days on end, and falls of snow are by no means unknown.[42]

There are no grounds for believing that the climate of this region has altered appreciably since the first centuries AD.[43] The extremes of winter weather in the region during late antiquity are certainly evident in contemporary literary sources, as will become apparent below. It is therefore surprising to find an eminent authority asserting that 'in contrast with the Arabs, who contented themselves with raids during the spring and summer, the Persians began their campaigns without consideration for the time of year'.[44] The only supporting evidence cited is Kavad's campaign of 502-3 which began in August and continued through the winter months. But this was the exception rather than the rule, and the difficulties with which he had to cope during the winter show why it was unusual.

The normal practice in northern Mesopotamia was for campaigns to begin at the end of the winter or during the spring. This is the case for nearly all other Persian and Roman invasions where a time of commencement is specified or can be deduced. There are a number of indications from the fourth century. Libanius states that Persian attacks during Constantius' reign regularly began in the spring (Or. xviii.206).[45] Shapur II carried out his threat to invade

---

[42] The information in this paragraph derives from the Admiralty, Naval Intelligence Division, Geographical Handbook Series, Syria (London, 1944), 169ff.; Iraq and the Persian Gulf (London, 1944), 166ff.

[43] Dillemann, Haute Mésopotamie, 67; E. Wirth, Syrien: eine geographische Landeskunde (Darmstadt, 1971), 98, 131–2.

[44] Pigulevskaja, Les Villes, 125.

[45] Cf. his remark (Or. lix.77) about Constantius wintering in Antioch, and then setting out to fight with the arrival of the campaigning season (ἡ ὡραια).

after the winter of 358–9;[46] with the arrival of late autumn that same year, however, further campaigning was not possible and the king is reported as contemplating returning to Persian territory (Amm. Marc. xix.9.1). Julian's expedition set out on 5 March 363 (xxiii.2.6),[47] and Shapur began another campaign at the end of winter in 371 (xxix.1.1); Valens, based at Antioch, responded by advancing in the spring of that year, and campaigned until the onset of winter (Zos. iv.13.2).

Evidence from the sixth century reveals the same pattern. In late 528, Roman and Persian forces agreed to call a halt to hostilities with the arrival of winter (Mal. p. 442/16–17). The battle of Dara in 530 took place in June, while that at Callinicum the following year was fought in April – both engagements coming soon after the initial invasion (Theoph. p. 180/30; Proc. *Wars* i.18.15). Khusro invaded at the beginning of spring in both 540 and 542 (Proc. *Wars* ii.5.1; 20.1), as did Belisarius in the intervening year (14.8). After a summer of campaigning, Maurice retired in the winter of 580–1, then resumed the following spring; the elder Heraclius' movements followed the same pattern in 586–7; campaigning had ceased in autumn 582; that of 586 began in spring, that of 591 (to restore Khusro II) at the beginning of the summer, and that of 588 ceased with the onset of winter.[48]

The disadvantages of continuing to campaign in the winter months are shown by the vicissitudes suffered by Kavad's troops during the siege of Amida from October 502 to January 503: '[Kavad] was weighed down by dejection and regret because the harshness of the winter overtook him; for the Persians were handicapped by their [inadequate] clothing, and their bows were slackened as a result of the moist air' (Zach. *HE* vii.3, vol. 2, p. 23/4–8). The Romans found themselves equally hindered by the conditions in their attempts to combat Kavad during the war of 502–5. The Roman general Celerius is reported as having had to give up his pursuit of Kavad in late 503 'because the winter season had come', while Patricius was unable to cross the River Kallath because it was flooded with winter rains (J. Styl. 65, 66). During the winter of 504–5, the Roman commanders tried in vain to continue their own siege to recapture Amida: 'When many days had passed . . . it became very cold, with much snow and ice, and the Romans deserted their camps one by one . . . Those who remained and did not go to their own places went to Tella and Rhesaena and

---

[46] For the threat, Amm. Marc. xvii.5.8; for its fulfilment, xviii.7.4, where the reference to the yellowing of grain and appearance of young grass is a clear indication of springtime (cf. Admiralty, *Iraq*, 456 – wheat ripens in early May).

[47] According to Soc. *HE* iii.21, Julian began at the very beginning of March, 'a little before spring', in order to catch the Persians while it was still cold (cf. Lib. *Or.* xviii.214).

[48] Th. Sim. iii.17.4–5 (580–1); ii.10.5–6 (586–7); i.9.11 (582); 15.1 (586); v.4.3 (591); Evag. *HE* vi.14 p. 233/2–3 (588). For the shorter campaigning season in Armenia, see Whitby, *Maurice*, 202.

Urha [Edessa], in order to find shelter from the cold' (J. Styl. 81). Similar difficulties were experienced by the Persian forces besieging Martyropolis in 531: 'the winter arrived . . . and the Persians became bedraggled with the rain and mud, and experienced hardships' (Zach. *HE* ix.6, vol.2, p. 98/2–4). In 360, Constantius II, too, was forced to abandon his attempt to recapture Bezabde[49] from the Persians by the arrival of steady winter rains which quickly turned the ground into a quagmire (Amm. Marc. xx.11.24–5).[50]

There are only a handful of other cases where campaigning seems to have been conducted during the winter. Although strictly lying prior to the period with which this study is concerned, it is generally thought that Septimius Severus captured Ctesiphon on 28 January 198, though the evidence is not as straightforward as the precision of the date might suggest,[51] and writing not long after this event, Dio takes it as given that the Parthians did not campaign in winter (xl.15.4). Gordian III's invasion in 243 seems to have taken place during the winter months, though at least one commentator has noted the oddness of the timing in the light of the likely climatic conditions.[52] Finally, at the other end of our period, Heraclius' final offensive against Khusro II began in September 627. 'In this year in the month of September, Heraclius with the Turks invaded Persia unexpectedly on account of the winter, throwing Khusro into perplexity when he learned of it' (Theoph. p. 317/11–13). September of course marks the beginning of autumn rather than winter, but it was clearly regarded as unusual to begin a major campaign so late in the year. The full force of winter was very late arriving that year – the first snow only fell on the Taurus on 24 February 628 (*Chr. Pasch.* p. 732/5–6). By this time, Heraclius had managed to defeat the main Persian army near Nineveh and sack the royal palace at Dastagerd. But the emperor cannot have known that the weather would favour him so well, and was taking a considerable risk in beginning operations

---

[49] The remains of Bezabde had long been thought to lie under modern Cizre, but have now been located about 15 km further up the Tigris at Eski Hendek (G. Algaze, 'A new frontier: first results of the Tigris-Euphrates Archaeological Reconnaissance Project, 1988', *JNES* 48 (1989), 241–8, at 249–52).

[50] Cf. the difficulties experienced by British forces in Mesopotamia during the Great War: A. J. Barker, *The Neglected War: Mesopotamia 1914–1918* (London, 1967).

[51] In support of the date, see A. R. Birley, *Septimius Severus*, rev. edn (London, 1988), 130–1, 249 n. 4; for a dissenting view which would place the capture of Ctesiphon in autumn 197, see Z. Rubin, 'Dio, Herodian and Severus' second Parthian war', *Chiron* 5 (1975), 419–41, at 431–7. The fact that 28 January coincides with the *dies imperii* of Trajan certainly gives grounds for suspicion (cf. C. B. Welles, R. O. Fink and J. F. Gilliam, *The Excavations at Dura-Europos. Final Report* vol. 5(1) (New Haven, 1959), 206). The claim of one source in this context (*HA Sept. Sev.* 16.2) that wars are better waged in this region during the winter is contradicted by its simultaneous acknowledgement of the practical problems which arise from such a course of action. The chronology of Trajan's eastern campaigns is notoriously difficult to unravel, but one of the few explicit statements (Dio lxviii.26.1) has him advancing from Antioch in the spring (116).

[52] Potter, *Prophecy and History*, 36, 201.

when he did. Theophanes' assumption concerning Khusro's reaction to the news shows that Heraclius' timing went against normal expectations, which are well summed up by Ammianus' comment on Roman thinking at the end of the winter in 360–1: 'the Persian king had reluctantly been forced back to his own territory by the hardships of the winter season, but with the return of mild weather, a more concerted attack was feared' (xxi.6.7).[53]

Environmental conditions usually imposed constraints on the timing of military action; they also imposed constraints on where it was practical for a large army to attack. The range of suitable routes was limited, which reduced uncertainty for the opposition. The main determinants were availability of water and suitability of terrain for large bodies of troops.

To the south lay the Syrian desert. In this sector, both empires lay open to attack by Arab raiders, but only one route was feasible for large armies, namely the route which followed the Euphrates along its course via Circesium. This route was employed by the Romans in 363 and possibly 581, and by the Persians in 252[54] and a number of times during the sixth century (531, 540, 542, 573).[55] Above the Euphrates, attacks were not possible across the sector of the frontier defined by the Khabour River from Circesium to the hills of the Jebel Sinjar because scarcity of water sources either side of the Khabour and a long belt of salt marshes to the east of the river rendered the passage of large bodies of men impracticable.[56] This did not, however, prevent Arab raiding parties from attacking through this sector (Proc. Bld. ii.6.15), which accounts for the fortifications along the Khabour attested in the Notitia Dignitatum.[57]

Conditions were quite different to the north of the Jebel Sinjar where a reasonably well-watered plain stretched northwards as far as the Tur Abdin massif.[58] 'This ground lying between the Sinjar range and the hill chain which along the right bank of the Tigris gradually recedes to the northeast [i.e. the Tur Abdin] offers itself as a great natural corridor both for trade and military

---

[53] By way of comparison, a quick survey of the Assyrian royal inscriptions, while revealing a handful of campaigns which occurred in the winter months, shows the great majority falling between March and September (based on twenty-eight cases where a month is specified, without, however, any claim to being exhaustive). I am grateful to Nicholas Postgate for this information.

[54] E. Kettenhoffen, Die römisch–persischen Kriege des 3. Jahrhunderts n. Chr. (Wiesbaden, 1982), 50–3, for the route, with J.-C. Balty, 'Apamée (1986): nouvelles données sur l'armée romaine de l'orient et les raids sassanides du milieu du IIIe siècle', CRAI (1987), 213–41, at 228–39 for the date.

[55] On the relative disadvantages of this route when moving upstream (explaining why the Persians rarely used it before the sixth century), see Whitby, Maurice, 197–9.

[56] D. Kennedy and D. Riley, Rome's Desert Frontier from the Air (London, 1990), 25 (salt marshes). In 573 Khusro approached Nisibis by advancing along the course of the Khabour and its headwaters (John Epiph. 4, FHG iv.275), but this was a case of movement in a south–north direction rather than east–west, with the river presumably providing his troops with water.

[57] Or. xxv.20 (Oraba), xxxvi.23 (Apadna), 28 (Thannuris); cf. Dillemann, Haute Mésopotamie, 256.

[58] Ibid., 50ff., for a detailed survey of the hydrography of this region.

invasion between the Mosul region and the Armenian foothills.'[59] This plain was the site of Nisibis and Dara and was the sector through which major Persian invasions were made during the reign of Constantius II in the fourth century, in 530 and the 580s, and in 604, as were Roman invasions in 572, 589 and 591. The Tur Abdin itself was not easily accessible to large bodies of men; Procopius wrote of its unsuitability for wagons and horses (*Bld.* ii.4.1).[60]

North of the Tur Abdin lay the Tigris, running from west to east at this point and fed by rivers from the Taurus mountains to the north. This region between the Tigris and the Taurus, known in antiquity as Sophanene and Arzanene, was the location of the Roman cities of Amida and Martyropolis. This was another avenue for invasion, though less convenient for the Persians because the southern spurs of the Taurus further east made access much more difficult from Mesopotamia for them.[61] The Romans exploited this handicap by invading through this sector in 420 and 578. Finally, further north lay the Armenian highlands. This too was difficult terrain, but was nevertheless the starting-point for Persian invasions in 502 and 575, and Roman invasions in 298 and 543. It is apparent, then, that there was a limited number of possible invasion routes in the east and that some of these were more convenient than others.

Along the empire's northern frontier, however, environmental parameters were less well defined. Its considerably greater length obviously made a big difference – more than three times longer, if the eastern frontier is defined in terms of the distance from the Caucasus to Circesium on the Euphrates – but this was not the only significant factor.

To take the question of timing first, invasions from the north were less seasonally constrained. Northern peoples were clearly prepared to campaign in cold conditions which Roman troops found trying (e.g., Pliny *Panegyric* 12.3–4; Amm. Marc. xxvii.1.1; xix.11.4), and of course the propensity of the Rhine and Danube to freeze over meant that winter sometimes afforded by far the best opportunity for large numbers to gain speedy access to imperial territory.[62] But it does not follow from this that large-scale invasions were only to be expected during cold winters. The sources often fail to specify the time of year at which attacks occurred, but many are known to have taken place outside the winter

---

[59] Sir Aurel Stein in S. Gregory and D. Kennedy (eds.), *Sir Aurel Stein's 'Limes Report'* (BAR s272, 1985), 102.

[60] For the Tur Abdin during late antiquity, see A. Palmer, *Monk and Mason on the Tigris* (Cambridge, 1990).

[61] Whitby, *Maurice*, 200–1.

[62] E.g., Dio lxxi.7.1 (middle Danube, 170s); Amm. Marc. xxxi.10.4 (Rhine, 378); Philostorgius *HE* x.6 (Danube, 380s); Claudian *In Rufinum* ii.26 (lower Danube, 395); Agath. v.11.6 (lower Danube, 558). This last writer explicitly remarks on the regularity of the phenomenon, while a brief reference to the Danube in another sixth-century work singles out for particular comment the river's tendency to freeze over in winter and support the passage of tens of thousands of mounted barbarians: Ps.-Caesarius, *Dialogues* 68, *PG* xxxviii.936; for this work's milieu, see R. Riedinger, *Pseudo-Kaisarios* (Munich, 1969).

season, showing that invaders were not solely dependent on the rivers turning to ice. The battle of Strasbourg (357) was fought in the summer (Amm. Marc. xvi.11.9), yet involved the crossing of the Rhine by tens of thousands of Alamanni beforehand (xvi.12.19). The invasion of the Quadi in 374 occurred during the harvest (xxix.6.6), as did that of the Avars in 583 (Th. Sim. i.4.2). The Huns invaded during the summer of 408,[63] a major Slavic incursion breached the Danube after the winter of 549–50,[64] while the massing of Avar forces for an invasion in 601 took place at the beginning of autumn (Th. Sim. viii.5.5). This is not to say that the rivers could therefore be crossed *en masse* at any time of the year: the early spring often witnessed sharp rises in river levels and flooding, ruling out any possibility of crossing.[65] But clearly the range of times when invasions were feasible was wider in the north than the east.

The question which arises from this – how large numbers were able to cross when these substantial rivers were not frozen – is closely related to the other aspect of our enquiry, available invasion routes. It is not specified how the invaders crossed in any of the instances just cited, but the number of possibilities is limited. One of these can be dismissed quickly. Unlike the Persians (e.g., Lib. *Or.* lix.103, 114; Proc. *Wars* ii.12.4), northern peoples are not known to have been adept at constructing bridges. The Avars were only able to do so with the assistance of skilled Roman prisoners (John Eph. *HE* vi.24), and it is a reasonable assumption that the Huns' efforts (Priscus fr. 6,2/7) also relied on captive craftsmen.[66] Moreover in both these cases tributaries were bridged (the Sava and Nischava), not the Danube itself.

There are various references in the sources to 'crossings' (*transitus*, διαβάσεις),[67] and one meaning given in the lexicons is 'ford'. One's instinctive reaction is to dismiss this as impossible on rivers the size of the Rhine and Danube, but in fact there are clearly attested examples on the Rhine. Ammianus refers to two occasions when the river was shallow enough at certain points for men to wade across (xiv.10.7; xvi.11.9; cf. Tac. *Ann.* iv.73). In the latter case, near Saverne (11.11), he remarks that the shallowness was due to the summer heat – a characteristic of the Rhine noted in other sources (Tac. *Histories* iv.26.1; *Pan.Lat.* ii(10).7.4,7; vii(6).11.1) – though in the other case, near Augst (10.6),

---

[63] Sozomen (*HE* ix.4.8–5.1) correlates this approximately (κατὰ ταὐτὸν) with the death of Stilicho (22 August).

[64] Proc. *Wars* vii.39.29–40.1, with Stein, *Histoire* vol. 2, 524.

[65] Cf. Admiralty War Staff, Intelligence Division, *A Handbook of the River Danube* (London, 1915), 28; note also the problems faced by Valens in 368, and by Goths who tried to swim across a rain-swollen Danube in 376 (Amm. Marc. xxvii.5.5; xxxi.4.5).

[66] Cf. Blockley, *Classicising Historians* vol. 1, 54.

[67] A *transitus* at Guntia (Günzburg) on the upper Danube (*Pan.Lat.* iv(8).2.1); διαβάσεις on the Rhine (Zos. i.30.2) and lower Danube (Men. fr. 15,1/23; Th. Sim. viii.2.3–4). There is a further reference to διαβάσεις at Th. Sim. vi.11.20, but it is not entirely clear whether the text is referring to crossing points or the action of crossing: see n. 69 in the Whitbys' translation. Cf. also Proc. *Wars* vii.14.2, viii.18.17.

the ford was accessible apparently even at a time when spring rains were heavy and rivers in flood (xiv.10.2, 7).

This phenomenon is entirely consistent with the original character of the Rhine, prior to human intervention during the nineteenth century. Particularly between Basel and Bingen, where it flows along a rift valley with a very gentle gradient, the river's natural tendency was to meander excessively, producing persistent silt deposition and multiple shallow channels ('braiding').[68] Thus, for example, in 1825 no fewer than 2,155 islands were counted along the 150 kilometre stretch from Basel to Baden-Baden (along which, incidentally, Ammianus' two occurrences were sited). Similar problems affected the lower Rhine, making navigation by craft other than small light vessels fraught with difficulties. During the nineteenth century various engineering projects involving the construction of barrages and canals helped to create a deeper and more direct channel. The faster flow that this produced meant that, along one stretch of the river, for example, erosion lowered the bed by 6 to 8 metres over the course of the next thirty years.[69] The shallower depth and slower current of the river in antiquity help to explain both the frequent freezing of the Rhine (cf. Herod. viii.4.3) and the fordability of the river at certain points and times.

Parts of the Danube were similar in character to the Rhine. Much of the middle and lower Danube runs through plains with an extremely gentle incline – an average fall of only 4 inches per mile (in contrast with the upper river which falls 3 feet per mile). The result is predictable – a meandering course, with a shallow bed and constant sandbanks and islands. Early this century, for example, one 10 kilometre stretch above Belgrade contained approximately 1,200 islands – a situation aggravated during the summer when 'a combination of evaporation and infiltration produces a lower level'.[70] Nor does this state of affairs seem to have changed dramatically even today. A fairly recent report on two dams which the Hungarian and Czechoslovak governments were proposing to construct on the Danube bend included the observation that 'stretches of the

---

68 Admiralty, Naval Intelligence Division, Geographical Handbook Series, *Germany* vol. 1 (London, 1944), 19–20; Mellor, *The Rhine*, 10, 20–1. Cf. the exasperated comment of a French military engineer in 1814: 'Everybody agrees that all boundaries should be as fixed and invariable as possible; yet what is more variable than the middle of the Rhine . . . ? The Rhine changes its course every year, sometimes two or three times' (quoted by P. Sahlins, 'Natural frontiers revisited: France's boundaries since the seventeenth century', *AHR* 95 (1990), 432–51, at 1442). I am grateful to Roger Tomlin for first directing my attention to the character of the river before the nineteenth century, and its significance.

69 Mellor, *The Rhine*, 11, 20, 22ff., including maps showing 'before' and 'after' on certain sections of the river.

70 Admiralty, *Danube*, 9, 386–7, 28 (quote). Cf. the account of a trip down the Danube from Budapest to Ruse in the early nineteenth century, in which the problems of meanders, shallows and sandbanks are only too evident: M. J. Quin, *A Steam Voyage down the Danube* (London, 1835).

Danube routinely drop to only a few feet in depth and become unnavigable'.[71] Nevertheless, literary sources from late antiquity provide no unequivocal references to the existence of fords on the Danube. There is a possible allusion to fordability in Ammianus (xix.11.4), in the context of the province of Valeria and hence the Danube bend. Anticipating an invasion by the Sarmatians in early 359, Constantius placed troops along the bank in that region, fearful because the warmth of spring had not yet melted the snows and so 'the river can be crossed everywhere' (*amnem undique pervium*). Tacitus (*Ann.* xii.12) uses a very similar phrase with reference to the Euphrates at Zeugma, *unde maxime pervius amnis*, which the standard dictionaries (s.v. *pervius*) take to mean 'fordable'; but it is conceivable that what Ammianus meant was that the river could still easily be crossed by boat, before the melted snow created flood conditions and rendered navigation hazardous.[72]

Boats are of course the remaining possibility for consideration, especially since many of the empire's northern neighbours were skilled in the use of watercraft. The Goths used boats with single banks of oars in the Danube delta during the fourth century (Themistius *Or.* x.137a), the Huns are known to have made use of hollowed-out tree trunks and rafts (Priscus fr. 11,2/72, 274–5),[73] and the sixth-century Slavs were noted for their ability to handle boats (Maurice *Strat.* xi.4/23ff.).[74] Small boats would undoubtedly have been used for small-scale raids, but were they a feasible proposition when it came to a large-scale invasion? Apparently so: Zosimus explicitly reports Sarmatians as attacking a strongly held town in the 320s after 'crossing the Danube in boats' (ii.21.1);[75] a large group of Goths, possibly of the order of 10,000 men,[76] made their own way across the Danube on hastily constructed rafts in 376 after the Roman authorities refused to include them in the main body admitted to the empire (Amm. Marc. xxxi.5.3), while in 386 another group of Goths, whose size was sufficiently large to warrant a ceremonial triumph after their defeat,[77] attempted to cross in hollowed logs (Zos. iv.39.1); Gepids transferred 12,000 Kotrigurs across the Danube in boats in 550 (Proc. *Wars* viii.18.15–17);[78] and

---

[71] *Time* (22 December 1986), 31.

[72] The reference to a *transitus* at Guntia (Günzburg) on the upper Danube (*Pan.Lat.* iv(8).2.1) has been taken to refer to a ford (H. Schönberger, 'The Roman frontier in Germany: an archaeological survey', *JRS* 59 (1969), 144–97, at 179), but this is not the only possible interpretation of the term.

[73] Log boats could also be rather more sophisticated than simply hollowed-out logs: K. Greene, *The Archaeology of the Roman Economy* (London, 1986), 20.

[74] For a survey of the literary and other evidence concerning Slavic watercraft, see L. Havlíková, 'Slavic ships in 5th–12th centuries Byzantine historiography', *BS* 52 (1991), 89–104.

[75] For the context, see T. D. Barnes, *Constantine and Eusebius* (Cambridge, Mass., 1981), 76.

[76] Heather, *Goths and Romans*, 13, 139.

[77] *Ibid.*, 13, for references.

[78] Aided in this instance by the fact that the Romans had lost control of the right bank of the river in this area at that time.

the Avars used large vessels to carry many troops in the late 570s, even if they did handle the craft clumsily (Men. fr. 25,1/18–24).[79]

But crossings by boat could not be made at any point along the rivers, which brings us back again to the references to 'crossings'. These were most likely not fords, but points along the rivers where crossing by boat was easiest, for there are certainly stretches of the Danube where the terrain along one or both banks would make embarkation and/or landing difficult, if not impossible, especially for large numbers of men. On the upper Danube between Passau and Linz, the river 'flows for some 60 kilometres through a kind of gorge, which provides a natural barrier to passage'.[80] Along a 300 kilometre stretch of the lower Danube, between Vidin (below the Iron Gates) and Ruse, the southern bank of the river for the most part consists of precipitous cliffs rising in places to heights of 100 metres or more. There are only a few points where the bank drops down to river level,[81] and these would have been obvious crossing-points in antiquity – hence the siting of Roman units at Bononia and Novae.[82]

Topographical features of this sort clearly helped reduce Roman uncertainty as to likely invasion points. However, there remained considerable stretches of both rivers where there were no such constraints. Certain sectors, such as the stretch leading up to the Danube bend, were undoubtedly seen as being more vulnerable,[83] but fortifications and units were distributed with varying densities along the whole length of the northern frontier.[84] Bases for river patrols along the Danube, as indicated for the early fifth century in the *Notitia Dignitatum*, were also distributed fairly evenly along the length of the river, the only major gaps being the headwaters in Raetia, and the Danube bend which was heavily fortified anyway. The *Notitia* does not provide comparable evidence for the Rhine (apart from units on the Bodensee: *ND Occ.* xxxv.32), but there was a base at Speyer in Valentinian's reign and there are allusions in literary sources to the presence of light patrol vessels (*lusoriae*) and other craft on the river in the third and fourth centuries.[85]

---

[79] Ammianus says that the Alamannic king Chonodomarius, fleeing after his defeat by Julian at Strasbourg in 357, was making for boats to cross the Rhine back to Alamannia when he was captured (xvi.12.58–9), which may imply that the large Alamannic forces at that battle had used boats to cross the Rhine before the battle.

[80] G. Altöldy, *Noricum*, tr. A. Birley (London, 1974), 147. Cf. Admiralty, *Danube*, 11.

[81] *Ibid.*, 18–19; F. Kanitz, *Donau-Bulgarien und der Balkan* (Leipzig, 1879–80), vol. 1, 2. I am grateful to Dr Roger Batty for drawing my attention to this latter work.

[82] Cf. R. F. Hoddinott, *Bulgaria in Antiquity* (London and Tonbridge, 1975), 128 ('Novae . . . controlled one of the easier Danube crossings').

[83] For the Danube bend, see Soproni, *Der spätrömische Limes*. Note also various references to the building of fortifications in 'suitable places': *ILS* 724 (Scythia), *CTh* xv.1.13 (Dacia ripensis), Amm. Marc. xxviii.2.1 (the Rhine); cf. *CIL* iii.3385.

[84] See the literature cited on p. 70, n. 103.

[85] For the Danube and Rhine fleets in late antiquity, see R. Grosse, *Römische Militärgeschichte von Gallienus bis zum Beginn der byzantinischen Themenverfassung* (Berlin, 1920), 72–7, supplemented by C. G. Starr, *The Roman Imperial Navy 31 BC–AD 324* (Ithaca, 1941), 161 n. 58, 164 n. 94,

Clearly, then, environmental parameters along the northern frontier gave far less help to the Romans in reducing uncertainty about likely times and lines of attack compared with the east, while its far greater length multiplied the number of potential danger points enormously. Moreover the constraint of adequate water supplies, which was such a crucial factor in determining the routes of large bodies of men in the east, was irrelevant in the north.[86]

Before leaving this subject, it is worth noting that, by contrast, the northern peoples themselves had significantly better-defined parameters within which to anticipate Roman expeditions north of the Rhine and Danube. With respect to timing, the Romans rarely operated in the winter (cf. Amm. Marc. xix.11.4). Arbogast is reported as having done so against the Franks in the late fourth century (Greg. Tur. *HF* ii.9), but being a Frank himself (in Roman employ) such a tactic will presumably have come naturally to him. When in the early seventh century, Maurice persisted in his attempts to make his troops fight north of the Danube during the winter, all that he ultimately achieved was provocation of the mutiny which resulted in his own overthrow and death.[87]

With respect to possible points of attack, Constantine's bridge at Oescus would have indicated an obvious point of access to barbaricum, as long as it stood.[88] At various points along the Danube and Rhine, too, forts situated on the far bank, often opposite legionary fortresses, acted as secure landing places to which troops could safely be ferried or where temporary bridges could be constructed with ease.[89] The Roman ability to erect temporary pontoon bridges was a valuable advantage, and is seen in operation on a number of occasions in the pages of Ammianus (xvii.10.1; 12.4; xxvii.5.2; xxix.4.2; xxx.5.13). Vegetius provides further detail, explaining how an expeditionary force always carried hollowed logs in carts, together with iron nails, cables and planks (iii.7, p. 81/3ff.; ii.25, p. 60/14ff.).[90] This technique, which had the potential to be

---

and P. Brennan, 'Combined legionary detachments as artillery units in late-Roman Danubian bridgehead dispositions', *Chiron* 10 (1980), 553–67, at 561 (though the reference in n. 29 to *CGL* should be v.604/56). My statement about the distribution of Danubian bases takes into account not only references to *classes*, but also to *milites liburnarii* and *nauclarii*.

[86] There is one instance in the late sixth century where Roman forces operating near the lower Danube are presented as having trouble finding water (Th. Sim. vii.5), but see Whitby, *Maurice*, 160, on this incident.

[87] *Ibid.*, 165–6, for the details, including the rationale behind Maurice's strategy.

[88] D. Tudor, *Les Ponts romains du Bas-Danube* (Bucharest, 1974), 135–66. Its fate is unknown, but the fact that Procopius makes no mention of it in his survey of the lower Danube defences under Justinian (*Bld.* iv.6–7) must mean it was no longer standing in the sixth century.

[89] For the Danube, see Brennan, 'Danubian bridgehead dispositions' (dealing with the Tetrarchic and Constantinian period; Justinian rebuilt some of these: Proc. *Bld.* iv.6.3–4; 7.7); Mócsy, *Pannonia*, 369–70; for the Rhine, see H. Schönberger, 'The Roman frontier in Germany', 180 (Deutz), 185 (Mannheim-Neckerau, Engers), 186 (Whylen); Johnson, *Fortifications*, 141 (Fig. 54), 255, 259.

[90] For knowledge of pontoon bridges in the late sixth century, see Maurice *Strat.* ix.1/34ff., xi.4/74ff., xiiB.21.

executed with considerable speed, sometimes enabled the Romans to achieve surprise (Amm. Marc. xvii.1.2–3; 12.4), provided they did not take too long over other preparations; but as already observed (p. 33), this was not always the case.

ETHNOGRAPHIC KNOWLEDGE

Assessing the quality of late Roman knowledge concerning the socio-political character of the empire's neighbours is, for a number of reasons, a highly problematic task, with the result that it is much less easy to arrive at satisfactory conclusions in this section. Late Roman historical writings contain many references to and descriptions of foreign peoples, which might seem to offer the prospect of being able to determine in some detail the extent of late Roman knowledge about the political and social organisation of the peoples with whom the empire dealt. However, these descriptions are heavily influenced by literary convention and inherited prejudice. There was a strong ethnographic tradition in Graeco-Roman historical writing running all the way back to the authoritative prototype of Herodotus, and it was taken for granted in late antiquity that historians with classicising pretensions would draw freely on this tradition when it came to describing foreign peoples. They were also heirs to a culture in which chauvinistic attitudes towards foreigners – 'barbarians' – were ingrained. As a result, ethnographic descriptions frequently reproduce stock themes concerning the social life and customs of barbarians, and stereotyped images of their character and temperament. Barbarians are regularly portrayed as the negative embodiment of Graeco-Roman values and ideals (e.g., they are usually treacherous, uncontrolled, arrogant, cruel, etc.), and their social life is delineated in terms of practices which invert the norms of Graeco-Roman society (e.g., consumption of meat and milk, polygamy, etc.).[91]

---

[91] For the classical Greek background, see F. Hartog, *The Mirror of Herodotus: the Representation of the Other in the Writing of History*, tr. J. Lloyd (Cambridge, Mass., 1988); E. Hall, *Inventing the Barbarian* (Oxford, 1989). For Roman assimilation of these conventions and attitudes, see generally (to the early fifth century) Y. A. Dauge, *Le Barbare. Recherches sur la conception romaine de la barbarie et de la civilisation* (Brussels, 1981), with treatment of more specific aspects or subsequent centuries by B. D. Shaw, '"Eaters of flesh and drinkers of milk": the ancient Mediterranean ideology of the pastoral nomad', *Ancient Society* 13/14 (1982/3), 5–31; E. Frézouls, 'Les deux politiques de Rome face aux barbares d'après Ammien Marcellin' in E. Frézouls (ed.), *Crise et redressement dans les provinces européennes de l'empire* (Strasbourg, 1983), 175–97; T. Wiedemann, 'Between men and beasts: barbarians in Ammianus Marcellinus' in I. S. Moxon, J. D. Smart and A. J. Woodman (eds.), *Past Perspectives: Studies in Greek and Roman Historical Writing* (Cambridge, 1986); U.-B. Dittrich, *Die Beziehungen Roms zu den Sarmaten und Quaden im vierten Jahrhundert n. Chr.* (Bonn, 1984), Chapter 4; M. Cesa, 'Etnografia e geografia nella visione storica di Procopius di Cesarea', *Studi classici e orientali* 32 (1982), 189–215; Cameron, *Procopius*, Chapter 12; *idem*, 'Agathias on the early Merovingians', *Annali della Scuola Normale Superiore di Pisa* 37 (1968), 95–140; *idem*, 'Agathias on the Sassanians', *DOP* 23/24 (1969/70), 69–183; Dagron, 'Ceux d'en face'.

These features mean that there are often very considerable difficulties in determining whether late Roman ethnographic descriptions contain authentic information about a particular people. Yet there is little doubt that Romans who observed other cultures at first hand during late antiquity (typically as envoys) were able to record what they found without obvious signs of significant contamination by the ethnographic tradition. The historian Olympiodorus is known to have included an account of his mission to the Huns in the early fifth century (fr. 19), but the archetype is Priscus' lengthy account of his participation in an embassy to the Huns in 449 (frs. 11,2; 12,1; 13,1 and 3; 14; 15,1).[92] From the sixth century, there is Julian's account of his mission to the Axumites (Mal. pp. 457–9), that of Nonnosus to the Arabs, Himyarites and Axumites (Photius Bibl. cod. 3) – both admittedly very fragmentary – and Zemarchus' concerning his to the Turks, as preserved in Menander (frs. 10,2–5) and (in much less detail) John of Ephesus (HE vi.23).

Furthermore, in the sixth century at least, there are clear indications of genuine interest in being informed about such matters – and at an official level. When envoys from the Turks first arrived in Constantinople during Justin II's reign, the emperor questioned them about their geographical location and political organisation, and the social organisation of those subject to them (Men. fr. 10,1/70–86). Moreover, Zemarchus, subsequently sent as envoy to the Turks, is said to have 'told the emperor everything' on his return (fr. 10,5/22). This is admittedly a rather vague expression, but since the account of Zemarchus' mission to which John of Ephesus had access contained comment on the population size of the Turks and on their 'institutions' (tekse cf. τάξις: HE vi.23, p. 324/13–17), Zemarchus' report to the emperor is likely to have included further background detail of this sort in addition to the content of his discussions with the Turkic ruler. It is also surely significant that the Strategikon, the practically oriented military treatise attributed to the emperor Maurice, includes a book (xi) devoted to the customs and tactics of contemporary foreign peoples (albeit with the greatest detail on the military aspect), and eschews the use of the term 'barbarian'.[93] Although the Strategikon betrays some residual influence of ethnographic stereotypes,[94] this tends to manifest itself in its explanations for observed phenomena rather than the phenomena themselves. Lacking classicising pretensions, it was less bound by traditional expectations when it came to deal with such subject-matter, while its practical purpose meant that it needed to give reasonably accurate factual information.[95]

---

[92] Clearly some features, most obviously his reported debate in Attila's camp with a former Roman 'gone native', may well be literary artifice or moralising (Blockley, Classicising Historians vol.1, 59).

[93] ἔθνος is the term employed throughout Book xi; elsewhere in the work, βάρβαρος features only twice, among the aphorisms in Book .viii.

[94] Dagron, 'Ceux d'en face'.

[95] I am grateful to Jonathon Shepard for particularly helpful discussion of some of these points.

It is indeed possible to separate out from some of the descriptions in classicising histories what would appear to be genuine information about particular peoples. For example, Procopius' description of the Slavs (*Wars* vii.14) has been ably defended against its critics and shown to contain broadly accurate details about their dispersed manner of settlement and primitive abodes (confirmed by archaeology), their lack of political centralisation, and preference in warfare for fighting on foot[96] – all details, it is worth adding, which the Romans could hardly have failed to observe in the course of campaigns against the Slavs and attempts to negotiate with them. And Agathias' excursus on Persian religion (ii.22–7), while weak or inaccurate on many of the finer points,[97] nevertheless shows adequate acquaintance with a number of the fundamental features of Zoroastrianism – reverence for water and for fire, the custom of exposing the dead, and the encouragement of consanguineous marriage. Yet it is apparent that he has not drawn on the Herodotean tradition for his information.[98] It would indeed be surprising if such features were not known, given, for example, that Zoroastrian communities existed in the eastern parts of the Roman empire until the fifth century AD,[99] and that the Roman–Persian peace settlement of 561/2 included reference to the Persian practice of exposing the dead (Men fr. 6,1/405–7).[100]

There is reason, then, to think that scepticism about the nature of Roman ethnographic knowledge can be carried too far. Nevertheless, it remains difficult to assess in detail how good Roman knowledge of a particular people was during particular periods of late antiquity. For a number of reasons, however, I would suggest that knowledge of Persian political and social institutions was generally better than that of northern peoples' (which is certainly not to say that it was free from the influence of stereotypes or prejudice). The first consideration which suggests this is the fact that, although late Roman writers generally continued to refer to the Persians as barbarians throughout late antiquity, they were prepared to recognise important similarities between Roman and Persian institutions which differentiated Persia from other barbarians. Procopius acknowledged the fact that, in contrast to most other peoples, Romans and Persians both possessed centralised political structures and respect for the rule of law (*Wars* i.3.5). Similarly, although the author of the

---

[96] Whitby, *Maurice*, 81 n. 36, *contra* Cameron, *Procopius*, 218–19. Cf. Matthews, *Ammianus*, 332–42 concerning the Huns, *contra* Shaw, 'Eaters of flesh'.

[97] For which, see Cameron, 'Agathias on the Sassanians', 74–111.

[98] *Ibid.*, 75.

[99] Boyce and Grenet, *Zoroastrianism* vol. 3 (for the period to the fourth century), and Priscus fr. 41/3 9 (for the fifth century, with specific reference to the role of fire).

[100] Cf., too, Menander's knowledge of the Persian festival of *Frurdigan*, also a result of diplomatic interchange (fr. 9,1/22–6). Christians within Persia will necessarily have been acquainted with Zoroastrianism, and some of this knowledge might well have been transmitted to the Roman empire in the course of the ecclesiastical interchange discussed on pp. 59–60.

Strategikon cannot resist jibes about the servile temperament of the Persians whose obedience to their rulers is motivated by fear, he comments on their orderly and planned approach to affairs (xi.1/28), and it has been plausibly argued that the whole chapter devoted to the Persians shows recognition of how similar many features of Persian organisation were to those of the Romans, compared with the other foreign peoples discussed in the subsequent chapters of Book xi.[101] Nor was this recognition only a sixth-century phenomenon: it can be seen being given concrete expression in the development of diplomatic protocol between the two empires from the fourth century onwards.[102] And at those points where practices and values diverged most obviously, in the sphere of religion, we have already seen that educated Romans were still familiar with the basic tenets of Zoroastrianism.[103]

Centuries of contact between the Mediterranean world and Iran is, of course, part of the explanation, and the relative durability of Persian institutions, as is the more intense degree of interchange between the two empires during late antiquity at both official and informal levels, compared with the northern frontier. Informal interchange has already been discussed (pp. 54–66); the greater frequency of diplomatic exchanges in the east will be discussed on pp. 169–70. Together, these provide a second reason for suggesting that Roman knowledge (at the official/elite level) of Persian political and social institutions was superior.

As indicated in the Introduction, the impact of this sort of background knowledge on the conduct of foreign relations tends to be imperceptible, so little can be said as to its practical consequences. There are, however, a few instances where its use can perhaps be detected (and not exclusively in dealings with Persia). These must serve as hints of what we might discover were our source materials fuller.

The first case involves knowledge of the predilections of the Persian kings. Physicians trained in the Roman empire enjoyed great prestige at the Persian court during the sixth century, and it has been persuasively argued that the use which the Roman government made of doctors as envoys in this period was partly an attempt to capitalise on this fact.[104] A second example concerns the political structure of the Avars. The *Strategikon* of Maurice recognised the vulnerability of the Avars to desertion on a large scale by the various peoples subject to their hegemony (xi.2/74–8), and it has also been argued that the

---

[101] Dagron, 'Ceux d'en face', 212–14 and n. 14.
[102] See Lee, 'Hostages', with references to earlier literature.
[103] Contrast the apparent deficiencies in knowledge about the religious practices of northern peoples: e.g., Matthews, *Ammianus*, 312, 329f., 340.
[104] Blockley, 'Doctors as diplomats'. The use which the Persian authorities made of Christians as envoys to the Romans (e.g. Proc. *Wars* ii.24.6; Men. fr. 16,1/39–50) was presumably based on similar reasoning.

Romans sought to exploit this knowledge in the final years of the sixth century, with some success.[105] The final instance relates to the religious practices of the Arab tribes. When the commanders of troops from the Lebanon expressed reluctance to join Belisarius on his invasion of Persia in 541 because they feared Arab attacks during their absence, Belisarius was able to reassure them that they need have no fear since around the time of the summer solstice (ἡ τροπὴ θερινή) the Arabs spent two months engaged in religious rituals and refrained from all hostile activity (Proc. *Wars* ii.16.18). Even if one suspects Procopius of trying to enhance Belisarius' image by privileging him with knowledge of something more widely known in those parts, this detail of Arab social life nevertheless finds strikingly precise confirmation in the account of Nonnosus from the 530s (Photius *Bibl.* cod. 3).[106]

It would of course be mistaken to suggest that Roman background knowledge of Persia was devoid of serious flaws: Roman failure to appreciate the limited character of Persian aims (see pp. 22–5) is a significant anomaly, though since intentions are by their very nature always difficult to divine, this is a more understandable failure. Nevertheless, in so far as it is possible to reconstruct Roman background knowledge about the empire's most important neighbours during late antiquity – and it is clear that the evidence is far from satisfactory – Roman knowledge of Persia, for all its limitations, does seem to have been better than their knowledge of any northern people. The Romans thus had a sounder framework with regard to Persia when it came to dealing with strategic intelligence, our other category of information and the subject of the next chapter.

---

[105] Whitby, *Maurice*, 164, 179.
[106] 'The other festival lasts for two months. They hold it after the summer solstice (μετὰ θερινὰς τροπὰς). During these festivals they maintain complete peace, not only with one another, but also with all the people dwelling among them.'

4

STRATEGIC INTELLIGENCE

THE concerns of this chapter may usefully be introduced by consideration of three episodes, each, as it happens, falling within a period of less than a decade during the middle of the fourth century and each recounted by the historian Ammianus Marcellinus.

The first concerns the activities during the mid-350s of the praetorian prefect of the east, Strategius Musonianus. He is reported to have investigated Persian plans through the agency of spies (*speculatores*), from whom he and an associate learned (*aperte cognossent*) that the Persian king Shapur II was currently engaged in fierce fighting with hostile peoples on a distant frontier of his empire. On the basis of this information Musonianus initiated secret negotiations with a Persian official, in the hope that these difficulties would incline the Persians towards a formal peace settlement with the Romans and put an end to the costly but inconclusive warfare of the previous two decades (xvi.9.2–3).

In the event, Musonianus' diplomatic initiative proved not only abortive, but positively counter-productive, leading on to the second episode. The Persians concluded from Musonianus' initiative that the Romans themselves were in difficulties, and since Shapur had been able, by early 358, to bring his own war to an end, he decided in turn to try to exploit Roman problems and sent envoys to demand territorial concessions as the price for peace. The emperor Constantius dismissed these demands, but since he was now preoccupied with problems on the Danube frontier, he sent embassies of his own with a view to delaying Shapur for as long as possible in the event that he should move to make good his threats (xvii.5). During the winter of 358–9, in fact, the Persian king busied himself preparing weapons, troops and supplies. News of these preparations reached Constantius initially in the form of rumours, subsequently supported by reliable reports (*nuntii certi*: xviii.4.1–2). This confirmation that Shapur was continuing his preparations prompted the emperor to take further steps for the defence of the eastern provinces, notably the promotion of the experienced Ursicinus to a senior position. Constantius' attempts at diplomatic delay, however, were fruitless and Shapur launched his offensive in early 359.[1]

The context of the third episode is the lower Danube frontier in 365:

> At the end of the winter, [the emperor] Valens was hurrying to Syria. He had already entered the territory of Bithynia when he learned from the reports of his generals (*docetur relationibus ducum*) that the Gothic peoples . . . were combining together and making preparations to invade the Thracian provinces. On discovering this, . . . he gave orders for sufficient reinforcements of cavalry and infantry to be sent to the places where the barbarian incursions were feared. (xxvi.6.11)

Ammianus is not explicit about the outcome of this episode, since he proceeds to concentrate on his main concern, the rebellion of Julian's cousin Procopius – some of the units sent to strengthen the lower Danube were induced, while passing through Constantinople, to support Procopius in his attempt to seize power. But since these particular units were not the sum total of the reinforcements – they are described as *inter alios* (6.12) – and Ammianus makes no mention of a Gothic invasion in 365,[2] it seems reasonable to concur in the assumption that 'the reinforcements . . . evidently deterred the Goths from carrying out their plan for the time being'.[3]

These three episodes possess a significant common feature – the acquisition by the emperor or his subordinates of information of strategic importance from beyond the empire's boundaries. There is no obvious reason to doubt the reliability of Ammianus' reports concerning any of the three. He himself was with Ursicinus at the imperial court in Sirmium when word of Musonianus' peace initiative was received and discussed (xvi.10.21), and the generals on the lower Danube will hardly have requested the diversion of troops by the emperor in 365 unless they were satisfied that the Gothic threat was genuine. Ammianus was certainly critical of aspects of Constantius' defence of the east, which raises the possibility that by saying the emperor knew in advance of the Persian invasion in 359, he was insinuating that he did not react with sufficient speed; yet the sheer detail he provides – including the embassies sent to forestall Persian aggression – can leave little doubt that the Romans really knew about

---

[1] For detailed discussion of all the foregoing events, see R. C. Blockley, 'Constantius II and Persia' in C. Deroux (ed.), *Studies in Latin Literature and Roman History* vol. 5 (Brussels, 1989), 465–90, at 479–83.

[2] As Roger Tomlin has argued (*CQ* 29 (1979), 470–8), Amm. Marc. xxvi.4.5–6, although occurring in the context of 365, presents an overview of the reigns of Valentinian and Valens, so that the passage's reference to Gothic raids more probably refers to 376–8 than to 365.

[3] Thompson, *Visigoths*, 18. Wolfram (*History of the Goths*, 66–7) has suggested that the Goths were in fact combining in defence against a possible Roman attack, but his argument is highly speculative; in particular, his claim that 'Valens sent only two elite units as reinforcements' overlooks Ammianus' statement that the units which defected to Procopius were only part of the Roman reinforcements.

Persian intentions. Ammianus himself shows how Constantius was genuinely preoccupied with the Sarmatian threat at the time (xix.11), and is critical of Constantius not for any slowness of response but rather for responding in ways which Ammianus regarded as ill-advised, such as the promotion of the lacklustre Sabinianus.

Given the reliability of Ammianus' reports of these episodes, attention can be directed to the crucial issue which they raise, that of their typicality – in two senses. First, with what sort of frequency did the empire acquire information of this sort? Secondly, how representative are they as to the content of information received?

Satisfactory answers to these questions require detailed analysis of a considerable body of disparate material. This chapter aims to provide that analysis. The reader should be warned at the outset that the need for a methodical, systematic approach does not make for easy reading; at the same time, the following analysis is of fundamental importance for the study as a whole. For the sake of clarity a brief summary of some of the conclusions is presented here; the implications of these conclusions are discussed at the end of the chapter.

With respect to the question of informational content, there are a number of points to be made. The three episodes were selected because they are broadly representative in so far as the first episode involved information about an enemy handicap, and the second and third, news of enemy military preparations. They are also representative of the geographical distribution of these two different categories of information. News of military preparations was received along both the eastern and northern frontiers, whereas receipt of information by the Romans concerning enemy handicaps seems to have been a phenomenon restricted to the east. Finally, they are representative of the limits of the intelligence acquired by the empire. Longer-range matters of importance, such as the replacement of the Parthians by the Sasanian dynasty, or the movements of the Huns and their impact on the Goths, were not anticipated by the empire.[4] But while information of the sort represented by our episodes from Ammianus was clearly of less significance by comparison, it clearly cannot be dismissed as unimportant.

Assessing the frequency with which strategic intelligence was acquired is by no means straightforward, but the evidence regarding enemy military prep-

---

[4] As emphasised by Millar, 'Emperors, frontiers and foreign relations', 19 (citing these two examples), apparently overlooking, however, the existence of a substantial stratum of information at the next level down, represented by the three episodes above. One might also justifiably ask, however, whether criticism of the Roman failure to anticipate the overthrow of the Parthian regime does not risk importing modern expectations (indeed, it would be interesting to know how well the CIA anticipated the collapse of the Soviet Union). Moreover, as Millar acknowledges (19 and n. 122) but underplays, the Romans certainly knew about the civil strife between rival claimants to the Parthian throne which presaged the fall of the regime, and were aware that this was to the advantage of the Romans (Dio lxxvii.12.2a–3).

arations suggests that here too a distinction between the eastern and northern frontiers needs to be drawn. It appears that the Persians were unable to prepare a major expedition against the Roman empire without a strong likelihood of the Romans receiving some forewarning of their plans. Along the northern frontier, a greater degree of uncertainty existed: sometimes, as in our third episode, there was advance warning, but on other occasions this seems to have been lacking, certainly to a greater degree than in the east. In this sense, the third episode is less typical than the second.

There is, however, a further dimension which complicates matters, yet cannot be ignored. Up to this point, the focus has been on the movement of information into the empire. But it is apparent that the traffic was not all one way. In spite of the inadequacy of sources presenting the points of view of the Persians and the various northern peoples, it is clear that these neighbours also sometimes acquired information of a similar sort about the Romans, and this feature also needs to be taken into account.

From this point, the clearest way of proceeding will be to deal first with the evidence relating to Persia, and then that relating to the north.

STRATEGIC INTELLIGENCE IN RELATIONS WITH PERSIA

The aim of this part of the chapter is to consider the theme of strategic intelligence in Roman-Persian relations from the early third to the early seventh centuries in as comprehensive a manner as possible. The first section below resumes our first introductory episode and presents further instances (in chronological sequence) where the Romans or the Persians seem to have known of one another's handicaps, or comparable items of news. The subsequent sections follow on from the second introductory episode and survey the evidence for knowledge of enemy military preparations.

Knowledge of handicaps

The purpose of this section is to show that Musonianus' acquisition of information about Persian troubles in the mid-350s was not an isolated instance in the history of Roman–Persian relations. Soon after this in fact – probably some time during 358 – a Roman officer, Antoninus, defected to the Persians, taking with him valuable information about Roman troop dispositions throughout the eastern half of the empire (Amm. Marc. xviii.5.1–2). This included details of Constantius' current commitments on the middle Danube, where he was dealing with unruly Sarmatians, news of which was believed to have spurred Shapur on with his preparations.

Throughout the second half of the fifth century, a constant bone of contention between the two powers was the Roman refusal to accede to

Persian demands for a financial contribution towards the defences in the Caucasus against barbarian raids.[5] On his accession to the throne in 491, Anastasius had to confront a concerted revolt by the Isaurians. 'When Kavad heard (*shma'*) this, he thought he had found his opportunity, and sent envoys to the land of the Romans, for he thought that they would be afraid and would send him gold, because the Isaurians had revolted against them' (J. Styl. 23), though in the event Anastasius rebuffed the Persian threat and called Kavad's bluff.[6] Although the author of the chronicle in which this statement occurs (its attribution to Joshua Stylites is probably incorrect)[7] is known to have been an inhabitant of Edessa and so was *prima facie* not so well placed to have known of this exchange, he was a contemporary of the events of the late fifth and early sixth century on which his chronicle concentrates and he specifically says that some of his knowledge derived 'from meeting with men who served as envoys to the two rulers' (25).

Kavad subsequently did engage in war with Anastasius (502–5). One lesson derived from this war by the Romans was the need for a strongly fortified position near the frontier in northern Mesopotamia, and the construction of a fort at Dara was ordered. It seems that the Romans would have pressed ahead anyway, but apparently they knew that the Persians were now busy with barbarian attacks in the north and so quickened the pace of construction in order to finish before the Persians were free to oppose them in force (Proc. *Bld*. ii.1.4–6; cf. Zach. *HE* vii.6, vol. 2, p. 36/3–4).

In 529 Justinian had to deal with a major insurrection by the Samaritan population of Palestine, provoked by his endorsement of anti-Samaritan legislation. A delegation of leading Samaritans approached Kavad with the offer of Samaritan support if he invaded Roman territory and Kavad seems to have been sufficiently tempted to go so far as to break off advanced peace negotiations with Constantinople – another example of the Persians acquiring knowledge of Roman difficulties. The activities of the Samaritan delegation came to light when they were apprehended and interrogated at the frontier while trying to cross back into the Roman empire, a report being sent to the emperor (Mal. p. 456/9–18; Theoph. p. 179/10–14).[8]

---

[5] For background and discussion, see R. C. Blockley, 'Subsidies and diplomacy: Rome and Persia in late antiquity', *Phoenix* 39 (1985), 62–74.

[6] Valash's attempt to extract money from Zeno in the early 480s (J. Styl. 17) may also have been prompted by knowledge of Zeno's preoccupation with the revolt of Illus, for Illus is said to have asked for help from Persia (John of Antioch fr. 214,2, *FHG* iv.620).

[7] See C. C. Torrey, 'Notes on the "Chronicle of Joshua the Stylite"', *Hebrew Union College Annual* 23 (1950/51), 439–50 (with references to earlier literature at 442); Brock, 'Syriac historical writing', 11.

[8] For the context, and discussion of the two accounts, see S. Winkler, 'Die Samariter in den Jahren 529/30', *Klio* 43–5 (1965), 435–57, especially 447–8; also K. Holum, 'Caesarea and the Samaritans' in R. L. Hohlfelder (ed.), *City, Town and Countryside in the Early Byzantine Era* (New York, 1982), 65–73.

Following Belisarius' success against the Vandals in Africa in 533, Khusro sent an embassy to Constantinople suggesting that he should receive a share of the booty, since the peace he had concluded with the Romans in 532 had released Roman troops for the expedition against the Vandals (Proc. *Wars* i.26.1–4) – which shows unequivocally that the Persian king knew of events in the Mediterranean world (though in this case, of a Roman success rather than a handicap). A possible source of this information might have been the Persian ambassador known to have witnessed Belisarius' triumph in Constantinople in 534 (Zach. *HE* ix.17, vol. 2, p. 133/17–18).

Khusro also learned of Roman commitments against the Goths in Italy in the late 530s. According to Procopius, the source of Khusro's information was a secret Gothic embassy sent by Vittigis to Khusro, requesting that the Persians relieve the pressure on the Goths by invading Roman territory in the east (*Wars* ii.2). The question naturally arises as to how Procopius could have known about this 'secret' embassy, but in fact he subsequently indicates his source: while travelling incognito through Thrace, the Gothic envoys had engaged a man fluent in Greek and Syriac to act as their interpreter in Persia; this man was later caught trying to cross back from Persia into the empire and, under questioning from the local Roman commander, revealed what had taken place (Proc. *Wars* ii.14.11–12).

When the inhabitants of Persian Armenia rose in revolt against Khusro in 572, Justin II tried to take advantage of the Persian preoccupation with this problem by mounting an attempt to recapture Nisibis. The obvious source of Justin's knowledge about Persian difficulties was the Armenian refugees who fled to the Roman empire, though in fact it is possible that the Roman government had been negotiating secretly with leading Persarmenians during the preceding years and so had known of the likelihood of revolt for much longer.[9]

It was customary, by the sixth century at least, for Roman and Persian rulers to inform one another of a change in occupant of the throne.[10] When Khusro I died in 579, however, his successor Hormizd refused to adhere to this courtesy; yet news of Khusro's death still promptly reached the Roman empire. The emperor Tiberius had dispatched envoys from Constantinople to Khusro early in 579; on reaching Antioch – that is, well before entering Persian territory – they learned of Khusro's death anyway (John Eph. *HE* vi.22), presumably since news of such an important event was bound to spread far and wide through ordinary channels.

A final case concerns another incident during the twenty years of warfare which resulted from Justin's action in 572. During negotiations in 582, the Persian envoy Andigan is reported to have tried to pressure the Roman envoy

---

[9] For sources and discussion, see Whitby, *Maurice*, 251.

[10] Helm, 'Untersuchungen', 388 n. 3 (who, however, overlooks the reference discussed here).

Zacharias into making concessions by telling him that Persian forces could no longer be restrained from invading Roman territory. In his account of these negotiations, Menander includes a very revealing statement by Andigan as to why he believed the Romans would succumb to this sort of intimidation: 'We know full well (ἐξεπιστάμεθα) that the Roman empire is resisting many enemies and bearing arms in many parts of the world, and its power has been dispersed against nearly every barbarian people; and the Romans, not unreasonably, know that our state is waging war against no other people except the Romans' (fr.26,1/46–51). Even if these were not the Persian envoy's precise words, there is good reason to think that Menander had a first-hand source for this episode in the person of the Roman envoy Zacharias.[11] Moreover, the Romans had indeed been suffering very severe setbacks at the hands of the Avars and the Slavs in recent years,[12] which supports the conclusion that Andigan's statement was based on more than mere surmise.

These further nine cases certainly show that our initial episode involving Musonianus was not unique. On the other hand, it might be objected that ten instances across four centuries still does not amount to much. The fact that most of them coincide with periods from which detailed narrative histories have survived creates a strong likelihood that, if we possessed comparable sources for other portions of these four centuries, the number of cases would multiply accordingly. But this sort of argument might be regarded with caution in some quarters. If, however, we turn to our other category – knowledge of military preparations – a more systematic approach is possible. In spite of the uneven quality and distribution of the surviving sources, one can draw up a reasonably complete catalogue of Roman invasions of Persia and Persian invasions of Roman territory — I leave aside for the moment the problem of distinguishing an invasion from a raid – and so have a yardstick of sorts against which to assess the frequency with which invasions were or were not anticipated. The approach adopted in what follows, therefore, has been, first, to examine all the cases for which there is explicit evidence concerning knowledge of military preparations (pp. 112–18), to see what sort of pattern emerges from these (pp. 118–20), and then to compare this against the catalogue of invasions (pp. 120–8).

Knowledge of military preparations

The explicit evidence can be grouped under two headings – those episodes where the sources actually refer to movement of information, and those where the movement of information is readily deduced from the responses it provoked.

---

[11] Blockley, *Menander*, 19.   [12] Whitby, *Maurice*, 87–9.

This latter category can be dealt with more succinctly, and mostly involves cases where the dispatch of an embassy by one or other power presupposes that they had received information about the other's forthcoming moves.[13] One such case is Constantine's planned expedition in 337. The surviving sources concerning this episode are meagre and there is much scholarly debate about Constantine's objectives.[14] But whatever they may have been, the Persians soon learned of Roman preparations, for an embassy arrived in Constantinople with the aim of dissuading Constantine from his plan,[15] though in the event it was only Constantine's own death which prevented the campaign from proceeding.

Julian's expedition in 363 is another example. Although there is no clear statement in any of the relevant sources that the Persians knew of Roman plans, it is readily apparent that they did from the fact that during the winter of 362–3 Julian received a request that he receive a Persian embassy so that differences could be settled peacefully (Lib. Or. xviii.164). Julian's abrupt rejection of this diplomatic move, and his return message – that Shapur would soon see him in person – show that Julian believed there was no point in trying to pretend that nothing was afoot. All this is confirmed by the strategy he adopted in March 363. By making a feint towards the Tigris before proceeding down the Euphrates, with the intention of misleading Shapur as to where his main thrust was directed,[16] Julian implicitly acknowledged that the Persians were expecting an invasion.

There are similar cases in the sixth century. Although initially the Romans do not seem to have believed that Khusro would break the peace of 532 (Proc. Wars ii.3.57; cf. Bld. ii.10.1), it is apparent that Justinian did eventually become aware of Persian intentions, for during the winter of 539–40 he sent an envoy to Khusro bearing a letter in which the emperor endeavoured to dissuade the Persian king from proceeding with his plans (Proc. Wars ii.4.14–26). With such a large proportion of his forces tied down in Italy, Justinian had no means other than diplomacy with which to deflect the Persian king. It is not necessary to accept that the actual text of the letter which Procopius purports to provide is genuine:[17] the embassy clearly was sent and its purpose was unequivocal.

The embassy of Sebokhth from Khusro to Justin II in 572 likewise shows that the Persian king knew of Roman plans. According to Menander, the embassy was sent because Khusro 'was afraid that, on account of the major [Roman] preparations, [Justin] might mount an invasion' (fr. 16,1/9–12), and Sebokhth's

---

[13] This point is argued in greater detail in Lee, 'Embassies as evidence'.

[14] See most recently T. D. Barnes, 'Constantine and the Christians of Persia', JRS 75 (1985), 126–36.

[15] Festus Breviarium 26; Eusebius Life of Constantine iv.57 [chapter heading] (p. 13/5).

[16] Dillemann, Haute Mésopotamie, 302; Ridley, 'Julian's Persian expedition', 318–19 and n.8; Matthews, Ammianus, 138–9.

[17] On the literary conventions governing letters in Procopius, see Cameron, Procopius, 148–9.

assiduous efforts to dissuade Justin from aggression against Persia support this interpretation.[18]

The final case is somewhat different from the four above, but nevertheless still conforms to the general rubric of knowledge being deduced from responses it provoked. Following the revolt in Persia of Vahram Chobin in 589 and the flight of the young Khusro II to Roman territory, the emperor Maurice was confronted by envoys from both men seeking his recognition and support. Once Maurice had made his decision to help Khusro regain his throne and had rejected Vahram's envoys, Vahram can have had no doubt that he faced an invasion from the west, as is shown by his immediate response in sending forces to cover the two major invasion routes from the Roman empire – that is, across the north Mesopotamian plain and down the Euphrates (Th. Sim. v.1.1–2). That the invaders knew Vahram was expecting them is shown by Khusro's ploy of dispatching a secondary force to seize Ctesiphon while the main army engaged Vahram (v.4.2).[19]

The episodes in this first group pose no obvious problems as regards reliability because none of them depends on an ancient source actually saying that information was acquired; the acquisition of information has been deduced from circumstantial evidence – in four cases, the dispatch of an embassy, and in the fifth, the rebuff of one. The second group of episodes which now follows does, however, raise the problem of reliability more acutely. When an ancient source says that 'the emperor learned of enemy preparations', one is bound to ask whether these statements can be taken at face value. Is it not conceivable that, as with the rhetorical speeches placed in the mouths of protagonists by ancient writers, we are perhaps also dealing with authorial licence here? In the discussion of each of the following episodes, therefore, attention will be given to ascertaining that it was possible for the author in question to have known about the movement of information he purports to record, and that the incident does not support any underlying polemic in the work, either for or against an individual.[20]

---

[18] Against the irrefutable evidence of the embassy, John of Epiphania's comment that the Persians still had no idea of Roman intentions when the invasion began (3, *FHG* iv.274) is hardly credible.

[19] For Theophylact's reliance on John of Epiphania, and the latter's sources for the Persian civil war, see Whitby, *Maurice*, 222–3.

[20] One other possibility which can be dealt with here is that of hindsight – that is, an author noticed that Roman forces intercepted Persian forces near the frontier, and so, in looking for an explanation beyond mere coincidence, inserted his own conclusion that the Romans intercepted the Persians *because* they knew they were coming. There are two difficulties with this explanation. First, in many of the instances discussed below the Romans are unable to meet Persian forces adequately in spite of knowing of their approach. These, then, cannot be deductions from mere coincidence. Secondly, even if an author *was* deducing that movement of information preceded the invasion, this must have been done in the belief that this was a reasonable assumption.

The first episode concerns Kavad's invasion of 502. Although the Roman response was slow, there is no doubt that there was some advance knowledge of the Persian threat. The chronicle attributed to Joshua Stylites states that the Roman ambassador Rufinus was dispatched to negotiate with the enemy 'when Anastasius the Roman ruler heard (*shma'*) that Kavad had assembled his forces'. This information must have reached Anastasius before the invasion began because Rufinus' instructions were to offer the Persian king money 'if Kavad was on the frontier and had not yet crossed into the land of the Romans' (50) – though this also suggests that the news had been received very late, leaving Anastasius little time to manoeuvre. This is somewhat surprising, for Kavad is reported to have sent requests to various Arab tribes and to the Armenians for contingents of troops to help in his war against the Romans (24), so that knowledge of his plans will have been widespread. The relative slowness of the Roman response can be explained partly by preoccupation with a Bulgar invasion of the Balkans and a major Arab raid into Phoenicia, Syria and Palestine that same year[21] – Kavad's invasion did not begin until 22 August (J. Styl. 47-8) – and partly by the fact that Kavad had threatened war on a number of occasions in the past without making good those threats (J. Styl. 19–20 and 23).[22]

That the author of this chronicle should have known about the receipt of the information by the Romans is not problematic for, as noted earlier, he specifically says that one of his sources was the Roman and Persian envoys whom he had met (25), whose number no doubt included Rufinus.[23] Nor is the apparent slowness of Anastasius' response cause for scepticism. One might have expected the emperor's receipt of prior warning to be emphasised by a writer critical of him, but in fact, as a fellow Monophysite, the author strives to present Anastasius in a very favourable light and the evidence in the chronicle that there was prior knowledge of Persian plans requires careful deduction from disparate comments (one might almost suspect an attempt to hide it). Indeed the chronicle's main theme is that Kavad's invasion was the instrument of God's judgement on the sin of Mesopotamia, a subject to which a concern with strategic intelligence is hardly relevant.

On his appointment as Master of the Soldiers (*magister militum*) in the east in 530, Belisarius assembled an army and advanced to Dara with a view to a possible offensive into Persia. But while awaiting Justinian's order to proceed, 'suddenly someone reported (ἀπήγγελλεν) to Belisarius and Hermogenes that

---

[21] Marcellinus *comes*, *Chronicle* s.a. 502; Theoph. p. 143/20–7.

[22] The fact that there had been no fighting with Persia for sixty years, and no really serious warfare between the two empires for a century and a half, presumably also gave some advantage to Kavad in terms of surprise.

[23] Apart from a certain Leo who took gifts to Kavad after the conclusion of peace in 505 (81), Rufinus is the only Roman envoy named in the chronicle.

the Persians were expected to invade Roman territory since they were keen to seize the city of Dara. When they heard this, they made ready their battle dispositions' (Proc. *Wars* i.13.12-13). The battle which ensued proved, of course, to be one of Belisarius' most famous victories. There is no reason to suspect the reliability of Procopius' account at this point. He was himself present at Dara, and, as Belisarius' secretary, was in an ideal position to know about such a report. As for any underlying *Tendenz*, it is hard to see how this brief allusion to advance warning of Persian preparations could have added anything to Belisarius' reputation.

During the same campaigning season, Kavad sent a second army to invade Roman Armenia. Procopius is once more explicit that the Roman commanders there, Dorotheus and Sittas, 'learning (γνόντες) that an enemy army was assembling in Persarmenia' (i.15.4), investigated the report further and then launched a successful pre-emptive attack on the Persian camp. Again there is no obvious reason why Procopius should have indulged in invention at this point. The whole episode shows the two generals in a positive light, whereas Sittas' exemplary conduct *vis-à-vis* Belisarius the following year[24] gave Procopius good reason to present Sittas in a poor light elsewhere.[25]

The next episode could with good reason have been placed in the preceding section, in so far as it involves knowledge of a handicap (with a difference) as well as knowledge of military preparations. In the part of the Caucasus closest to the Black Sea lived the Lazi, a client kingdom of the Roman empire until disaffection resulting from maltreatment at the hands of corrupt Roman officials prompted them, during the winter of 540–1, to invite the Persians to deliver them from Roman hands:

> Khusro assembled a large army and was preparing for the invasion without, however, revealing his plan to the Persians (apart from those sole individuals with whom he usually consulted concerning secret affairs). He also instructed the [Lazian] envoys to tell no one what was afoot. Instead, he made out that he was setting off for Iberia [the region east of Lazica] to set affairs there in order since, he said, a Hunnic tribe had attacked the Persian empire in that region.
>
> At this time Belisarius arrived in Mesopotamia where he assembled the army from round about, and he was sending men into Persian territory to spy . . . On their return, the spies were adamant that the enemy would not be mounting an

---

[24] Cameron, *Procopius*, 146, 158.

[25] The sequel to this episode requires brief comment. After this setback, the Persian general managed to regroup his forces – 30,000 in all – and proceeded to advance unchallenged into Roman territory. It is highly improbable that the Romans should have been aware of the initial gathering of Persian forces and not of this subsequent one. The Persians apparently outnumbered the Roman forces two to one and significantly Procopius says the Persians 'caught up with (καταλαμβάνουσι) their enemy near Satala' (i.15.9–11). Rather than a surprise Persian invasion, this suggests a controlled Roman retreat until the terrain allowed them to offset their numerical inferiority.

invasion for the meantime, for Khusro was preoccupied elsewhere with a war against the Huns. When he heard this, Belisarius wanted to invade enemy territory immediately with the whole army. (Proc. *Wars* ii.15.35–16.4)

Khusro's ploy succeeded in deceiving the Romans as to the purpose of his preparations and he was able to take the Roman forces in Lazica virtually unawares (ii.16–17). The most significant feature of this episode, however, is the expectation attributed to him by Procopius that he could not conceal from the Romans the fact that he was preparing for a major expedition. Indeed the success of his plans depended on the certainty of such information reaching Roman ears. Of course one is bound to ask how Procopius knew of Khusro's plan to deceive the Romans with disinformation, but this is not as problematic as might appear. An obvious explanation for the discrepancy between the spies' adamant reports and what actually happened was that Khusro had deliberately spread a false report about his intentions, and Procopius clearly assumed that his readers would find this credible.[26]

Following Justin II's invasion in 572, Khusro used the winter of 572–3 to assemble forces in Ctesiphon, and in the spring of 573 he advanced against the Roman forces now besieging Nisibis. According to one source, Khusro made a point of moving his army towards Nisibis through uninhabited country 'so that his movement would not become known to the Romans by any means' (John Epiph. 4, *FHG* iv.275) – a remark of considerable significance in the context of pp. 150–3 below. In spite of Khusro's precautions, however, information about his preparations and approach was certainly communicated to Justin:

> The bishop of Nisibis had become a close friend of Gregory [patriarch of Antioch] . . . and was particularly discontented as a result of the maltreatment which the Christians had suffered continually at Persian hands, and longed for his city to be subject to the Romans. So he supplied Gregory with news (γνῶσιν) of all that was taking place in enemy territory, informing him of everything as it happened. The latter immediately passed this on to Justin and notified him as quickly as possible of Khusro's advance. (Evag. *HE* v. 9, p. 204/29–205/8)[27]

Justin, however, ignored this information, preferring to believe other reports to the effect that Khusro was dead or dying (Evag. *HE* v. 9, p. 204/20–2).[28] The

---

[26] Procopius was not himself present in the east in 541, but was probably there the following year (Cameron, *Procopius*, 163–4) when he could have made enquiries from those directly involved in events. For the problems raised by Procopius' alternative account of these events in the *Secret History*, and a proposed solution which preserves the integrity of the *Wars* account in most respects, see Lee, 'Procopius'.

[27] The reliability of this passage is discussed in detail in A. D. Lee, 'Evagrius, Paul of Nisibis, and the problem of loyalties in the mid-sixth century', *JEH* (forthcoming).

[28] Given Khusro's previous willingness to use disinformation in 541, it would not be surprising if these reports of his death had also been initiated by the king himself; one of his own generals had successfully used the same ploy against the Romans in the 550s (Agath. ii.19.5–20.3), and Khusro's own advancing years would have lent credibility to such a rumour.

Roman forces at Nisibis were not reinforced or prepared for Khusro's arrival, and taken by surprise, they fled in disarray. It is worth stressing, however, that this disaster – which included the loss of Dara soon after – was not a consequence of lack of accurate information.[29]

In 584 Persian forces were planning to attack Roman installations on the Tur Abdin through the pass of Maïacarire on the southern side of the plateau. The Roman commander Philippicus somehow learned (ἐπύθετο) of Persian intentions (Th. Sim. i.13.4) and exploited this knowledge to good effect. Once the Persian forces had set off from Nisibis for the assault on the Tur Abdin, Philippicus led Roman forces by another route and began plundering the region around Nisibis until the Persians hurried back to oppose him, whereupon he retired again into Roman territory north of the Tur Abdin.[30] Theophylact's knowledge of this incident is readily accounted for – John of Epiphania, on whose account his history was based, worked for Gregory of Antioch, whom Philippicus knew well[31] – nor can Theophylact be suspected of inventing the movement of information with a view to enhancing Philippicus' reputation: the incident does present Philippicus in a favourable light, but Theophylact's portrayal of him is elsewhere critical.[32]

The pattern of information-movement

The eleven episodes discussed in the previous section – plus the second introductory episode, Shapur's invasion in 359 – leave many questions unanswered. For example, the time lag between acquisition of the information and the actual invasion usually cannot be determined with precision, and the means by which the information was acquired is often not specified (this subject will be considered in Part III). Nevertheless, in all twelve a common phenomenon is present: the empire that was to be invaded knew of enemy plans in advance. In eight cases, however, the defending empire was unable to prevent the invasion in spite of having this information. This inability was due to one of two reasons. On four occasions, effective response was hampered by preoccupation with a military problem elsewhere, whether it was the Sarmatians on the

---

[29] It should also be noted that the success of Khusro's secondary force in 573, which continued up the Euphrates and captured Circesium and Apamea, was not the result of surprise but of the withdrawal of the Ghassanid Arabs from the sector of the Roman frontier which it was their responsibility to defend, apparently (John Eph. HE vi.3–4) because of Justin's successful alienation of them through a bungled attempt to assassinate their chief (though note the reservations of Whitby, Maurice, 257–8).

[30] For the difficulties in determining Philippicus' moves precisely, see the Whitbys' translation, 39 n. 72.

[31] Whitby, Maurice, 222, 231.

[32] P. Allen, Evagrius Scholasticus the Church Historian (Louvain, 1981), 248, qualified by Whitby, Maurice, 231.

middle Danube in 358–9, Bulgars and Arabs in 502, the Goths in Italy in 539–40, or the Armenians in revolt in 572. It is worth emphasising that in three of these cases, there is clear evidence that the invader knew of the handicap (the exception being Kavad in 502). In the other four, when no such handicap existed, the invader acted in a way designed to upset or deceive enemy expectations; hence Julian's feint in 363, Khusro's ploys in 541 and 573, and the dispatch of the secondary force to capture Ctesiphon in 591. In other words, failure to prevent the invasions was ultimately due to the invader offsetting the handicap of advance warning by either creating or exploiting a temporary advantage. Both strategies provide implicit confirmation that movement of information was a genuine phenomenon.

Of the four cases involving no exploitation or creation of a temporary advantage, Constantine's planned invasion of 337 is unusual in not being carried out.[33] It is not known that Persia was facing any severe problems elsewhere at the time, but there is a sixth-century report concerning a memorandum of Constantine's in which he apparently indicated his intention of taking the Persians by surprise, possibly by attacking from Lazica (John Lydus *De Magistratibus* iii.33–5).

The remaining three episodes – the two invasions of 530 and the attack of 584 – are quite different, for in none of these was there any advantage to be exploited, nor does there seem to have been any attempt to create one. Their outcomes are highly instructive: both invasions in 530 failed in the vicinity of the frontier, and that of 584 ended up having to deal with a Roman counter-offensive.

The pattern for the movement of strategic intelligence between the two empires which the cases discussed above suggest may be summarised as follows:

(a) Advance warning of an invasion always appears to have reached the enemy. Every planned invasion had to reckon with this fundamental disadvantage.

(b) In order to offset this disadvantage, it was necessary to have some sort of temporary advantage at the time of invasion, whether it was a case of exploiting a pre-existing enemy handicap, or of creating an advantage by upsetting enemy expectations in some way.

(c) When no off-setting advantage was sought by the invader, the invasion was met by a substantial enemy force before it had penetrated far into enemy territory. The fact that an invading force was intercepted need not necessarily have guaranteed that it was turned back, though this was what happened in the three instances discussed above. The outcome of the ensuing engagement

---

[33] Aurelian is reported to have been preparing for an invasion of Persia at the time of his death in 275 (*HA Aur.* 35.4–5), but no further details are known and the source in question is notoriously unreliable anyway.

depended on another whole set of factors, such as the respective abilities of the commanders in a pitched battle. As far as movement of information is concerned, however, the crucial point is that the invaders were intercepted close to the frontier, and by a substantial force.

The other invasions

The episodes discussed above represent about one quarter of all known invasions in both directions throughout the four centuries of Roman–Persian relations. This shows that the phenomenon of advance warning was not rare, but the real test of typicality will be the extent to which the remaining three-quarters of the catalogue of invasions is consistent with the pattern outlined at the end of the preceding section. Before we examine this question, however, a terminological point must be dealt with – the definition of 'invasion' used in compiling the catalogue. Smaller-scale raids need to be excluded, for by their very nature it would be unreasonable to expect them to have been anticipated. However, ancient sources are often imprecise about the scale of an attack, and even when numbers of troops are mentioned, the figures are sometimes clearly inflated.[34]

The only practical criterion for discriminating between large-scale invasions and smaller-scale raids is that of who led the forces in question. If an expedition was led by the Persian king or Roman emperor, then presumably it was of importance and so by implication sizeable in terms of men and logistic support. After 395, of course, no emperor campaigned in person until Heraclius, so for the latter half of our period a Roman invasion has to be redefined as any expedition led by a *magister*, the highest ranking officer. There are also two periods during the sixth century when this criterion must be modified with respect to the Persian king. During the final years of his reign, a period of renewed warfare with the Romans (528–31), Kavad was in his late seventies and early eighties – at his death in 531 he was 82 (Mal. p. 471/9) – and so all expeditions were led by subordinates; for the sake of completeness these must be counted as invasions at the risk of including smaller-scale affairs (unless obviously such – e.g., Zach. *HE* ix.5). Similar reasoning applies to Persian offensives after 576, for, following the dismal failure of his campaign in that year, Khusro decreed that henceforth no Persian king was to lead a campaign in person.[35] Whether or not out of respect for this law, Khusro's immediate successor Hormizd does not seem to have led any expeditions himself. However, Hormizd's successor Khusro II clearly did not feel bound by his

---

[34] Cf., e.g., Cameron, *Procopius*, 148.

[35] Three sources report this decree with some variations as to the precise details (Whitby, *Maurice*, 266–7); this does not, however, affect the point made here.

grandfather's injunction, though the greater demands of his campaigns in the early seventh century meant the deployment of multiple armies and therefore use of a number of generals.[36]

We can now turn to the remaining invasions which, as indicated, constitute about three-quarters of the total. Evidence concerning these remaining invasions includes little mention of information-movement, but this is not surprising since nearly all of them are markedly less well documented than those already discussed; it certainly does not mean that there was no information-movement. Nor does the fact that the majority of the remaining invasions achieved at least initial success mean that advance warning was absent. As the cases already discussed make plain, invasions were sometimes still initially successful in spite of advance warning when the invaders exploited or created some sort of advantage. A particular instance can therefore only be regarded as conclusive proof of the absence of information-movement when *both* (a) the invasion penetrated the other empire without meeting early and substantial opposition *and* (b) the defending empire was not handicapped in some major way or the invader did not create an advantage.[37]

Turning first to Persian invasions which achieved at least initial success, a large number did occur at times when the Roman empire was handicapped in some important respect. Ardashir's successful advance in 230 took place when the eastern armies were in a state of mutiny (Dio lxxx.4.1–2), while his capture of Nisibis and Carrhae in 238 coincided with the final turbulent months of the reign of Maximinus Thrax.[38] Shapur I's invasion of 252 occurred at a time when the Romans were preoccupied with a multiplicity of problems along the northern frontier,[39] and that of 260 followed on from major Alamannic and Gothic incursions during 259–60.[40]

---

[36] Clearly my concern here is with the size of an attacking force and not its aims. The campaigns of Shapur I in 252 and 260, or that of Khusro I in 540, for example, are sometimes referred to by modern historians as 'raids', but this is a comment, not on the size of the Persian forces, but on the fact that both kings withdrew their armies during the same campaigning season and seem to have been more interested in carrying off booty and captives than in permanent occupation of territory.

[37] Because the discussion that follows treats the invasions on a topical basis rather than in chronological sequence, an appendix at the end of this chapter provides a chronological listing of all the invasions included in this chapter.

[38] X. Loriot, 'Les premières années de la grande crise du IIIe siècle: de l'avènement de Maximin le Thrace (235) à la mort de Gordien III (244)', *ANRW* II.2 (1975), 657–787, at 716–17 with n. 471.

[39] For the date and discussion, see Balty, 'Apamée', 228–39.

[40] E. Demougeot, *La Formation de l'Europe et les invasions barbares* vol. 1 (Paris, 1969), 493–9 (Alamanni); Potter, *Prophecy and History*, 313–14 (Goths). Ammianus (xxiii.5.3) recounts an incident from one of Shapur's invasions – it seems more likely that it belongs to the earlier one (see note *ad loc.* in Budé edition) – in which the inhabitants of Antioch, enjoying a performance in the theatre, were taken completely unawares by the Persians. This might be seen as a clear indication that the Romans had no advance warning of that particular Persian invasion, but such a conclusion does not necessarily follow. Large Roman armies are known to have met Persian

During the reign of Constantius II in the fourth century, Shapur II made three attempts to capture the important frontier fortress of Nisibis. On none of these occasions did he achieve his goal, but a Persian army was nevertheless on Roman soil for an average of two to three months at a time. Shapur's first attempt, however, coincided with Constantius' absence in Constantinople in the middle of 337 in order to attend to the division of power after Constantine's death.[41] In 346 Constantius was again absent in Constantinople for a number of months in order to settle religious tensions with his brother Constans.[42] The third attempt, in 350, followed soon after the usurpation of Magnentius in Gaul forced Constantius to withdraw forces from the east and prepare for a major expedition to the west.[43]

In the following century, Yazdgerd II invaded Roman Armenia in 440. The sources for this episode are very limited, but according to one chronicle, the invasion occurred at a time when other peoples – Arabs and Tzani – were troubling the frontiers, and when the Isaurians were again in revolt.[44]

In the sixth century, Khusro's invasion in 542 coincided with the period when the plague was raging in Constantinople and the east,[45] and it is probable that Justinian's initially slow response to the invasion was due to preoccupation

---

forces on both occasions – at Barbalissos in 252, and near Carrhae and Edessa in 260 (see *Res Gestae Divi Saporis* ss. 4 and 11). On both occasions the Romans were defeated, but the inhabitants of Antioch, knowing that such substantial forces had gone forward to meet the enemy, would therefore have had every reason to be surprised by the sudden appearance of Persian troops outside their city.

[41] For the date, see Barnes, 'Constantine and the Christians of Persia', 133, where he also comments that 'Shapur took immediate advantage of this unexpected change in the political and military situation . . . There was no long interval between the arrival of the news that Constantine was dead and Shapur's invasion of Roman territory.'

[42] Seeck, *Geschichte* vol. 4, 84–6, 421. Barnes has challenged Seeck's conclusions about Constantius' presence in the capital between May and August ('Imperial chronology, AD 337–350', *Phoenix* 34 (1980), 160–6, at 164 n. 15), but his position is inconsistent. He argues that this absence 'seems most improbable for a year when the Persians besieged Nisibis for three months', but fails to consider the possibility that they decided to mount the siege at this time precisely because Constantius was absent – a proposition he is happy to endorse for the siege of 337 (see preceding note).

[43] Seeck, *Geschichte* vol. 4, 95. Julian *Or.* i.22 [27a] makes an explicit connection, though this has been thought unlikely by Lightfoot 'Facts and fiction', 113, on the grounds that 'preparations for a spring offensive must have been made long before the news reached the Persian court'. Magnentius' acclamation occurred on 18 January 350, but we do not know that the siege began in the spring; it could have begun in May or June, which would allow time for the news to travel and the preparations to be made.

[44] Marcellinus *comes*, *Chronicle* s.a. 441. Although the entry occurs under 441, the fact that Marcellinus can first register a Persian war which began in 440 (for references, see B. Croke, 'Dating Theodoret's *Church History* and *Commentary on the Psalms*', *Byzantion* 54 (1984), 59–74, at 65 n. 24) under 441 means there is no reason why the attacks of the Arabs, Tzani and Isaurians which are likewise first registered by Marcellinus under 441 could not also have occurred the previous year.

[45] Justinian's 7th Edict of 1 March 542 (*Corpus Iuris Civilis* vol. 3, 763–7) shows that the plague had reached the capital by February.

with the dire effects of the pandemic. 'There seems little reason to doubt that the bubonic plague interfered directly with Justinian's [military] plans in 542 and 543, [and] created a manpower shortage of considerable dimensions during the next two or three years.'[46] This would also account for the Roman failure to aid Edessa against Khusro in 544, a year moreover when there were incursions into the Balkans by the Bulgars and Antae.[47]

In 576 Khusro made a major inroad into Roman territory through Armenia, but the account of Menander (fr. 18,6) reveals a number of factors which account for the slow Roman response. First, Khusro helped create an advantage by attacking earlier in the year than was normal Persian practice in Armenia. Secondly, a major portion of Roman troops from this sector were busy further north dealing with unruly Sabirs and Alani, and pay for the eastern troops was late and had not yet come. 'Therefore Khusro invaded Persarmenia without fear or difficulty, for no one offered resistance' (Men. fr. 18,6/48–9).

The Persian attacks on Monocarton and Martyropolis in 585 coincided with the incapacitation of the Roman general Philippicus by severe illness (Th. Sim. i.14.5-10),[48] and the invasion of 588 happened while the army in the east was mutinying over their rations being reduced by a quarter (iii.1ff.; Evag. HE vi.9).[49]

The success of Khusro II's campaigns in the early seventh century owed much to critical thrusts coinciding with the internal discord which accompanied the beginnings of the reigns of Phocas and of Heraclius. Apart from the generally unsettled conditions created by their seizures of power in 602 and 610, both men faced determined opposition from army commanders in the east. In late 603, the Roman general at Edessa, Narses, revolted against Phocas. One source says he wrote to Khusro asking him to invade Roman territory (Theoph. p. 291/29–292/1); the launching of a Persian offensive towards Edessa in 604 suggests that there had in fact been communication between Narses and Khusro. But even if this was not the case, it is clear that Khusro knew of Phocas' usurpation from its formal announcement by a Roman envoy in early 603 (Th. Sim. viii.15.2–7), and was seeking to exploit the ensuing turmoil. Furthermore, Narses' revolt, which successfully resisted the first two armies sent against it by Phocas, seriously impeded the Roman response to the Persian

---

[46] Teall, 'Barbarians', 319. For literature on the plague, see Cameron, *Procopius*, 40 n. 42, to which add J. Durliat, 'La peste du VIe siècle. Pour un nouvel examen des sources byzantines' in G. Dagron (ed.), *Hommes et richesses dans l'empire byzantine* vol. 1 (Paris, 1989), 107–19.

[47] Proc. *Wars* vii.11.15f., 14.11, with Stein, *Histoire* vol. 2, 522 n. 3, 577 n. 1 for the date.

[48] Some troops may also have been required to deal with Arab raids in the south: Whitby, *Maurice*, 280.

[49] For the background to this unrest, see W. E. Kaegi, *Byzantine Military Unrest, 471–843* (Amsterdam, 1981), Chapter 4. Both Evagrius (*loc. cit.*) and Theophylact (iii.3.8) imply that the Persians invaded at this time because they knew of the mutiny.

offensive which resulted in the loss of all of northern Mesopotamia to Persia by 609.[50]

Heraclius' overthrow of Phocas in 610 meant a continuation of this turmoil. In particular, one of Phocas' brothers, Comentiolus, continued to hold out against Heraclius during late 610/early 611 at Ancyra in Anatolia:

> The revolt of Comentiolus had a momentous effect upon the implementation of any new defence plans by Heraclius for Asia Minor, Syria or the Armenian areas. It delayed Heraclius' efforts to consolidate his authority and to normalise transportation of military supplies, and most of all to organise some reasonable strategy against the Persians . . . It is not surprising that the Persians decided to open a major offensive . . . at such a vulnerable moment in the spring.[51]

Further aided by factional violence in many major centres, the Persian offensive captured Antioch along with other important Syrian cities, and allowed initial Persian penetration of Asia Minor[52] Given their successful circumvention of the traditional focus of Roman defences in northern Mesopotamia and the disarray in the rear ensuing from civil war, the rapid sweep of Persian armies through Palestine, Egypt and the rest of Asia Minor is more easily understood. Their initial successes in 611 were particularly critical with respect to this last region: 'the physical structure and pattern of urban settlement in Anatolia goes a long way to explaining the speed and depth of penetration of . . . the Persians in the seventh century . . . Quite simply, once the frontier [between Syria and Anatolia] . . . had been breached, there was then very little to prevent a speedy advance towards the urban concentrations of the west and the coasts.'[53]

After the Romans had regained control of much of Asia Minor by the early 620s, the Persians launched two further offensives into Anatolia, in 624 and 626.[54] These invasions sought to exploit the temporary handicap Heraclius had imposed on himself: in an attempt to gain a decisive advantage in the war, the emperor adopted the strategy of leaving Asia Minor exposed to attack while he tried to strike towards the heartlands of the Persian empire. His partial success in 624 soon forced the Persian army to withdraw from Anatolia and come to the aid of other Persian forces in the Caucasus. The strategy almost came unstuck in 626 when the co-ordinated Persian-Avar assault on Constantinople came close to capturing the capital.

Many Persian invasions which were not intercepted at the outset did there-

---

[50] Cf. Kaegi, *Unrest*, 141.
[51] *Ibid.*, 144.
[52] A. N. Stratos, *Byzantium in the Seventh Century* vol. 1, tr. M. Ogilvie-Grant (Amsterdam, 1968), 104–5; C. Foss, 'The Persians in Asia Minor and the end of antiquity', *EHR* 90 (1975), 721–47, at 722–3.
[53] Hendy, *Byzantine Monetary Economy*, 108–9.
[54] See Stratos, *Seventh Century* vol. 1, Chapters 12–14.

fore coincide with significant Roman handicaps. A few others owed their success to what appears to have been deliberate creation of an advantage. Khusro's use of unexpected timing in 576 has already been noted. Earlier that century, the invasion of 531, commanded by the Persian noble Azarethes and guided by the Arab Mundhir, came up along the Euphrates, from which direction, Procopius says, there was no recollection of the Persians having mounted an invasion before (*Wars* i.18.2–3).[55]

As for successful Roman invasions, a number occurred when the Persians faced internal difficulties of their own. Gordian III's invasion in 243–4, though finally a failure, did achieve initial success and coincided with the new king Shapur's preoccupation with campaigns in the eastern parts of his empire.[56] Carus' invasion in 283 occurred while Vahram II was trying to deal with the revolt of his brother Hormizd (*Pan.Lat.* iii(11).17.2; Eutropius ix.18.1; *HA Car.* 8.1). The Roman invasion of 421 coincided with a revolt of Armenian satraps against the Persians – a revolt which lasted for three years.[57] The Romans tried to counter-attack in 543 when the plague began to take its toll in Persian territory (Proc. *Wars* ii.24), and Maurice's first campaign, in 578, followed soon after a Roman prisoner in Persia had apparently tried secretly to urge the Romans to attack while the Persians were facing problems – possibly Turkish pressure in the north.[58]

There are also some cases where Roman invading forces sought to create an advantage. The first was Maurice's invasion of 581 when, according to Theophylact, he invaded Persia through the uninhabited part of 'Arabia' (Beth Arabaye, i.e. northern Mesopotamia) 'in order to steal a victory by the cleverness of the undertaking' (iii.17.6). The second was Heraclius' invasion of 627–8, already noted on pp. 93–4, which took Khusro II by surprise by beginning in September, late in the normal campaigning season (Theoph. p. 317/11–13). If one views Severus Alexander's campaign in 232 as an invasion in its own right rather than a response to Ardashir's attack in 230, then this possibly provides another example, in so far as he may have had in mind a strategy of deception similar to that of Julian in 363.[59]

---

55 This statement has been queried by I. Kawar (Shahid) who, drawing attention to the incursion by Mundhir in 529 (Mal. p. 445), suggests that the route adopted in 531 may therefore have been used on a previous occasion ('Procopius and Arethas', *BZ* 50 (1957), 39–67, at 370). But as Shahid himself recognises, Malalas does not specify the route taken in 529. Furthermore, the incursion of 529 was a plundering raid led by an Arab; the attack of 531 must therefore have been the first time in living memory that a Persian-led force invaded from that direction (Shapur I's invasion of 252 had in fact used this route: see p. 94 n. 54).

56 Frye, *Ancient Iran*, 296.

57 Moses Khorenats'i, *History of the Armenians* tr. R. W. Thomson (Cambridge, 1978), iii.56 (p. 326); for the context, see K. Holum, 'Pulcheria's crusade AD 421–22 and the ideology of imperial victory', *GRBS* 18 (1977), 153–72, at 167–8.

58 Men. fr. 20,1/29–33, with Whitby, *Maurice*, 269.

59 Potter, *Prophecy and History*, 22.

What of the remaining cases where the invasion does not seem to have coincided with some sort of handicap or the invader did not seek to create an advantage? Nearly all of them fail to satisfy the other condition for conclusive proof of absence of information-movement – namely, that the invasion penetrated the other empire without meeting early and substantial opposition. For in those that follow, the invading force was intercepted in the vicinity of the frontier. It might be objected that the meeting of opposing forces near the frontier is exactly what one would expect irrespective of the quality of intelligence. But such a criticism, while no doubt valid for the clash of small-scale units posted on or near the frontier, is inadequate when it comes to explaining the interception of one large-scale army by another which is typical of the cases discussed below. The number of occasions when an invasion was *not* met near the frontier – all the cases already referred to in this section – only serves to reinforce this point.

Cases where the invading force was met near the frontier include Constantius II halting the Persians near Singara in the 340s.[60] In 578 the Persian general Tamkhusro attempted to forestall Maurice's first invasion by making a pre-emptive strike at Roman bases before Maurice had completed his preparations; in the event, the disruption created was insufficient to prevent the Roman campaign from proceeding.[61] Tamkhusro's attack in 582 was turned back at Constantina (Th. Sim. iii.18.1–2), and there was also an inconclusive engagement on the Nymphius in that year – it is not clear which side was the aggressor but neither side gained an advantage anyway (i.9.4–11). Philippicus met and turned back the Persian advance in 586 at Solachon, again close to the frontier (Th. Sim. i.15–ii.3).

The Persian force of 30,000 men which crossed the border in 528 can also be included in this category, for although they inflicted a defeat on the Romans, a substantial Roman force did nevertheless confront them at Thannuris, in the vicinity of the frontier, as shown by the extent of Persian losses, which forced them to retire in spite of having been the victors (Mal. pp. 441–2). Uncertainty about the location of the frontier in 296 makes confirmation difficult, but one source reports Galerius as having received instructions 'to leave the [imperial] boundaries and advance into Mesopotamia to hold off the Persian attack' of Narseh (Aurelius Victor *De Caesaribus* 39.33), which implies that the ensuing battle lost by Galerius took place beyond Roman territory. Another Persian invasion, in 371, which resulted in a Roman victory at Vagabanta, is problematic because the location of Vagabanta remains uncertain, but the relevant

---

[60] For the debate about the date, see most recently Blockley, 'Constantius II and Persia', 476 n. 63; W. Portmann, 'Die 59. Rede des Libanios und das Datum der Schlacht von Singara', *BZ* 82 (1989), 1–18.

[61] John Eph. *HE* vi.14 with Whitby, *Maurice*, 269.

account implies that the Persians were turned back without achieving anything (Amm. Marc. xxix.1.1–3).[62]

Heraclius' campaigns of the mid-620s present an analogous problem, in so far as the boundary, which during this period had been pushed back dramatically north-west into Anatolia, was much less clearly defined, if it could be said even to exist. Nevertheless, his campaigns of 622 and 625 are consistent with the other cases noted above of an offensive being met by substantial opposition before advancing far. In 622, Heraclius began his campaign eastwards from Cappadocian Caesarea, but was very soon confronted by large Persian forces. The emperor eventually achieved some sort of success against these forces, though it seems likely that George of Pisidia exaggerated the significance of a comparatively minor incident.[63] It is hardly surprising that the Persians should have been aware of Roman moves, for Heraclius had spent three months assembling and training his army in Caesarea, and had apparently feared Persian intervention before his preparations were complete (George of Pisidia De Expeditione Persica ii.57–9). Similarly, in 625 Heraclius attempted to invade Persia from the Caucasus but soon found himself facing two armies. The Romans gained some sort of advantage in the ensuing battles, but were prevented from striking into Persia itself as Heraclius apparently had intended.[64]

The foregoing analysis leaves very few Roman–Persian invasions unaccounted for; that is to say, there are very few cases which meet the conditions specified at the beginning of this section for demonstrating the absence of information-movement.[65] Indeed the remarkably high degree of consistency between the pattern established from the explicit evidence and the remaining cases where there is no explicit allusion to the movement of information cannot be mere coincidence. It suggests that the first and second episodes discussed in the introduction to this chapter were very typical, and that

---

[62] One suggested identification is with the Bagavan valley in Armenia (almost certainly well beyond the Roman frontier at that time): Dillemann, *Haute Mésopotamie*, 259; E. Kettenhofen, 'Toponyme bei Ps.-Pawstos', *Handes Amsorya* 103 (1989), 65–80, at 69 (I owe this latter reference to Chris Lightfoot).

[63] N. Oikonomides, 'A chronological note on the first Persian campaign of Heraclius (622)', *BMGS* 1 (1975), 1–9.

[64] Stratos, *Seventh Century*, vol. 1, 159–65.

[65] Galerius' invasion in 298 is perhaps one such case, though various explanations offered for its success – that attacking through Armenia gave him some sort of tactical advantage (Barnes, *Constantine*, 18), that treachery against the Persians by the Armenian nobility aided him (Dillemann, *Haute Mésopotamie*, 210 n. 3) – could place it in the category of creating an advantage. Tamkhusro's attack in 577 is perhaps another, though in John of Ephesus' account (*HE* vi.10) the Roman forces did receive warning from a spy (*skulka*, cf. σκούλκα) which they complacently disregarded after their major successes of the previous season – but this has a suspiciously moralising tone. Maurice's second campaign in 580 is a further possible case, but the only account (Th. Sim. iii.17.3–4, with Whitby, *Maurice*, 272) is extremely brief; similar considerations apply to Comentiolus' attack in 589 (iii.6.1–4, Evag. *HE* vi.15, with Whitby, *Maurice*, 289–90). Even if genuine, a handful of exceptions does not seriously impugn the overall conclusion.

information of this sort moved between the two empires with remarkable consistency. The implications of this for the history of Roman–Persian relations will be considered in the Conclusion to this chapter; at this stage, we now turn to compare this with the position regarding information-movement along the empire's northern frontier.

STRATEGIC INTELLIGENCE IN RELATIONS WITH NORTHERN PEOPLES

The concern of this part of the chapter is to examine the typicality of our third introductory episode – the reported Gothic threat on the lower Danube in 365. In dealing with the northern frontier, however, a number of problems present themselves which are less evident with respect to the east. One is the more restricted range of evidence, a difficulty which arises partly because the writers who furnished such detailed narratives of eastern affairs are not as prolific concerning the north. Ammianus devotes a significant proportion of his history to events on the Rhine and Danube, but his accounts often lack the extra-ordinary detail and immediacy which characterise the chapters dealing with the east, where he had been much more involved personally. Procopius only incorporates occasional chapters on the state of the Danubian frontier in the later books of the *Wars*. On the other hand, Theophylact Simocatta maintains a good balance between east and north, and though only fragmentary, the fifth-century history of Priscus is invaluable for relations with the Huns. There is, however, no body of literature for the north comparable to the Syriac material which is so useful for the east. The fourth-century *Passion of St Saba*, which provides valuable insights into Gothic society, is analogous but unique, and there are no narrative histories comparable to the *Chronicle* of Ps.-Joshua Stylites.

Another problem is that of distinguishing between invasions and raids, for which there is no relatively straightforward solution such as existed for the east. This matters less in discussing episodes where information-movement is readily apparent, but where the Romans failed to anticipate an attack, it is important to be able to determine its scale. Of course part of the empire's difficulty with the northern peoples was that the latter often favoured a type of warfare which relied heavily on operating in small groups rather than full-scale armies – a restriction imposed on them by logistic problems as much as anything else.[66] This is not, however, to say that large-scale invasions were uncommon, as will become apparent.

The demography of northern peoples has long been a subject of debate. The scattered figures provided in ancient sources are often clearly inflated – as even ancient writers themselves were sometimes prepared to acknowledge (e.g., Amm. Marc. xxxi.10.5) – and recent discussions have tended to minimise

---

[66] Thompson, *Early Germans*, 146–9; Musset, *The Germanic Invasions*, 172.

population size.[67] Certainly the notion that the empire's defences failed to prevent invasions from the north because of sheer weight of barbarian numbers is no longer tenable,[68] but this does not mean that they could not bring together forces of a size that should in theory have been detectable by the Romans. Those who have argued for smaller numbers have still been prepared to accept the likelihood of armies of between 20,000 and 40,000 men.[69] Nevertheless, when it comes to specific incursions, the sources are all too vague about the size of the enemy force – and understandably so. Ammianus, for example, frequently uses the term *globus* in the context of barbarian attacks but it is never clear to what scale of force he is referring.[70] Nor can the solution employed with respect to the Persians – that an invasion was any expedition led by the monarch – always be applied here. The sources too often fail to specify who led a particular incursion, and, as observed on p. 27, many northern peoples still had a plurality of kings, so that even if an attack is known to have been led by a king, this is not necessarily a guarantee that the attack was on a large scale.

Though no simple answer is available, however, a range of possible criteria can nevertheless be suggested. Where sources are vague about the size of the attacking force, they sometimes provide greater detail about the size of the forces required to deal with the attack, and/or the rank of the individual who led the Roman response. If it was an an emperor or *magister*, then it can reasonably be assumed that the forces were substantial, and that the enemy incursion was therefore also on a large scale. If the sources speak of very large numbers of barbarians, such as 100,000 or more, it seems reasonable to accept that we are dealing with a large-scale invasion without giving credence to the figure itself. Finally, if the sources indicate that the incursion was made by a combination of peoples, then it is likely that larger numbers will have been involved.

Productive use of these criteria, however, requires a degree of elaboration which is often lacking in the ancient sources. All too frequently our knowledge of a particular attack derives from a cryptic statement in a chronicle or from an imperial victory title. Such evidence does not provide sufficient detail to be able

---

[67] E.g., Jones, *Later Roman Empire*, 194ff.; R. Wenskus, 'Bevölkerungszählen', *Reallexikon der germanischen Altertumskunde*, 2nd edn, vol. 2, 359–61; Goffart, *Barbarians and Romans*, Appendix A; Wolfram, *History of the Goths*, 7; cf. J. B. Bury, *History of the Later Roman Empire* (London, 1923), vol. 1, 104–5, for sensible remarks earlier this century. These views have been expressed primarily with reference to the settled northern peoples of the third and fourth centuries, but the situation will have been no different with respect to nomadic pastoralists in the fifth and sixth centuries, who are invariably outnumbered by settled agriculturalists (Anderson, *Passages from Antiquity*, 221–2).

[68] Musset, *The Germanic Invasions*, 171; Todd, *Northern Barbarians*, 192.

[69] Jones, *Later Roman Empire*, 196. Cf. W. Goffart, 'Rome, Constantinople, and the barbarians', *AHR* 86 (1981), 275–306, at 284: 'it would probably be wrong to estimate the size of any tribe in more than five figures'.

[70] E.g., at xiv.2.5, he differentiates between men who are *globis confertos* and those who are *dispersos*, but elsewhere (xxxi.5.17) *latrocinales globi* are contrasted with major incursions.

to answer the necessary questions (viz., Was it a large-scale incursion? Did the Romans fail to anticipate it?) Progress can therefore only be made through analysis of those instances where adequate detail is available. I shall first examine the evidence for information-movement in both directions across the northern frontier (pp. 130–6); I shall then consider evidence which is ambiguous or suggests an absence of information-movement (pp. 136–9).

Evidence for information-movement

Some years before the episode in 365 involving the Goths, Constantius II was disturbed by 'news (*nuntii*) of an alarming and serious nature', informing him of turmoil among the Sarmatian tribes living beyond the middle Danube. A few years earlier he had transplanted one particularly troublesome Sarmatian tribe, the Limigantes, to regions well removed from Roman territory (Amm. Marc. xvii.13.30), but in the winter of 358–9 he received news at Sirmium that they had left their new homeland and after attacking a neighbouring Sarmatian tribe, were now moving once more towards the Danube (xix.11.1). Receipt of this information in advance allowed Constantius to take appropriate defensive measures and forestall what was regarded as an imminent invasion. The fact that an invasion did not occur prompts the question of whether there was a real threat in the first place, but the attendant circumstances leave little room for doubt. It is clear from Ammianus' account of Constantius' dealings with the Limigantes on the Danube in early 359 (xix.11) that the tribe had indeed moved back towards the empire, while Constantius would hardly have diverted himself and part of his army to the middle Danube at a time when he knew of an imminent Persian invasion unless he believed the danger was genuine. The fact that he did forestall this threat serves to confirm the movement of information.

In the same year, Julian, then Caesar (i.e. 'junior emperor') with responsibility for Gaul, feared an attack from some of the Alamannic tribes. In order to ascertain what they were planning and how he might pre-empt them, he sent one of his tribunes secretly among them. This man, whose name (Hariobaudes) betrays his Alamannic origin and who Ammianus says was fluent in the Alamannic language, successfully completed his mission and provided Julian with information which enabled him to make a pre-emptive strike (xviii.2.2,7,15). Irrespective of its reliability, the information which Hariobaudes brought back clearly crossed the frontier.

Only one instance of prior knowledge is known from the fragmentary sources of the fifth century, it concerns the activities of one of Attila's sons in the mid-460s: 'Dengizich made war on the Romans and advanced towards the bank of the Danube. When Anagastes, the son of Ornigisclus, who was responsible for the defence of that part of the river in Thrace, learned (μαθὼν) this, he sent some of his men to enquire what they were wanting by preparing for war' (Priscus fr. 48,1).

For the sixth century, it is only when the detailed account of Theophylact Simocatta becomes relevant that further examples come to light. In the early 590s, it was reported (ἠγγέλθη) to the Roman general Priscus that the Avar khagan was preparing to attack his forces and had also instructed his Slavic allies to cross the Danube. Priscus managed to defuse this potentially dangerous situation through astute diplomacy (vi.11.5ff.). The reality of the Avar threat is supported by Priscus' dispatch of an envoy to the khagan, as also is that of the Huns in the preceding paragraph by Anagastes' sending of men to Dengizich.

In late 601 the Roman general Peter heard (ἠκηκόει) that Avar forces were gathering near the Iron Gates on the Danube. Peter moved his forces to this area and negotiated with the Avar general, and in this way discouraged the Avars from attempting to invade (Th. Sim. viii.5.5–7). As in earlier incidents, the movement of troops and a diplomatic exchange lend credence to the reported acquisition of information.

Instances of information-movement from the north into the empire are therefore limited in number. However, there is never any suggestion in the sources which describe these incidents that the movement of information was a rare or extraordinary phenomenon. The sources in which they do occur are those which provide detailed accounts of the episodes with which they deal, which suggests that, were similarly detailed accounts available with respect to the northern frontier for other periods of late antiquity, the number of instances would be multiplied accordingly. In other words, the limited number of instances is more likely to be a reflection of the paucity of detailed sources than of the infrequency of information-movement.

The evidence for information-movement across the northern frontier can be augmented by considering cases where the information seems to have moved in the other direction. On repeated occasions during the mid-fourth century, the Romans found that they were rarely able to mount an expedition to the north of the empire without news of their plans preceding them. Sometimes enemy forces anticipated the projected foray by preventing the Romans from crossing the river in question. Constantius tried to lead a force into southern Alamannia in 354, but was opposed by a large Alamannic army occupying the opposite bank of the Rhine at the point where he had intended to place a temporary bridge. This experience was duplicated soon after when a second attempt was made at another point. The Romans themselves recognised that information was somehow passing to the enemy: a rumour gained currency that certain Alamannic officers in the Roman force had deliberately forewarned their kinsmen (Amm. Marc. xiv.10.6–8). Julian encountered the same problem when he tried to cross the Rhine in 358. He too found a strong concentration of enemy forces facing him on the opposite bank, and Ammianus even suggests that Julian's plans were known throughout Alamannia (xviii.2.7–8). In the preceding year, also, the *magister* Barbatio had actually managed to make some progress in throwing a pontoon bridge over the Rhine, only to see it destroyed by a battery of logs felled upstream by the wily Alamanni (Lib. *Or.* xviii.50).

Absence of opposition to a Roman crossing did not, however, mean that surprise had been achieved, as Valens discovered in 367. When his forces advanced into Gothia he found that the object of his efforts had melted away, for 'they knew in advance of his coming move' (Amm. Marc. xxvii.5.2) – alerted, no doubt, by the construction of a camp and bridge. Similarly, Valentinian found enemy settlements deserted when he invaded Alamannia in 368 (xxvii.10.7), while many of the Quadi had withdrawn into the mountains in anticipation of his coming in 375 (xxx.5.13) – hardly surprising given that the emperor had spent three months making preparations on the southern bank of the Danube (5.11).[71]

Similar episodes are known from the late sixth century. In 593, Priscus organised an expedition against the Slavs. According to Theophylact, the Avar khagan 'learned by report' (ἀκοῇ. . . διέγνωκε) of Roman troop movements and, thinking that these moves were directed against themselves, sent envoys to forestall the attack (vi.6.2–14). Had Theophylact only asserted Avar knowledge of Roman moves, one might be sceptical, but the sending of the embassy and its meeting Priscus south of the Danube shows that they must have had knowledge. Similar reasoning validates an incident from two years later when Priscus, after crossing the Danube with an army, was met by Avar envoys demanding to know his intentions (vii.7.3). In 599, Priscus combined with Comentiolus with a view to crossing the Danube at Viminacium. Once more the khagan heard (ἠκηκόει) of Roman moves, as is shown by the appearance of Avar forces at Viminacium to oppose their crossing (viii.1.11–2.4).

Although there are no known cases of the Romans having knowledge of handicaps among any northern people during the late Roman period, it is apparent that the northern peoples themselves sometimes knew of Roman preoccupations which they could exploit to their own advantage. The best documented instance of this occurred in 378, when Gratian was planning to transfer a major portion of his forces to the Balkans to assist Valens against the Goths. A member of the imperial guard (a *scutarius*) at Gratian's court was of Alamannic origin and, returning home on leave at this time, happened to

---

[71] Cf. the remarks of Col. D. H. Gordon from his experience of the north-west frontier in India earlier this century: 'even employing skilful means of deception and rapid night marches, no inhabitants were ever encountered – all had managed to make a safe get-away' ('Fire and sword: the techniques of destruction', *Antiquity* 27 (1953), 149–52, at 149).

mention the impending movement of troops. Once Gratian had set off, the Alamanni attempted to invade Gaul. At first they were repulsed, but, Ammianus says, because they knew the bulk of the army was now elsewhere, they regrouped, tried again and this time broke through. Gratian was forced to turn back to deal with this invasion, leaving Valens to face his fate at Adrianople (Amm. Marc. xxxi.10). In an incident of significantly less dramatic proportions from the late 350s, some Franks are reported to have used their knowledge of Julian's absence on campaign in Alamannia to carry out raids into northern Gaul, until they learned of his return (xvii.2.1).

In both these cases, Ammianus is explicit about the movement of information, though only in the first can this be positively verified. The *scutarius* is reported to have been punished later by Gratian (xxxi.10.20), so his role in the transmission of the information had obviously emerged somehow. There are, however, many other cases where, although there is no explicit mention of information-movement in the sources, the coincidence between Roman handicap and invasion from the north is too consistent to be just coincidence. Nowhere is this consistency more striking than in the major Hun invasons of the late fourth and fifth centuries. The invasion of 395 occurred when most of the eastern army was still absent in the west after dealing with the usurper Eugenius. Uldin's attack in 408 took place during the months following the death of Arcadius and the accession of the child-emperor Theodosius II. The invasion of 422 happened while the empire was committed to conflict with Persia. Invasion was threatened in 434 if certain conditions were not met, at a time when Roman forces from the east were fighting the Vandals in Africa. The invasion of 441 occurred while the empire was once again fighting Persia, and also mounting an invasion against Vandal Africa. And the invasion of 447 took place in the aftermath of a period during which the empire had suffered earthquakes, famine and pestilence.[72]

A similar pattern has been observed with respect to the invasions of Gaul in the third century:

Each time civil wars or the assembling of large armies against the Persians or the Goths resulted in the departure of *vexillationes* [detachments] from the Rhine legions, the German *limes* was attacked: in 253–254, when Valerian took the army gathered in Raetia-Noricum to Italy to overcome the usurpation of Aemilianus . . . ; in 258, when Gallienus left Cologne and the Rhine to go and re-establish in Pannonia the order upset by the usurpation of Ingenuus; in 269 again, when the Gallic emperor Postumus was planning a descent on Italy and was himself preoccupied with usurpers; finally, and above all, in 274–275, when Aurelian,

---

[72] For references (except 408), see Thompson, *Attila*, 26–8, 31, 70–1, 78–9, 90. In 408, Arcadius died on 1 May (Soc. *HE* vii.1.1), and Sozomen correlates Uldin's invasion approximately (κατὰ ταὐτὸν) with the death of Stilicho (*HE* ix.4.8–5.1), which occurred on 22 August (Zos. v.34.7); cf. Seeck, *Geschichte* vol. 5, 408–9.

conqueror of the last Gallic emperor Tetricius, turned his back on the Rhine and collected a large army with which to defeat the Persians.[73]

Some modern historians have noted this extraordinarily consistent sequence without explicitly acknowledging the obvious conclusion. E. A. Thompson, for example, twice comments on the manner in which 'the Hun chose his time so well', and E. M. Wightman has observed how the Germanic peoples 'developed an acute sense of exploiting the empire's weaker moments'.[74] The clear implication of the remarkable consistency with which northern peoples exploited the empire's weaker moments is that they often knew when the empire was at a disadvantage. In all likelihood, this will usually have been a deduction from the movement of troops away from the adjacent frontier rather than their knowing why those troops were being moved;[75] yet even this is information of significance crossing the frontier.

One or two scholars have in fact considered this possibility, only to draw sceptical conclusions. J. W. Eadie has done so with specific reference to one third-century invasion on the Rhine: 'The suggestion that the transfer of troops from southern Germany may have provoked the Alamannic attack in 259/60 is neither necessary nor persuasive. As the Alamanni had been raiding Roman territory for several decades, there is no need to suppose that they were responding to any particular opportunity in 259/60.'[76]

Was it in fact the case that the major breakthroughs came, not because the invaders knew of Roman handicaps, but because they were continually trying to breach the frontier irrespective of whether the Roman defences were weakened or not? Such a proposition is certainly difficult to sustain for the Hun invasions of the fifth century. Although the fragmentary nature of Priscus' history means that there are major gaps in our knowledge of this period, a number of chronicles provide annual entries throughout and there is no mention of Hun attacks other than those referred to above between 395 and

---

[73] Demougeot, La Formation, vol. 1, 466 (though J. F. Drinkwater, The Gallic Empire (Stuttgart, 1987), 101ff., disagrees with her chronology).

[74] Attila, 70, 82; Gallia Belgica (London, 1985), 193. Cf. E. Luttwak's comment on the third century: 'sanguinary turmoil at the very core of the imperial system was bound to invite aggression from without' (The Grand Strategy of the Roman Empire (Baltimore, 1976), 128); Drinkwater, Gallic Empire, 23 ('the barbarians, apparently sensing their opportunity [in 260], poured across the northern frontier'); and Wolfram, History of the Goths, 43, 45, 63, 65.

[75] For specific comment in the sources on the movement or absence of units from the Balkans at the time of Hun invasions: Jerome Ep. 77.8 (395); Soc. HE vii.8.15, Theoph. p. 104/1–4 (420–2). It is significant, however, that northern peoples never seem to have created temporary advantages in the way that the Persians did – a reflection of their lower levels of organisational ability?

[76] 'Barbarian invasions and frontier politics in the reign of Gallienus' in W. S. Hanson and L. J. F. Keppie (eds.), Roman Frontier Studies 1979 (BAR s71, 1980), vol. 3, 1045–50, at 1048.

447, apart from an attack in 404/5.[77] Indeed, it is known, for example, that during the years after 435 Attila and Bleda were occupied in establishing supremacy over other tribes outside the empire (Priscus fr. 2/44–6). Had there been other successful Hun attacks on any scale, they would surely have received mention, as too would any success by Roman forces in turning back a major attack near the frontier. As for the statement that 'the Alamanni had been raiding Roman territory for several decades [before 259]', although the sources are again poor, the only Alamannic attacks attested in the third century prior to 259 are those in 213–14, 233–4, 253–4 and 257.[78]

A. E. Wardman has also commented on this possibility:

> It is all too easy to think of Germans and Goths as waiting for news of a Roman military departure from a frontier area so that they could take advantage of a part stripped of its defences. The model suits a conflict where there is an effective way of gathering and disseminating information, but probably not the fourth century; in any case the invaders were not usually free to wait their time, they were compelled by other tribes.[79]

There are a number of difficulties with this argument. First, the point that northern peoples had no effective means of gathering such information[80] overlooks the possibility that information can travel through the informal channels which will be discussed in Chapter 5; although I would not necessarily regard it as a typical example, the *scutarius* in 378 is a case in point. It was not so much a case of the Romans 'not tak[ing] information leaks all that seriously';[81] the problem was that major strategic moves such as the transfer of units were not easy to hide.

Secondly, Wardman offers as an alternative model the traditional 'domino' view of the invasions – that barbarians invaded because of pressure from other barbarians, who in turn had been forced on by yet others. The general validity of this view has been vigorously challenged by Walter Goffart, who has shown that the model of one tribe pushing another into the empire is not supported by

---

[77] 404/5: Maenchen-Helfen, *Huns*, 62–3. Thompson, *Attila*, 83, also refers to an invasion in 443, but see the discussion of the relevant sources by B. Croke, 'Anatolius and Nomus: envoys to Attila', *BS* 42 (1981), 159–70. Cf. also B. Croke, 'Evidence for the Hun invasion of Thrace in AD 422', *GRBS* 18 (1977), 347–67, who shows (347–52) that there were no major Hun attacks between 423 and 434.

[78] See the exhaustive collection of texts referring to the Alamanni in C. Dirlmeier (ed.), *Quellen zur Geschichte der Alamannen* (Sigmaringen, 1976–84), 6 vols., especially vol. 6, 102–3 (chronological collation of sources for 213 to 260). Note also the reservations about Eadie's conclusions expressed by M. P. Speidel, 'Exploratores. Mobile elite units of Roman Germany', *Epigraphische Studien* 13 (1983), 63–78, at 78 n. 65.

[79] 'Usurpers and internal conflicts in the 4th century AD', *Historia* 33 (1984), 220–37, at 230–1.

[80] Eadie seems to have a similar point in mind when he writes 'it is difficult to believe that they would have had knowledge of troop movements in Mainz or Strasbourg, towns that were some distance from the territory they had occupied' (1048).

[81] Wardman, 'Usurpers', 230.

the available evidence. 'The onset of the Huns in the 370s did impel some Goths to abandon their land and seek admission to the Roman Empire, but hardly another movement of the invasion period fits this pattern of one people being pressed onwards by another.'[82] The 'domino' model presupposes an 'image of a crowded barbaricum, full of people being driven frantic by newcomers continually shoving in upon them'.[83] Such a picture tacitly assumes the existence of vast numbers of barbarians, which does not accord with current views on barbarian demography noted earlier.[84]

Thirdly, these expressions of scepticism fail to address the sheer consistency of coincidence between invasions and Roman problems, which in my view strongly favours the conclusion that northern peoples often knew about changes in military dispositions along the northern frontier arising from difficulties elsewhere in the empire.

Uncertain and negative evidence

This conclusion has relevance to the frequency with which the Romans had advance warning of attacks by northern peoples. As the earlier discussion of the eastern frontier showed, the Romans failed to prevent an invasion many times, in spite of having advance warning, because of a handicap of one sort or another. Invasions which coincided with handicaps cannot therefore be used as evidence that there was no advance warning. This applies to the Hun invasions and those of the third century in Gaul already discussed. It is also relevant to a number of other periods, such as the Alamannic invasions of the early 350s, which occurred at the time when the usurper Magnentius had stripped the Rhine of most of its troops for his contest with Constantius (Julian Or. i.28 [35a]). The various attacks across the Danube during Justinian's reign, and during the 570s, 580s, and early seventh century, took place while the bulk of Roman forces were committed in the west or the east.[85] This, for example, is how Agathias accounts for the lack of opposition to the invasion of the Kotrigur Huns in 559 (v.11.6–13.8). None of this is to say that the Romans had prior warning of such

---

[82] *Barbarians and Romans*, 17. See also the astute remarks of G. Walser, 'The crisis of the third century: a reinterpretation', *Bucknell Review* 13 (1965), 1–10, at 4–5.

[83] Goffart, *Barbarians and Romans*, 17, citing (16 n. 22) Ferdinand Lot who actually used the analogy of a crowded room.

[84] Archaeological investigation has shown that certain parts of the Rhineland, for example, became deserted during the fifth century after their inhabitants crossed into the empire, which also gives the lie to the notion that they were forced off their territory by others (W. Janssen, 'Some major aspects of Frankish and medieval settlement in the Rhineland' in P. Sawyer (ed.), *Medieval Settlement: Continuity and Change* (London, 1976), 41–60, at 47–9, 59–60).

[85] Justinian: Whitby, *Maurice*, 79–80; 570s: Lemerle, 'Invasions et migrations', 289; 580s: John Eph. *HE* vi.25; post-602: Stratos, *Seventh Century* vol. 1, 66–7, 143, 178ff.

invasions; only that their status is uncertain, and that the available evidence lacks sufficient detail to resolve the ambiguity.

Nevertheless, there remain a number of episodes where an attack on a large scale was not anticipated and where there is no other obvious explanation to account for Roman failure to meet it. Such was the case with the Sarmatian attack across the Danube in 323. A number of features suggest that this was more than a small-scale raid: they are described as trying to besiege a town (Zos. ii.21), Constantine himself led the eventual response, and the subsequent fighting took place across a sizeable area;[86] yet there were no extenuating circumstances to account for the slow Roman reaction. Similar considerations are relevant to an attack on Raetia by the Alamannic tribe of the Juthungi in the late 350s (Amm. Marc. xvii.6): contrary to their normal practice, the invaders attempted to besiege towns, the incursion had to be dealt with by the *magister* Barbatio, and he took with him a strong force (*valida manus*) – a phrase Ammianus uses elsewhere to describe an expedition led by the emperor Constantius (xvii.12.4) and the army entrusted by Julian to Procopius in 363 (xxvi.6.2). Yet the Romans failed to anticipate the Juthungian attack and there were no other known circumstances at the time to explain the inadequate response.

Valentinian's relations with the Alamanni began on a bad note, thanks to his *magister officiorum* Ursacius who insulted them by giving smaller and less valuable gifts when their envoys came for their regular 'hand-out' in 364 (Amm. Marc. xxvi.5.7). At the beginning of January 365 the affronted Alamanni replied by invading northern Gaul in three groups, the first eventually inflicting a heavy defeat on four units led by the *comes* Charietto (xxvii.1). Valentinian was still on his way west at the time, but Ammianus says he did not learn of the invasion until he was nearing Paris around 1 November 365 (xxvi.5.8). However, this is far too long a time lag (ten months) for such news to have taken in reaching the emperor; the news that reached Valentinian around 1 November must have been, not that of the invasion in January, but of Charietto's much more recent defeat.[87] It is apparent therefore that there was a considerable lapse of time between the invasion and the first Roman effort to contain it; that is, Roman forces had been taken by surprise. Yet there can be no doubting that this was a major offensive and not a case of small-scale raiding: it required the *magister* Jovinus finally to defeat the invaders; Ammianus reports that his army inflicted losses of 6,000 dead and 4,000 wounded on one of the three invading groups;

---

86 T. D. Barnes, 'The victories of Constantine', *Zeitschrift für Papyrologie und Epigraphik* 20 (1976), 149–55, at 152 (for the source problems); *idem, The New Empire of Diocletian and Constantine* (Cambridge, Mass., 1982), 75 (fighting on the Danube at Campona, Margum and Bononia, i.e. along quite an extensive front).

87 R. S. O. Tomlin, 'The emperor Valentinian I' (Oxford D.Phil. thesis, 1974) Appendix 7, 492–8, on whose reconstruction I rely here. I am grateful to Roger Tomlin for permission to cite his dissertation.

and Jovinus' efforts were rewarded with the consulship in 367 (Amm. Marc. xxvii.2).[88]

In 374 a Roman officer in the province of Valeria on the middle Danube contrived the murder of Gabinius, king of the Quadi. This action, however, only served to provoke an invasion. The invasion was clearly on a substantial scale: the Quadi operated in combination with the Sarmatians (Amm. Marc. xxix.6.8), and although their forces worked in a number of separate groups (6.6,13), one such group was able to overcome two legions (6.13–14). Valentinian would certainly not have journeyed in person from Gaul to Pannonia if this had been a case of minor border raids.[89] Yet Ammianus is explicit that the invasion took the province by surprise (6.6), which would seem to be confirmed by the fact that the first reports of it came, not from the military command there, but from the civilian governor Probus (xxx.3.1).[90]

Radagaisus' invasion across the Danube in 405–6 also belongs to this category. Although the astronomical figures provided by some sources (e.g., Zos. v.26.3) must be grossly inflated, this was equally clearly an invasion on a grand scale which Stilicho only managed to contain with an army of thirty *numeri* (26.4).[91] The invaders reached Italy apparently without opposition, yet there was no other pressing problem to distract the Romans at this time. In particular, Stilicho had defeated Alaric and the Goths in northern Italy in 402, and after concluding an agreement, the latter had retired to the Balkans again, where they remained quiescent until after Stilicho's death in 408.[92]

According to Menander, the Avar move against Sirmium in the late 570s/early 580s caught the Romans by surprise because 'their movement happened suddenly and unexpectedly' (fr. 25,1/57–8). In the autumn of 597 Avar forces under the leadership of the khagan invaded Moesia and 'the surprise of the Avar attack allowed them to advance as far as Tomi on the Black Sea'[93] where they were able to blockade a Roman army (Th. Sim. vii.13.1–2). This last fact, and the description of the ensuing battle with Comentiolus, leaves no doubt that this was a large enemy force which the Romans nevertheless failed to apprehend until it had penetrated some considerable way into Roman territory; yet the 590s was a decade when, following Roman help in restoring

---

[88] The major Saxon incursion into northern Gaul in 370 (Amm. Marc. xxviii.5.1–3 – its eventual defeat receives mention among the achievements of Valentinian's reign: xxx.7.8) may provide another example, but it is not certain by which route the invaders came: if it was a seaborne attack (as suggested by Ammianus' phrase *Oceani difficultatibus permeatis*), then this failure to anticipate it would be much more excusable, even with the existence of the 'Saxon shore' defences.

[89] He had sent a subordinate to investigate the governor's reports before making the decision to move, so was aware of the scale of the problem before he set out (xxx.3.2).

[90] Tomlin, 'Valentinian', 234.

[91] Jones, *Later Roman Empire*, 197, suggests that this represented an army of about 20,000 men.

[92] Seeck, *Geschichte*, vol. 5, 330–4.

[93] Whitby, *Maurice*, 162.

Khusro II to the Persian throne, there were no distractions on the eastern frontier and the empire was able to concentrate its attention on the lower Danube.

Clear cases of absence of information-movement across the northern frontier are therefore limited, like instances where the Romans did have forewarning. Again, however, this is more likely to be a reflection of the lack of detailed sources dealing with these regions for major periods of late antiquity. The pattern that emerges from the available evidence suggests that the situation in the north differed from that in the east. On occasion, information of great military and diplomatic interest undoubtedly traversed the northern frontier. The Romans sometimes did receive advance information of imminent barbarian invasions and were able to take preventive measures, though perhaps as often invasions occurred without any apparent prior warning. As in the east, information also moved in the other direction. Northern peoples sometimes seem to have known of troop movements consequent upon troubles elsewhere in the empire, and sometimes exploited this knowledge. However, instances where information was not available seem to have been proportionately greater in the north than the east. Information-movement appears to have been less regular in the north, and the scope for uncertainty greater.

CONCLUSION

Throughout late antiquity, information of strategic significance moved across both the eastern and northern frontiers of the Roman empire and in both directions: this is the most obvious conclusion arising from the evidence discussed in this chapter. The type of information involved undoubtedly had its limitations, but the suggestion that the empire's frontiers were information barriers[94] needs qualification, at least with respect to the late Roman period. Comparable judgements concerning specific frontiers also require reappraisal, again in so far as they concern late antiquity. For example, the view of N. C. Debevoise (apropos of relations with Parthia) that 'Roman intelligence was notoriously bad in the East' has recently been re-endorsed by Benjamin Isaac in his important study of the eastern frontier, apparently with reference not only to the Parthian period but also the Sasanian.[95] Unlike Debevoise, who did not support his assertion with any systematic analysis,[96] Professor Isaac argues his position in some detail, but still overlooks much of the evidence discussed on

[94] Millar, 'Emperors, frontiers and foreign relations', 19.
[95] *Limits of Empire*, 402.
[96] Isaac cites no specific reference in Debevoise, *A Political History of Parthia* (Chicago, 1938), but a statement almost identical to the one quoted above appears at 82, where, however, the only supporting evidence is Trajan's failure to anticipate the revolts of 116 (n. 43, referring forward to p. 234).

pp. 109–18 above. A similar opinion has been offered with reference to the Rhine and Danube frontiers:

> It can be argued that every successful raid on a large scale must have involved a good deal of activity which the Romans should have identified and reacted against either by pre-emptive attacks or by appropriate defensive concentrations. It is difficult to believe that there were many of the former and the raids at all periods seem to testify to a dangerous slowness on the part of the Romans.[97]

This view was expressed in a paper explicitly aimed at raising questions rather than offering answers; it certainly has the merit of identifying the problem, nor is it without some validity for the late Roman period, to the extent that the Romans often *were* slow to react to invasions from the north. Nevertheless, it underestimates the availability of information, both as regards the Romans sometimes receiving advance warning of attacks and taking pre-emptive measures, and as regards invasions from the north sometimes exploiting occasions when the empire was vulnerable.

Obviously certain aspects of the analysis presented in this chapter remain unsatisfactory, notably the fact that it deals with late antiquity as a whole, without differentiating diachronic variations in the availability of information within that period. Elsewhere in this study it has been suggested that the imperial government's interest in foreign relations increased over the course of late antiquity, raising the possibility that acquisition of intelligence also increased with the passage of time. The problem is that the evidence is simply not detailed enough to be able to plot variations in the availability of information from century to century, forcing one to concentrate on broad patterns across the *longue durée*. The one variation that is clear is at the regional level: in so far as one can gauge on the basis of the evidence about prior knowledge of invasions, strategic intelligence seems to have traversed the eastern frontier with greater frequency than the northern frontier. One of the aims of Part III will be to account for this variation. This is, however, an appropriate point at which to consider the implications of this finding for the larger picture of late Roman foreign relations.

Let us turn first to Roman–Persian relations. Advance knowledge of impending invasions sometimes enabled effective preventive measures to be organised, but far more often the defending empire was unable to meet an invasion adequately. From this, it might be supposed that, in the final analysis, the regularity of information-movement counted for little. Such a conclusion, however, is unwarranted, for two reasons. First, most of the successful invasions owed their success to knowledge of enemy handicaps, that is, to information-movement. It has been argued (pp. 21–5) that, though not intent on large-scale

---

[97] Warmington, 'Frontier studies', 295.

territorial aggrandisement, each empire feared the intentions of the other and
was determined to keep the other on the defensive. Thus each was inclined to
seize opportunities when they could strike with relative impunity. Knowledge
of such opportunities was the result of the acquisition of strategic intelligence,
which was therefore a factor influencing the pattern of aggression throughout
Roman–Persian relations.

But aggression between the two empires also needs to be placed within a
broader perspective – a perspective from which it is apparent that the amount
of warfare between the two empires over the centuries was in fact comparatively
limited. A. H. M. Jones observed that 'in the 240 years which passed between
the accession of Diocletian and that of Justinian there was . . . a state of war
between Rome and Persia for less than forty, and in most of these forty years
there were no hostilities, but truces, official or unofficial, during which
negotiations were pursued'.[98] And concerning the sixth century, which Jones
saw as a period of more intense warfare between the two empires than earlier
centuries, another scholar has commented: 'The invasions of 540 and 573 were
very unpleasant but they were also passing incidents. Looking at the century as
a whole, nomads and Persians were kept out. The frontier areas in Syria and
Palestine at any rate were in a flourishing condition. Agricultural expansion was
the rule. The system only collapsed under Phocas.'[99] Various explanations have
been given to account for this comparative lack of warfare between the two
empires. Jones focused on the role of internal problems, Liebeschuetz has
emphasised the role of fortifications as a deterrent;[100] others have stressed the
'realism' of both Romans and Persians as to what was possible in this region.[101]
It is always difficult to determine what *prevents* something from happening, but
I would suggest that the likelihood of information about an expedition by one
empire reaching the other may also have acted as a constraint and contributed
to the general stability of the eastern frontier during late antiquity.

The pattern of information–movement across the northern frontier does not
stand in total contrast to the east, but it is significantly different. Information of
considerable military and diplomatic interest undoubtedly reached the Romans,
but not with the same frequency as in the east. There was greater scope for
uncertainty, and it is difficult not to see this as having contributed to the greater
instability which characterised the empire's northern frontier during late

---

[98] *Later Roman Empire*, 1030–31.
[99] Liebeschuetz, 'The defences of Syria', 499. It was really the fact that Phocas' was but the first of
an unprecedented series of revolts – Phocas against Maurice, Narses then Heraclius against
Phocas, Comentiolus against Heraclius, and all in the space of a decade – which created the
conditions for the enormous but short-lived Persian gains of the early seventh century; clearly
these circumstances were exceptional.
[100] Cf. Whitby, 'Roman defences in upper Mesopotamia'.
[101] Frézouls, 'Les fluctuations', 200, 224–5; E. W. Gray, 'The Roman eastern *limes* from
Constantine to Justinian', *Proceedings of the African Classical Association* 12 (1973), 24–40, at 27, 33.

antiquity. Moreover, information clearly passed in the other direction also, for northern peoples often seem to have known when sectors of the empire's northern defences were weakened as a result of Roman problems elsewhere. This can further our understanding of why northern peoples sometimes achieved success against the empire in spite of being numerically and organisationally inferior to the Romans. In these ways, then, variations in the availability of strategic intelligence can be seen to have had important implications for the broader pattern of Roman foreign relations during late antiquity.

APPENDIX

CHRONOLOGICAL CATALOGUE OF
ROMAN–PERSIAN INVASIONS (230–628)[102]

THIRD CENTURY

1	230	Ardashir invades Mesopotamia
2	232	Alexander Severus invades Persia
3	238	Ardashir captures Nisibis and Carrhae
4	243–4	Gordian III invades Persia
5	252	Shapur I invades Syria
6	260	Shapur invades Syria and Cappadocia
7	283	Carus invades Persia
8	296	Narseh invades Syria
9	298	Galerius invades Persia

FOURTH CENTURY

10	337	Constantine plans to invade Persia
11	337	Shapur II besieges Nisibis (1)
12	344/8	Constantius II and Shapur clash at Singara
13	346	Shapur besieges Nisibis (2)
14	350	Shapur besieges Nisibis (3)
15	359	Shapur invades Mesopotamia
16	363	Julian invades Persia
17	371	Shapur invades Armenia

FIFTH CENTURY

| 18 | 421 | Romans invade Persia |
| 19 | 440 | Yazdgerd II invades Armenia and Mesopotamia |

SIXTH CENTURY

| 20 | 502 | Kavad invades Armenia and Mesopotamia |

[102] See pp. 120–1 for the definition of 'invasion'.

21	528	Persians (under 'Xerxes') invade Roman territory
22	530	Persians defeated at Dara
23	531	Persians invade and win battle at Callinicum
24	540	Khusro I invades Syria
25	541	Khusro invades Lazica
26	541	Belisarius invades Persia
27	542	Khusro invades Syria
28	543	Romans invade Persarmenia
29	544	Khusro besieges Edessa
30	572–3	Romans invade Persia
31	573	Khusro captures Dara
32	576	Khusro invades Armenia
33	577	Tamkhusro invades Armenia
34	578	Maurice invades Persia (first campaign)
35	580	Maurice invades Persia (second campaign)
36	581	Maurice's abortive thrust down the Euphrates
37	582	Tamkhusro defeated and killed near Constantina
38	582	Inconclusive engagement on frontier at the Nymphius
39	584	Abortive Persian attack on the Tur Abdin
40	585	Abortive Persian attacks on Monocarton and Martyropolis
41	586	Battle at Solachon
42	588	Persian attacks on Constantina and Martyropolis
43	589	Comentiolus invades Persian territory
44	591	Khusro II invades Persia with Roman help

SEVENTH CENTURY

45	604	Khusro invades Mesopotamia
46	611	Persians invade Cappadocia
47	622	Heraclius' first campaign
48	624	Persian thrusts into Anatolia
49	625	Heraclius' second campaign
50	626	Persian siege of Constantinople (with Avars)
51	627–8	Heraclius' third and final campaign

PART III

SOURCES OF INFORMATION

5

DIFFUSION OF INFORMATION

THE preceding part of this study has shown that information of strategic and wider significance was obtained by the empire during late antiquity, and that there was a significant difference between the levels of information that the Romans possessed about the Persians on the one hand and northern peoples on the other. This third and final part of the study considers the question of how this information was acquired, and suggests reasons for the difference between east and north. Officially initiated information-gathering through agencies such as spies and embassies is one obvious subject requiring investigation, and this will be taken up in Chapter 6. But it is apparent that some information entered the empire (as well as leaving it) through informal channels: the interaction of ordinary inhabitants on either side of the empire's boundaries, already discussed in detail in Chapter 2, did not occur without the transmission of news. This phenomenon is the concern of the present chapter.

All too often in the cases discussed in Chapter 4 the agency by which information was acquired is not specified. As has been seen, late Roman writers frequently employ generalised expressions to the effect that an official or officer 'heard' or 'learned' an item of information, without specifying the source of this knowledge. Although organised information-gathering agencies such as spies and envoys will undoubtedly have been responsible for some of this knowledge, there are cases where information of importance apparently filtered across political boundaries through informal channels before coming to the attention of the authorities.

Such was the case with news of Shapur II's preparations during the winter of 358/9, word of which first reached Constantius in the form of rumours, subsequently confirmed by 'reliable reports', presumably from Roman spies (Amm. Marc. xviii.4.2). In describing how the generals Sittas and Dorotheus acquired information about Persian plans to invade Roman Armenia in 530, Procopius (*Wars* i.15.4) uses a characteristically imprecise expression in saying that they 'learned that an army was gathering'; however, he goes on to say that the generals sent two men to investigate further, which implies that the initial report derived from informal channels. News of the death of Khusro I in 579 provides a further example. As noted on p. 111, it was customary by the sixth century for Roman and Persian rulers to inform one another of a change in occupant of the throne, a courtesy, however, to which Khusro's successor Hormizd refused to adhere. Nevertheless, Roman envoys to Khusro who set out from Constantinople in early 579 still learned of the king's death in Antioch, well before entering Persian territory (John Eph. *HE* vi.22). Since Hormizd had refused to inform the Romans officially, this important news must have reached Roman territory by ordinary word of mouth.[1]

An illustration of this phenomenon operating in the opposite direction is provided by the fourth-century Syriac writer Aphrahat, who lived in Persia, in the monastery of Mar Mattai near Nineveh. T. D. Barnes has recently argued that Aphrahat's fifth *Demonstration* should be dated to early 337 and that it was written in anticipation of Constantine's forthcoming Persian campaign, which Aphrahat hoped would result in the placing of a Christian ruler on the Persian throne. As argued in the previous chapter, the presence of a Persian embassy in Constantinople in 337 shows that Shapur was aware of Constantine's invasion plans (though the source of this knowledge is not specified). If, however, Barnes' interpretation of the evidence in Aphrahat is valid, then Constantine's preparations were known of not just at the royal court in Ctesiphon, but also at the monastery of Mar Mattai (and so presumably more widely in Persia), where it can only have been known as a result of news carried by ordinary individuals.[2] At a much more localised level, there is an incident from 587 when a Roman force from a fort on the Tur Abdin tried to mount a surprise attack on the nearby Persian fort of Beiudaes. Upon arriving in front of the fort, however, the Roman troops found its people ready for them, for 'the local inhabitants had advance knowledge of the Roman attack' (Th. Sim. ii.18.9).

A very interesting but more ambiguous case concerns Isho'yahb, the bishop of Persian Arzanene in the 580s. According to one source, 'the king Hormizd knew him and loved him, for it was he who provided the king with information concerning the movements of the Roman armies' (*Chr. Seert* ii.42, *PO* xiii.438, tr. Scher and Griveau). The ambiguity concerns the question of how Isho'yahb acquired his information. It is conceivable that Isho'yahb set up and operated his own private network of informers across the frontier, but geographical location and ecclesiastical position would probably have been sufficient to provide him with such information. Arzanene was adjacent to the boundary with the Roman

---

[1] Cf. the way in which Theodosius II deliberately suppressed news of the death of Honorius in 425 (Soc. *HE* vii.23.1), implying that, had he not done so, word of it would very quickly have spread.

[2] Barnes, 'Constantine and the Christians of Persia'. At no point in his article does Barnes explicitly draw this conclusion, but his argument implicitly assumes it.

empire across which there will have been regular interchange in the ordinary course of events, and his position as bishop in particular will have given him access to cross-frontier clerical traffic of the type discussed in Chapter 2. 'It is easy to believe that, from his episcopal town, situated on the borders of the Roman empire and of Persarmenia, he could readily acquire valuable indications concerning the military preparations and strategic combinations of the Byzantine generals.'[3]

All of the foregoing instances involve information of political or military importance, and as such are of obvious relevance to the concerns of this study. But given the inherent difficulties in documenting so ephemeral a phenomenon as the transmission of news by word of mouth over long distances, it is worth further illustrating it by adding a few incidents from late antiquity which involve the movement of information of other sorts. The fact that such information can have been of no conceivable interest to governmental authorities serves to underline that it must have been transmitted as the result of ordinary human interaction, independently of any organised information-gathering agencies.

One such incident concerns a holy man who, at some time during the first half of the sixth century, came to the Roman frontier city of Martyropolis where he performed some astonishing miracles of healing. 'But while he was busy in that city, people from the land of the Persians heard [about him] because he was near there, and they brought to him two women – one oppressed by an evil spirit, the other unable to bear children' (John Eph. *Lives* 1, *PO* xvii.11–12).[4] There was no question of such news reaching Persian territory as a result of deliberate information-gathering, but the response shows that the movement of information was genuine. On a grander scale there is the large number of Persian pilgrims who travelled to Syria in the fifth century to witness Simeon Stylites (Theod. *HR* xxiv.11, 13, 20): again, their presence in Syria presupposes the movement of news about Simeon from Roman territory into Persia.

INFORMATION DIFFUSION IN PRE-INDUSTRIAL SOCIETIES AND IN LATE ANTIQUITY

Given that news could be transmitted through informal channels in late antiquity, the next step is to try to gauge the scale of the phenomenon. A simple quantitative totting-up of examples would not be representative, since in the nature of things such incidents will tend not to have been recorded in the literary sources. A more helpful approach is to consider the factors which affect

---

[3] Labourt, *Le Christianisme*, 201.

[4] Cf. John's comment elsewhere that two stylites near the frontier city of Amida 'were regarded with awe . . . News of them travelled as far as the land of the Persians' (*Lives* 4, *PO* xvii.59).

the extent to which information circulates informally in pre-industrial societies generally, and then assess the presence or otherwise of these factors in late antiquity. Movement of information in pre-industrial societies is dependent on the movement of people – 'one of the most efficient forms of communication among humans is change of location' – and the transmission of information is determined by the degree of human interaction in a given region, for 'all interactions imply information flow'.[5] The validity of these self-evident axioms will be obvious with respect to non-literate societies such as the various northern peoples dealt with in this study. In such societies all communication must by definition have been oral and therefore dependent on person-to-person contact, but they also apply to societies which had acquired some degree of literacy, as was the case with Roman and Persian society. Oral communication remained the primary or sole medium for the vast majority of the population anyway, but even when information was conveyed in written form, its transmission still relied on individuals physically carrying the written message from one geographical point to another and giving it to someone else. So even though acquisition of literacy (by at least an elite) significantly differentiated the societies of the Roman and Persian empires from those of northern peoples, the circulation of information in all these societies was still governed by these same fundamental axioms.[6]

What are the implications of these axioms for the passage of information across political boundaries? First, the frequency with which information is transmitted will correlate with the frequency with which individuals traverse the boundary in question. Secondly, ease of mutual linguistic understanding will obviously have a crucial bearing on the effectiveness with which individuals from one state or people can interact with those from another.

Before information can be carried across a boundary, however, it must already be circulating within one or other state (or people). Since circulation of information in predominantly oral societies depends on the intensity of human interaction, it is necessary to consider the factors influencing the levels of human interaction within societies. Human interaction is a subject which has attracted increasing interest from regional geographers since 1945. The proposition which gave impetus to research on this subject was in fact developed by a non-geographer, the American physicist J. Q. Stewart. In the 1940s and 1950s he formulated a set of ideas which he termed 'social physics', because 'he noted certain regularities in various aspects of population

---

[5] Renfrew, 'Trade as action', 32, 53.

[6] The one medium of communication in the ancient world which did not depend on direct human interaction was fire signals, but these performed a very specialised function and were limited both in use and in the content they could convey: W. Riepl, *Das Nachrichtenwesen der Altertums* (Leipzig, 1913), 74ff.; cf. R. Rebuffat, *Mélanges de l'école française de Rome* (Antiquité) 90 (1978), 829–61.

distributions, regularities which were akin to the laws of physics'.[7] One such regularity is now generally referred to as the social gravity model. By explicit analogy with Newton's law of gravity, Stewart proposed that the amount of human interaction between two geographical points was, first, directly proportional to the 'social mass' (i.e., population) at those points, and secondly, inversely proportional to the distance between them.[8] 'The general uneven distribution of population varies the opportunity for contacts. In other words, the potential for information transfer is spatially biased by areas of high population density through which information can travel quickly, in contrast to low-density areas through which information transfer . . . can occur only slowly.'[9]

Although the Newtonian analogy served only as a heuristic device and provided no genuine theoretical explanation, the model has nevertheless been found to accord with empirical data on all manner of human movement. Significantly for this study, the model 'holds over time and cross-culturally'.[10] A sophisticated mathematical theory has in fact now been produced to provide the model with secure theoretical foundations, and with it a wide range of applications in regional planning,[11] but for the purposes of this study the model's relevance derives from its highlighting of two fundamental determinants of human interaction – the size of human settlements and their proximity to one another (i.e., settlement density). One simple example which illustrates the model's validity is provided by epidemiology, an axiom of which is that 'disease spreads . . . in proportion to the density of population of the regions crossed'.[12] The title of the book from which this quotation comes draws an analogy between the spread of germs and ideas which makes explicit the relevance of this axiom to the movement of information: prior to the invention of mass media, ideas also required human contact in order to be diffused, and did so to greater effect in centres of population.

---

[7] R. J. Johnston, *Geography and Geographers: Anglo-American Human Geography since 1945*, 2nd edn (London, 1983), 66.

[8] *Ibid.*, 101–2. The earlier literature that developed from Stewart's proposal is surveyed by G. Olsson, *Distance and Human Interaction* (Philadelphia, 1965), 43ff., while a discussion of more recent developments is provided by T. R. Tocalis, 'Changing theoretical foundations of the gravity concept of human interaction' in B. J. L. Berry (ed.), *The Nature of Change in Geographical Ideas* (DeKalb, Ill., 1978), 65–124. Details of the gravity model and its numerous applications can be found in any textbook on spatial geography.

[9] J. C. Lowe and S. Moryadas, *The Geography of Movement* (Boston, 1975), 267.

[10] B. H. Mayhew and R. L. Levinger, 'Size and density of interaction in human aggregations', *American Journal of Sociology* 82 (1977), 86–110, at 93.

[11] Johnston, *Geography*, 102; Tocalis, 'Changing theoretical foundations', 116ff.

[12] A. Siegfried, *Germs and Ideas: Routes of Epidemics and Ideologies*, tr. J. Henderson and M. Claraso (Edinburgh and London, 1965), 19. Cf. J.-N Biraben and J. Le Goff, 'The plague in the early Middle Ages' in R. Foster and O. Ranum (eds.), *Biology of Man in History* (Baltimore and London, 1975), 48–80, at 61: 'The geography of the epidemics confirms the existence of urban centres since contagion cannot spread without them.'

Such conclusions are hardly startling, though their application in historical studies has been limited to date. A number of incidents from late antiquity indicate the specific relevance of the gravity principle to the particular historical context with which this study is concerned. In 350 the emperor Constans, who had responsibility for the western half of the empire, was murdered by one of his officers, Magnentius. Although the other emperor, Constantius II, inflicted a serious defeat on Magnentius at Mursa in Pannonia in 351, he was only able to deliver the *coup de grâce* in southern Gaul in mid-353. While the fate of the empire remained uncertain Constantius resorted to every available strategy that might undermine Magnentius' position, including the dubious one of encouraging the Alamanni to invade northern Gaul so as to place pressure on the usurper from the rear. As a result, when Julian was given responsibility by Constantius for the west in 355 he found much of northern Gaul either devastated or occupied by Alamannic settlers. Indeed their activities had created a band of territory between themselves and the Romans which was devoid of settlement (Julian *Letter to the Athenians* 7 [279ab]), and 'destruction layers from a number of sites...give some substance to the claim that Julian found a wide strip west of the Rhine laid waste'.[13] This area of wasteland had significance for the movement of information: 'When he took up winter quarters far from the Rhine the Caesar was to be informed of any enemy attacks by relays of messengers, the word passing from one place to the next. Previously the extent of the wasteland had deprived us of all knowledge of their plans' (Lib. *Or.* xviii.52, tr. Norman). Absence of human habitation had created a genuine information barrier which had to be overcome through special temporary arrangements. The implication is that under normal circumstances, information would have filtered through, and that the prerequisite for such movement was the existence of human settlements.

Khusro I showed an appreciation of this principle when, in 573, he moved his army from Ctesiphon 'through uninhabited country so that his movement would not become known to the Romans by any means' (John Epiph. 4, *FHG* iv.275). The emperor Maurice seems also to have realised this, for he made a point of invading Persia in 581 through uninhabited parts in order, says Theophylact, to achieve surprise (iii.17.6). It is also of interest that the *Strategikon* attributed to Maurice made the following recommendation: 'If the army is small, care should be taken not to pass through inhabited parts, whether in our territory or that of the enemy, lest it be observed by spies and the news is passed

---

[13] Wightman, *Gallia Belgica*, 210, with the literature cited at n. 26 – to which may be added the further references given in the Rheinische Landesmuseum Trier publication *Trier – Kaiserresidenz und Bischofssitz: Die Stadt in spätantiker und frühchristlicher Zeit* (Mainz, 1984), 48.

to the enemy; rather it should proceed through other areas' (i.9/60–4).[14] Given, then, that the size and density of settlements will have affected the amount of human interaction in particular regions, and therefore the circulation of information there, it will be important to consider settlement patterns in the relevant frontier regions.

The intensity of information-movement is of course also dependent on the content of the information itself. Some information will only be of interest to a small number of people or a specific locality. Other news will be of much wider relevance, which will help to ensure that it is diffused over a larger area. This finds support in sociological studies of the diffusion of rumour, which have confirmed the otherwise self-evident truth that the motivation to pass on news depends on its degree of importance to people.[15] The criterion of 'newsworthiness' therefore also needs consideration.

It would seem, too, that in predominantly oral societies, greater importance attaches to the verbal exchange of news between individuals than is the case in societies where other sources of information (e.g. newspapers) are available. From his experience in the Pacific island of Tikopia, the anthropologist Raymond Firth observed that 'a vast amount of ordinary news is passed on by word of mouth daily. This is so especially within any village, and between villages in the same district . . . Exchange of news is part of regular social intercourse.'[16] In other words, the absence of a plurality of information sources tends to generate a greater interest in any news individuals may know, while individuals who possess news of broader interest may have considerable incentive to disseminate it, since doing so often serves to enhance their status in the local community.[17] It is these factors which probably account for the remarkable speed with which news has been observed to spread through communities almost solely reliant on oral transmission.[18] 'News is both pulled and pushed . . . through all societies: the uninformed anxious to obtain news, the informed eager to give it away. Even without the benefit of sophisticated information technologies, the news, driven by these complementary desires, can attain impressive speeds.'[19]

---

[14] Why the author should recommend this for *small* armies is not readily apparent, but perhaps he assumed that a large army could not expect to travel without attracting attention even away from cities and towns.

[15] G. Karlsson, *Social Mechanisms* (Stockholm, 1958), 29–31, where further literature is cited. Cf. M. Stephens, *A History of News: from the Drum to the Satellite* (New York, 1988), 30–5.

[16] 'Rumor in a primitive society', *Journal of Abnormal and Social Psychology* 53 (1956), 122–32, at 123.

[17] J. M. Stycos, 'Patterns of communication in a rural Greek village', *Public Opinion Quarterly* 16 (1952), 59–70; I. J. Sanders, *Rainbow in the Rock: the People of Rural Greece* (Cambridge, Mass., 1962), 211.

[18] E.g., J. K. Campbell, *Honour, Family and Patronage* (Oxford, 1964), 313; J. Cutileiro, *Portuguese Rural Society* (Oxford, 1971), 137–8.

[19] Stephens, *History of News*, 20, with many further illustrations of these points at 13–26.

One might expect that circulation of information in this manner would give rise to excessive proliferation of rumours. Rumour is certainly evident in such societies, but a leading study of rumour has criticised 'the widespread tendency to confuse rumor with oral transmission and to assume that all such reports are unreliable'.[20] Firth, for example, stressed 'the great amount of accurate reporting arising from these social contacts',[21] while another anthropologist has expressed a similar view concerning another predominantly oral society:

> The Trucial Coast, when I was there . . . , would have seemed an ideal place for rumour. There were no newspapers and there was no local broadcasting. The majority of people were illiterate. Local people quite often misunderstood the news they heard broadcast in Arabic from foreign radio stations because of differences of pronunciation and idiom. And there were all sorts of changes and crises. And yet rumours were few and far between.[22]

It cannot therefore be assumed that information circulating informally in pre-industrial societies will have been consistently subject to gross distortion.

A number of factors, then, will influence the intensity with which information circulates within and between predominantly oral societies – cross-frontier interaction, mutual linguistic intelligibility, settlement density, and 'newsworthiness'. Some of these factors have already received attention in a different context, in Chapter 2. Levels of cross-frontier interaction in the east and the north received detailed consideration, and it was argued that levels of interchange were higher across the boundary with Persia than across the empire's northern boundaries. It was also observed that Syriac functioned as a *lingua franca* along the Fertile Crescent during late antiquity, whereas no language in the north appears to have performed a similar function on a comparable scale. Both of these factors will have exercised a major influence on the frequency with which news moved into and out of the empire through informal channels, and must go a long way towards accounting for the differences in availability of information in east and north which emerged from Part II.

It is not easy to define in an exhaustive manner what items of information qualify as newsworthy; this will vary according to the particular circumstances of individuals and societies. However, one consideration of newsworthiness has concluded that certain subjects have been of enduring interest to a wide audience throughout history – above all 'warning of a clear and present danger', and more generally 'reports of accidents, earthquakes, military expeditions,

---

[20] T. Shibutani, *Improvised News: a Sociological Study of Rumor* (Indianapolis, 1966), 21.

[21] Firth, 'Rumor', 123.

[22] P. Lienhardt, 'The interpretation of rumour' in J. M. H. Beattie and R. G. Lienhardt (eds.), *Studies in Social Anthropology* (Oxford, 1975), 104–31, at 127.

sports, weather, death and violations of the law'.[23] Much of the material considered in Chapter 4 falls under these headings. The most common item of information recorded in the surviving sources from late antiquity was news of military preparations, which of course had potentially serious implications for the security of individuals and so will undoubtedly have been of wide interest. The incident involving news of the death of Khusro I has also been noted: this does not fall into the category of danger, but clearly the death of a ruler (and especially one as long-lived as Khusro) was a highly newsworthy event, as also was the unexpectedly rapid conquest of the Vandals by Belisarius in 533 (see below p. 162). Newsworthiness does not, however, serve to differentiate east and north in the same way as the other factors under consideration since news of, say, military preparations will have been of interest whether one was living in northern Mesopotamia or on the lower Danube. The importance of news-worthiness lies rather in helping to understand why certain categories of information had the potential to become widely diffused.

The final factor to be considered – settlement density – is, however, of importance in accounting for the different levels of available information in the east and the north. First, what was the nature of settlement patterns in the western parts of Sasanian Persia and in the Roman provinces adjacent to the frontier with Persia? The high level of urbanisation in Roman Syria, to which the Hellenistic period had bequeathed an urban infrastructure, is undisputed.[24] The city of Antioch itself had walls 10 kilometres long enclosing approximately 2,000 hectares in the fourth century, and must have had a population of at least 150,000,[25] while the limestone plateaux to the west of the city had a dense concentration of towns and villages.[26] Furthermore, these settlements seem to have been growing in size during late antiquity: 'the very centuries, fourth and fifth, which saw the decline of the urban economies of the west, saw something of a boom in the east, especially in Syria, where archaeological remains clearly point to expanding urban settlement in some areas'.[27] Libanius' description of the way in which the villages around Antioch held a cycle of reciprocal fairs (Or. xi.230) illustrates how settlement density could generate regular human interaction within a region.

East of the Euphrates, in the provinces of Mesopotamia and Osrhoene, the distribution of cities became less dense. Nevertheless, while acknowledging lack of habitation in parts, the fifth-century bishop Theodoret could characterise Osrhoene as a province with 'many large and populous cities' (HR ii.1), and

[23] Stephens, History of News, 31, 33.

[24] A. H. M. Jones, The Cities of the Eastern Roman Provinces, 2nd edn (Oxford, 1971), Chapter 10.

[25] Liebeschuetz, Antioch, 92–6.

[26] G. Tchalenko, Villages antiques de la Syrie du nord (Paris, 1953–8).

[27] H. Kennedy, 'From polis to madina: urban change in late antique and early Islamic Syria', Past and Present 106 (1985), 3–27, at 4.

Jones provides the names of twenty-five cities in these provinces.[28] At the end of the fourth century, John Chrysostom described the conditions along the route followed by the patriarch Abraham through northern Mesopotamia to Palestine, and contrasted the isolation and dangers Abraham must have experienced with the very different circumstances of the present day. Contemporary travellers through the same regions enjoyed the safety of frequent cities, estates and inns, often manned by armed guards, and these features in turn encouraged many people to travel (*Ad Stagirum* ii.6, *PG* xlvii.458).[29]

Further north in Armenia, the density of cities was significantly lower, with Jones' catalogue providing the names of twenty-three cities in the whole of this region.[30] This stands in contrast with the sixty-five cities he lists in Syria, Euphratensis, Osrhoene and Mesopotamia[31] – provinces representing a combined area roughly equivalent to that within which the Armenian cities were scattered. One would therefore expect information to have circulated at a lower level of intensity in Armenia.

The evidence for settlement in Sasanian Persia is uneven in quality. The most systematic surveys have been carried out by R. M. Adams, who has used surface survey techniques to cover both the Diyala River basin and the central Euphrates floodplain.[32] These regions lie respectively to the east and south-east of Ctesiphon and are therefore of less direct relevance to the present concern. Nevertheless, Adams' conclusions do highlight significant trends in Sasanian Persia. His surveys cover broad chronological sweeps of Mesopotamian history and so throw into relief major changes from period to period, and dynasty to dynasty. The surveys show that the Sasanian period marked the high point of urban settlement in both these regions. The Diyala plains were found to contain 107 urban sites and a further 308 villages (as against corresponding figures of 26 and 38 for the Seleucid/Parthian era), while the Euphrates floodplain contained 80 urban sites and 141 villages (compared with 59 and 95 respectively for the preceding era).[33] Moreover, besides this dramatic growth in the number of urban sites, 'the size of individual urban centers apparently increased substantially'.[34]

---

[28] *Cities*, 542 (Tables 31–2).

[29] Ref. cited by Hunt, *Holy Land Pilgrimage*, 55. Cf. the archaeological remains and inscription indicating an inn (πανδοκεῖον) on one of the routes between Batnae and Edessa in the mid-third century: C. Mango, *OJA* 5 (1986), 223–31.

[30] *Ibid.*, 539 (Table 24), 540 (Table 27), 542 (Table 32).

[31] *Ibid.*, 542–4 (Tables 31–5).

[32] Adams, *Land behind Baghdad* and *Heartland of Cities*. For a discussion of some of the strengths and limitations of the techniques employed by Adams (and others), see J. A. Brinkman, *JNES* 43 (1984), 169–80 (though this paper focuses on Adams' treatment of pre-Sasanian periods).

[33] *Land behind Baghdad*, 72 (Table 19); *Heartland of Cities*, 178–9 (Tables 15–17). The criterion employed was surface area: villages were defined as sites ranging from 4 to 10 hectares in size, while urban sites were anything from 10 hectares to 200 or greater (*ibid.*, 194 (Table 19)).

[34] *Land behind Baghdad*, 73.

These trends are consistent with other characteristics of Sasanian rule. Their development of a centralising administration facilitated the organisation of large-scale irrigation projects (cf. Amm. Marc. xxiv.3.10). Under peaceful conditions, these achievements in hydraulic engineering brought new areas under cultivation and so increased agricultural production. Indeed Adams has concluded that, for the Diyala basin at any rate, there was 'a relatively complete utilisation of the irrigable area that was available'.[35] Greater food resources in turn supported population growth, which was actively encouraged by some kings, who offered incentives for marriage and child-bearing.[36] Many Sasanian monarchs also promoted urbanisation through the founding of royal cities, as noted in Chapter 1 (pp. 17–18).

Other regions of Sasanian Persia have not received the same systematic archaeological coverage as the Diyala valley and central Euphrates floodplain. It is apparent, however, that the area extending westwards from Ctesiphon to the Euphrates was densely inhabited by Jewish communities. A recent gazetteer of Jewish communities in Sasanian Persia lists over 150 locations, most of which lay within this more restricted region.[37] In the midst of this lay Ctesiphon itself, part of a vast urban sprawl covering an area of approximately 15 square kilometres and straddling the Tigris not far below the entry point of the Diyala.[38]

Northwards along the Euphrates, settlement became restricted to the immediate environs of the river as waterless terrain closed in on both sides. Ammianus' description of Julian's descent along the Euphrates in 363 shows the string of settlements along the river's course (xxiv.1–6). That at Anbar (Peroz-Shapur), for example, seems to have covered an area of approximately 60 hectares.[39] There were no towns of any size between the two rivers north of a line between Anbar and Ctesiphon, again owing to the lack of major water supplies. Settlement, however, remained dense in the corridor of fertile land lying between the Tigris and the Zagros mountains to the east. One major route northwards from Ctesiphon passed through a succession of settlements along the Tigris itself, while the other followed the course of the Diyala upstream before branching north through Kirkuk and Irbil.[40] Christian communities were heavily concentrated in this area between the Tigris and the Zagros.[41] Indicative of the large numbers who moved around and through this region is

---

[35] Ibid., 74.
[36] J. A. Neely in T. E. Downing and M. Gibson (eds.), Irrigation's Impact on Society (Tucson, Ariz., 1974), 39.
[37] Oppenheimer, Babylonia Judaica.
[38] Ibid., 179–235; Matthews, Ammianus, 140–3.
[39] Calculated from Fig. 3 in A. Maricq, 'Découverte aérienne d'Anbar' in his Classica et Orientalia (Paris, 1965), 147–56, at 151.
[40] See CHI vol. 3, 759–61 (C. Brunner).
[41] Morony, Iraq, 336 (Fig. 7).

the crowd which witnessed the martyrdom of Mar Pethion in 447 near a point along the second route: 'A great number of people gathered at that place: some were there to see the sad death because they were at leisure, others were present because the road of the Great King lies along the foot of the mountain there.'[42]

The generally high levels of settlement density along the Fertile Crescent mean that there existed the precondition for a significant level of human interaction, and therefore of information circulation. The regions adjacent to the northern boundaries of the empire, where there was a much lower level of urban development, stand in sharp contrast to this. Roman occupation of some areas beyond the Rhine and Danube up to the third century (notably Dacia) had seen the beginnings of urbanisation in these regions, but of course this was not sustained after Roman withdrawal. Late Roman literary sources never mention anything larger than villages among the northern peoples of the fourth century and archaeological investigations have produced nothing to contradict this.

It must be conceded that such investigations have been unable to engage in thorough surveys of broad areas of the type carried out by R. M. Adams in Iraq – the topograpy and modern settlement patterns of the relevant areas, especially in western Europe, have militated against such projects. Nevertheless, the available evidence, incomplete as it is, does point to a marked contrast between northern barbaricum and Sasanian Iraq, with respect both to the size of individual settlements and their density of distribution.

To take the latter criterion first: too small a number of sites in western Europe are known to make any estimate of settlement density practical,[43] but the situation is better in eastern Europe. For many decades Romanian and Soviet archaeologists have been investigating settlements and cemeteries belonging to the so-called 'Sîntana de Mureş/Černjachov' culture of the third and fourth centuries, which has been associated with the Gothic occupation of the regions north of the lower Danube and the Black Sea. There are various statements as to how many settlements have been discovered, though it is not always clear whether particular statements refer to those on both Romanian and Soviet soil, or only to one or the other. A total of about 800 sites had been found in Romania by the mid-1970s,[44] while more recent figures of more than 2,500 and 3,000 settlements have been given for the Černjachov culture, as it is referred to by archaeologists working in the Ukraine and Moldavia.[45] If it is assumed that

---

[42] *AB* 7 (1888), p. 40/6–9.

[43] Though archaeologists take it for granted that societies to the north of the empire generally had 'a dispersed pattern of settlement which lacked identifiable central places' (Fulford, 'Roman and barbarian', 83).

[44] Ionita, 'The Goths in the Carpatho-Danubian area', 77.

[45] O. Pritsak, *Oxford Dictionary of Byzantium* (1991), s.v. 'Černjachovo'; Kropotkin, 'Centres', 47. It is unclear whether Kropotkin's figure of over 3,000 refers only to Soviet territory or takes in

the figure of more than 3,000 refers only to settlements found on Soviet territory, then a combined total of about 4,000 sites results for Romania plus the Ukraine and Moldavia. The area over which Sîntana de Mureş/Černjachov sites have been found comprises roughly the eastern half of Romania (about 120,000 sq. km), Moldavia (33,700 sq. km), and about half of the Ukraine (about 300,000 sq. km), giving an overall total of about 450,000 square kilometres, and an average of one settlement for about every 110 square kilometres (though of course the settlements tended to cluster along the courses of rivers). Even if it is postulated that the number of actual settlements is double the number so far found, a density of one site per 55 square kilometres still differs markedly from densities of approximately one site per 20 square kilometres in the lower Diyala valley, and one site per 30 square kilometres in the central Euphrates flood-plain.[46] Alternatively, we could discard the Romanian figures as being some-what out of date and not reflecting further discoveries which presumably have been made in the intervening fifteen years, and calculate the average density on the basis of the more up-to-date Soviet figures; in other words, about 3,000 sites over an area of about 330,000 square kilometres. But this still gives an approxi-mate average density of one settlement per 110 square kilometres, or one per 55 square kilometres if a doubling of the number of sites is again postulated. These calculations are obviously very crude, but this is offset by the magnitude of the disparity between the results for east and north.

The same limitation applies to using the area of individual settlements as an index of their population size. 'The underlying assumption is that there is a correlation between population size and settlement space. Although it would be difficult to quarrel with this assumption, there is a problem in determining the nature of the correlation.'[47] This problem is acute when we are trying to estimate actual population figures for particular settlements, but becomes less so when used, as here, in the comparison of broad trends in different regions. Unfortunately, the number of settlements which have been fully excavated are limited in number, especially in western Europe.

To take this region first, along the North Sea coast of Germany, excavations of a third-century village at Flögeln have revealed seven farmyards out of a

Romanian sites as well: in his Fig. 1 (p. 40) and Fig. 3 (45), the boundary of the Černjachov culture encompasses eastern Romania, but the actual sites indicated on both maps lie within Moldavia and the Ukraine.

[46] These figures have been calculated from Adams' two studies. Sites of 4 hectares or greater were used (220 in the Diyala, 415 in the lower Euphrates). The size of the Diyala survey area was 8,000 square kilometres (*Land behind Baghdad*, vii), while that of the lower Euphrates comprised 6,250 square kilometres intensively surveyed, plus 800 square kilometres which received a limited survey (*Heartland of Cities*, 42, 37).

[47] F. A. Hassan, *Demographic Archaeology* (New York, 1981), 64. Cf. S. E. van der Leeuw in Brandt and Slofstra, *Roman and Native*, 33.

probable total of ten; the excavated area amounts to 3.2 hectares,[48] giving an overall area of about 5 hectares. Although Feddersen Wierde, in the same district as Flögeln, has been investigated intensively, excavations have not revealed the full limits of the village; however, the size of the clay mound (*Wurt*) on which it was established is no greater than 4 hectares in area,[49] providing an upper limit for the extent of the settlement. Further inland and closer to the imperial frontier is the village of Wijster. Excavations over an area of 3.6 hectares uncovered the boundary of the village to the north and south-west, but not in the other directions;[50] however, scholars do not countenance a maximum possible size of much more than twice the excavated area.[51] Deeper in Germany, the well-defined site at Bärhorst covered 4 hectares,[52] while that at Tornow-Borchelt measured 2.7 hectares.[53] In the Jutland peninsula, the site of Hodde was 1.9 hectares in size,[54] that at Vorbasse covered 7.5 hectares in the third century, and 10 hectares in the fourth,[55] and four other settlements in the region ranged from 1.8 to 10 hectares.[56] Although this constitutes a very limited catalogue, archaeologists nevertheless accept that it represents the right order of magnitude for barbarian settlements north of the Roman empire during late antiquity.[57] As such there is once again a clear contrast with the numerous Sasanian sites ranging from 20 to 200 hectares – 34 sites in the central Euphrates floodplain, and 48 in the lower Diyala valley.[58]

In eastern Europe, some sites belonging to the Sîntana de Mureş/Černjachov culture have been fully exacavated, and this has revealed a number of sites larger than 10 hectares. One discussion of the evidence from the Ukraine and Moldavia mentions six settlements of about 20 hectares in area, two of 25 hectares, and one (Budesty) of 35 hectares;[59] another lists the names of eleven sites of 20 hectares or greater, one site between 15 and 20 hectares, two between 10 and 15, then seventeen between 5 and 10.[60] Although the number of settlements larger than 10 hectares contrasts with what has been found in

---

[48] P. Schmid and W. H. Zimmermann, 'Flögeln', *Probleme der Küstenforschung im südlichen Nordseegebiet* 11 (1976), 1–77, at 73–4.

[49] W. Haarnagel, *Die Grabung Feddersen Wierde* (Wiesbaden, 1979), 26.

[50] W .A. Van Es, *Wijster* (Groningen, 1967), 40–1.

[51] Todd, *Northern Barbarians*, 84.

[52] *Ibid.*, 97.

[53] J. Herrmann, *Die germanischen und slawischen Siedlungen und das mittelalterliche Dorf von Tornow, Kr. Calau* (Berlin, 1973), 16.

[54] Schmid and Zimmern, 'Flögeln', 69 (citing literature in Danish).

[55] S. Hvass, 'Vorbasse', *Journal of Danish Archaeology* 2 (1983), 127–36, at 130.

[56] Todd, *Northern Barbarians*, 94.

[57] *Ibid.*, 99; R. Hachmann, *The Germanic People*, tr. J. Hogarth (London, 1971), 83; P. S. Wells, *Farms, Villages and Cities: Commerce and Urban Origins in Late Prehistoric Europe* (Ithaca and London, 1984), 189.

[58] Adams, *Land behind Baghdad*, 72 (Table 19) and *Heartland of Cities*, 179 (Table 17).

[59] A. Häusler, *Zeitschrift für Archäologie* 13 (1979), 42.

[60] Kropotkin, 'Centres', 41 (Table).

western Europe, these larger settlements are clearly the exception rather than the rule, and their numbers are still significantly smaller than those in the areas of the Persian empire for which evidence is readily available. The evidence discussed in this paragraph derives from the third and fourth centuries, but the subsequent occupation of the Danubian plains by the nomadic Huns and Avars in the fifth and sixth centuries will hardly have acted as a stimulus to urban development.[61]

Levels of urbanisation in the Roman provinces adjacent to the northern boundaries of the empire may be treated much more briefly, for there is no doubt that these regions were among the least urbanised in the empire. Roman occupation of northern Gaul, Pannonia and northern Thrace during the early empire undoubtedly served to stimulate the growth of towns and cities, but even so they remained relatively under-urbanised.[62] These regions suffered particularly from the unsettled conditions of the mid-third century, when the empire experienced foreign invasions on an unprecedented scale and chronic political instability and civil war, and these served to retard further development, while apart from fresh growth in those cities favoured as imperial capitals, the overall picture in the fourth century is one of stagnation if not contraction.[63] Of these regions, only northern Thrace remained part of the empire by the sixth century, and here there was never any lasting reversal of fourth-century trends; the only part which retained a concentration of cities was the Black Sea coast.[64]

INFORMAL CHANNELS

This investigation of the factors influencing the diffusion of information through informal channels has indicated a number of features of the frontier region shared with Persia which would have served to facilitate the movement of information at significantly higher levels than in the frontier regions along the northern boundaries of the empire. Throughout this investigation, the phrase 'informal channels' has been used as shorthand for individuals who carried items of news, or sequences of individuals through whom news was passed. But what sorts of individuals acted as 'informal channels'? They comprise the categories of people discussed in Chapter 2 in the context of cross-frontier interaction:

---

[61] One study of Moldavia in the fifth to seventh centuries gives 8–10 ha. as the usual size of settlements: Teodor, *Carpathian Region*, 4.

[62] Cf. N. J. G. Pounds, *An Historical Geography of Europe* (Cambridge, 1990), 56 (Fig. 2.11).

[63] Wightman, *Gallia Belgica*, Chapter 10; Mócsy, *Pannonia*, Chapter 9, especially 308–19; A. G. Poulter, 'Roman towns and the problem of late Roman urbanism: the case of the lower Danube', *Hephaistos* 5/6 (1983/4), 109–32.

[64] Hendy, *Byzantine Monetary Economy*, 69–75, notes the limitations of the onomastic evidence, but concludes that other indicators specifically confirm the thin spread of cities in northern Thrace; cf. Whitby, *Maurice*, 66–80 (noting, at 76, 'the tendency of the population of this region to withdraw south from the exposed Danube plains to the sheltered valleys of the Stara Planina').

pilgrims, students, clerics, merchants, mercenaries and the like – anyone with some reason to travel into or out of the empire. Apart from the Roman deserter Antoninus (Amm. Marc. xviii.5.1–3), whose carrying of intelligence to the Persians was a carefully planned and conscious act anyway, there are few explicit examples where such individuals can be observed actually acting as informal channels in the context of either the eastern or northern frontiers – the Alamannic *scutarius* in 378 (Amm. Marc. xxxi.10) is a rare exception.

Merchants can, however, be seen doing this in a somewhat different context, in an incident recounted by Procopius (*Wars* iii.24.10–12). Some merchants set sail from Carthage on the same day in 533 that the city was captured from the Vandals by Belisarius. They reached Spain quite quickly, and there the fact that they possessed news of these dramatic events in north Africa somehow came to the attention of the Visigothic king Theudis, who swore them to silence on the matter (which implies that he expected them otherwise to spread about such major news). Soon after, a Vandal embassy arrived at Theudis' court seeking an alliance. The embassy did not prejudice its chances of success by disclosing to Theudis the desperate predicament in which the Vandals now found themselves; but thanks to the merchants, Theudis was already aware of this and so did not commit himself to supporting them, and in this way the merchants' information saved the Visigoths from becoming embroiled with Justinian, at least for the time being. At a less significant level, Roman forces operating in Alamannia in the 370s killed some slave-traders (of unspecified ethnicity) upon whom they chanced, for fear that they would run off and warn the Alamanni (Amm. Marc. xxix.4.4). It is also significant that on his mission to Syracuse in 533, Procopius himself learned what he needed to find out for Belisarius through a merchant; the merchant himself did not have the answers, but he knew where to find them (*Wars* iii.14.7ff.).[65]

There are of course a number of comments by writers in antiquity to the effect that information retailed by merchants was not to be trusted. The geographer Ptolemy cited with approval the following opinion of merchants: 'they are preoccupied with trade and are not interested in searching out the truth; they frequently exaggerate distances greatly for the sake of boasting' (*Geog.* i.11.7), Strabo expressed similar reservations (685–6, xv.1.3–4), while the fourth-century historian Eunapius, lamenting the difficulties of obtaining

---

[65] Sparta learned of Persian naval preparations in the early fourth century BC from a Syracusan merchant (Xenophon *Hellenica* iii.4.1), and the Britons knew about Caesar's invasion plans from traders (*Gallic War* iv.21); merchants helped to disseminate widely the reputation of late antique holy men (P. Brown, JRS 61 (1971), 90 n.123). For examples from earlier periods of Roman history, see Riepl, *Das Nachrichtenwesen*, 444–7, 464–5, and for reliance on merchants for information in other pre-industrial societies, see D. Lerner, *The Passing of Traditional Society* (Glencoe, Ill., 1958), 322; I. Wilks, *Asante in the Nineteenth Century* (Cambridge, 1975), 31–2; M. Adamu, *The Hausa Factor* (Ibadan, 1978), 94.

accurate information about events in the western Mediterranean, remarked that the traders who had been there all told lies (fr. 66,2/13–14). Such complaints should not necessarily be accepted uncritically – for example, if Eunapius had difficulty finding out the truth, how did he know the traders he consulted were lying? Indeed the complaints carry a hint of prejudice which perhaps reflects a more general suspicion of this 'unproductive' social group.[66] At any rate, both Strabo and Ptolemy elsewhere acknowledge their debt to merchants for information (118, ii.5.12; *Geog.* i.17.3–4), as also does Tacitus (*Agricola* 24.2), while the elder Pliny noted that the account of Sri Lanka given by an embassy from that land agreed with the earlier reports of Roman merchants (*Natural History* vi.88).

A more significant constraint on the circulation of information through merchants and other informal channels was the lack of speed with which individuals travelled. There must have been a likelihood that such news as travellers carried became out of date before it came to the attention of the relevant authorities. However, a number of considerations suggest that this need not have been a consistently fatal flaw. First, 'the timeliness of intelligence depends on the relative speed of information and its subject matter, not on the absolute speed of each separately'.[67] Travel in antiquity may have been slow by modern standards, but if individuals travelled slowly, large armies travelled even more slowly[68] – a point of considerable relevance given that the most common type of information discussed in Chapter 4 concerned military preparations. Secondly, as argued elsewhere, indications of campaign preparations must have been evident well before an army set out;[69] news of these preparations will therefore have had a significant head start on the advance of the army itself. Finally, it was not a case of news having to make its way by informal channels all the way from, say, Ctesiphon to Constantinople. One would expect it to come to the attention of local authorities at some earlier stage after entering the other empire, from which point the information could be communicated to the capital and to local military commanders by the speedier method of courier.[70]

---

[66] On the disdain for merchants common to many pre-industrial societies, see P. D. Curtain, *Cross-cultural Trade in World History* (Cambridge, 1984), 5–6, and for the Graeco-Roman world in particular, M. I. Finley, *The Ancient Economy*, 2nd edn (London, 1985), Chapter 2.

[67] M. Van Creveld, *Command in War* (Cambridge, Mass., 1985), 22.

[68] D. W. Engels, *Alexander the Great and the Logistics of the Macedonian Army* (Berkeley, 1978), 154–5.

[69] Lee, 'Campaign preparations'.

[70] For the use of couriers by the Persian government, see, e.g., Zach. *HE* viii.5, vol. 2, p. 77/23 (*buradara*, cf. βερηδάριοι); Men. fr. 6,1/327; *Synodicon Orientale*, ed. and tr. J.-B. Chabot (Paris, 1902), p. 256 n. 4 . For the Roman 'public post' (*cursus publicus*), see Riepl, *Das Nachrichtenwesen*, 180ff., 241ff.; there is uncertainty about Procopius' claim (*SH* 30.1–11) that Justinian curtailed the *cursus publicus*, but if he did do so, it is noteworthy that he specifically says the route to the Persian frontier was left intact (30.10). On one occasion in the late fourth century, the journey

This of course raises the question of how such information came to the attention of local authorities. Although the sources are not very helpful in providing explicit examples, there are some incidents which show that Roman authorities in frontier regions did take an interest in questioning individuals who were crossing, or had crossed, the border. One incident arises in the context of the Samaritan revolt of 529/30, to which reference was made in Chapter 4. A party of leading Samaritans travelled to Ctesiphon to request Kavad's help and offer their knowledge of local conditions to assist with any Persian military action:

> The Romans learnt of the Samaritan betrayal when certain of their men of substance were captured on their return from Persian territory, and were recognised after their journey to Kavad . . . There were five Samaritans who were recognised. On being captured, these were taken before the *magister militum per Orientem* and were examined in his presence. They confessed to the treachery which they were planning. The report on them was read to the emperor Justinian. (Mal. p. 456/9–18, tr. Jeffreys, Jeffreys and Scott)

Theophanes' account of the same incident (p. 179/10–14) offers the further significant detail that they were apprehended at 'Ammadios', which is taken to be the village of Amoudis,[71] lying about 10 kilometres south of Dara and so just inside the Roman border with Persia. This suggests some concern on the part of the Roman authorities to question travellers crossing the border. It is also noteworthy that a written report about the incident was forwarded to Constantinople.

A second incident from about a decade later corroborates this. Reference was also made in Chapter 4 to the secret embassy from the Goths to the Persian Khusro in the late 530s, which travelled incognito through Roman territory in the guise of a bishop and his entourage (Proc. *Wars* ii.2.2–3). In 541 the man whom the Gothic envoys had hired in Thrace as an interpreter in Greek and Syriac returned from Persian territory and was apprehended by Roman troops in the neighbourhood of the city of Constantina. As with the Samaritans, interrogation by a Roman officer resulted in the interpreter revealing what had taken place (Proc. *Wars* ii.14.12). Constantina is further into Roman territory than Amoudis, but still very much in the vicinity of the border.

·

from Antioch to Constantinople was completed in five and a half days (Lib. *Or.* xxi.15–16), although this was regarded as very fast. Note also that the incident described in Pet. Pat. fr. 8 (*FHG* iv.186–7) does not support the conclusion that communications between the lower Danube and the emperor could take four months (as Millar, 'Emperors, frontiers and foreign relations', 11, seems to imply): the import of the anecdote is that the governor deliberately told the Carpian envoys to return in four months in order to annoy them; for delay as a diplomatic weapon in a later period, see J. Shepard, 'Information, disinformation and delay in Byzantine diplomacy', *Byzantinische Forschungen* 10 (1985), 233–93.

71 Dillemann, *Haute Mésopotamie*, 159 n. 5.

From the fourth century the case of the Roman deserter Antoninus is instructive. He actually went to the trouble of purchasing an estate adjacent to the Tigris (which was then the boundary with Persia) so as to be able to cross into Persia without going through a border post (Amm. Marc. xviii.5.1–3). Clearly he anticipated the possibility of being asked embarrassing questions by Roman troops or officials at such posts (a reasonable surmise given that he was taking his whole family with him). One might also note the experience of the hermit Malchus and his female companion in the mid-fourth century who, following their escape from captivity among the Arabs, finally reached the safety of a Roman camp, presumably one of those along the *strata Diocletiana*. Having given an account of their experiences to the local tribune, they were sent on to a higher officer (the *dux Mesopotamiae*) (Jerome *Life of Malchus* 10, PL xxiii.60) – all of which may perhaps be a further indication of an interest on the part of the military in questioning travellers from beyond the empire.[72]

All this evidence is suggestive, without proving the point conclusively. However, even if the late Roman authorities did not make a regular practice of questioning all those entering the empire, such information would also have been acquired as a result of the ordinary daily interaction of Roman soldiers and officials with the local inhabitants of the cities and towns of frontier regions, from whom they could easily have picked up items of news which originated from travellers. 'Soldiers in cities daily rubbed shoulders with civilians; but even in their camps, the same was true. Camps ordinarily were planted, for strategic reasons, near centres of travel – bridgeheads, cross-roads, mountain passes, or other natural focuses of trade and traffic.'[73] The linguistic dimension will again have been of importance here. In particular, it is worth remembering that many of units listed in the *Notitia* for the eastern provinces are described as *indigenae* and therefore of local origin, which in turn means that many would presumably have spoken and understood Syriac – an important consideration in terms of their being able to pick up news circulating in these parts.

This does not exhaust the subject of diffusion of information through informal channels, but it is an appropriate point at which to consider the other side of the coin, organised information-gathering, and how it relates to the role of informal channels.

[72] Cf. Augustine *Epp.* 46–7 concerning seasonal labourers entering the empire across the frontier in north Africa, who were required to give an oath to the soldiers at the relevant border post.
[73] R. MacMullen, *Soldier and Civilian in the Later Roman Empire* (Cambridge, Mass., 1963), 119.

6

INFORMATION-GATHERING

ALTHOUGH spies are the agency which no doubt springs most readily to mind in the context of information-gathering, embassies could also make a major contribution in this area. This is a point made very effectively in the *Siasset-namah*, or 'Book of Government', composed in the eleventh century by an Arab official, but drawing on sources from the Sasanian period. It is worth quoting at length:

> It should be realised that when kings send ambassadors to one another, their purpose is not merely the message or the letter which they communicate openly, but secretly they have a hundred other points and objects in view. In fact they want to know about the state of the roads, mountain passes, rivers and grazing-grounds, to see whether an army can pass or not; where fodder is available and where not; which are the officers in every place; what is the size of the king's army, and how well it is armed and equipped; what is the standard of his table and company; what is the organisation and etiquette of his court and audience-hall; does he play polo and hunt; what are his qualities and manners, his designs and intentions, his appearance and bearing; is he cruel or just, old or young; is his country flourishing or decaying; are his troops contented or not; are his peasants rich or poor; is he avaricious or generous; is he alert or negligent in his affairs; is his chamberlain competent or the reverse, of good faith and high principles, or of impure faith and bad principles; are his generals experienced and battle-tried or not; are his boon companions polite and worthy; what are his likes and dislikes; when drunk is he jovial and good-natured or not; is he strict in religious matters and does he show magnanimity and mercy or is he careless; does he incline more towards jesting or to gravity; and does he prefer boys or women. So that if at any time they want to win over that king, or oppose his designs or criticise his faults, being informed of all his affairs they can think out their plan of

campaign, and being aware of all the circumstances, they can take effective action.[1]

Although it is hard to match such an eloquent and detailed statement of the value of envoys in this role, it is a function well-attested in a variety of historical periods and contexts – in Anglo-French relations in the fourteenth century, papal missions to the Mongols in the thirteenth,[2] and closer to late antiquity, Byzantine embassies to the Arabs, such as that of Daniel of Sinope who was sent to the caliph in 714 'on the pretext of discussing peace, . . . with instructions to investigate carefully their movements against the Roman empire and their strength' (Theoph. p. 384/1–4).

The most explicit testimony to late Roman awareness of the potential of embassies for information-gathering comes from Procopius in his account of the activities of the Persian ambassador Isdigousnas in Constantinople during 551 (*Wars* viii.15.20):

> Alone out of all envoys, this man did not have the experience of being watched over. Both he and the large body of foreigners who accompanied him were allowed, over a long period, to mix and converse with whoever they wished, and to wander all over the city, buying and selling whatever they wanted to . . . as if in one of their own cities. There was no Roman following or accompanying them at all, or bothering to keep an eye on them as is normally done.

It is not known why this envoy was allowed such freedom, but clearly it was regarded as unusual. This is also implicit in the careful process by which foreign embassies were admitted to the empire and conveyed to Constantinople in the fifth and sixth century, as described in a passage attributable to Peter the Patrician and preserved in the *De Caerimoniis* (i.87–90) of the emperor Constantine Porphyrogenitus.[3] Likewise, Julian detained an Alamannic envoy in Gaul in the mid-350s on suspicion of spying (Lib. *Or.* xviii.52–3). The Persians showed a similar concern to control the movements of Roman envoys. Menander Protector shows Roman ambassadors being received on the frontier at Nisibis (fr. 9,1/25–8; 23,9/13–5), being escorted by royal officials to the

---

[1] Nizam al-Mulk, *Siasset-namah* xxi.2, tr. H. Darke (London, 1960), 98–9. For the background to this work, see A. K. S. Lambton, 'The dilemma of government in Islamic Persia: the *Siyaset-Nama* of Nizam al-Mulk', *Iran* 22 (1984), 55–66, where his reliance on Sasanian political theory and anecdotes is noted (56, 59).

[2] J. R. Alban and C. T. Allmand, 'Spies and spying in the fourteenth century' in C.T. Allmand (ed.), *War, Literature and Politics in the Late Middle Ages* (Liverpool, 1976), 73–101, at 77–9; John of Plano Carpini, *History of the Mongols* in C. Dawson (ed.), *The Mongol Mission* (London and New York, 1955), 3, 66, 68.

[3] For the date and authorship see J. B. Bury, 'The ceremonial book of Constantine Porphyrogenitus', *EHR* 22 (1907), 207–27, at 212–13.

capital, and being assigned a guard during their stay in Ctesiphon (fr. 23,9/34ff., 107),[4] and oriental sources confirm these practices.[5]

These constraints will have had some impact on the ability of embassies to gather information, but unless their hosts were to blindfold them for the duration – which would have been both impractical and contrary to the generally accepted principle of treating envoys with honour – members of a mission will have been able to pick up intelligence of value simply through alert observation. The opportunities afforded for acquiring information under the heading of background knowledge are indicated by Libanius (*Ep.* 331.1), writing about the experiences of his relative Spectatus who participated on an embassy to Ctesiphon in 358:

> Spectatus has returned to us from his embassy, regarded by many as fortunate – by some, because he saw so much land and mountains and rivers, by others, because he witnessed the way of life of the Persians, the customs and laws by which they live; others considered it a great thing to have seen the king himself and the jewels with which he was adorned.

That ambassadors to other, even more exotic, destinations took careful note of the nature of the societies they encountered is apparent from accounts such as that of Priscus' mission to Attila and that of Nonnosus to the Arabs, Himyarites and Axumites. As already noted (pp. 38–9), the substance of negotiations was undoubtedly of interest to the Roman government; it is more difficult to prove that there was also official interest in background details of this sort, but the way in which Justin II closely questioned envoys from the Turks about their geographical location and political and social organisation (Men. fr. 10,1/70–86) suggests that there was.

The government was obviously interested in whatever intelligence of a strategic nature envoys could acquire. The Persian government's extraordinary efforts to prevent Roman envoys in 579 from completing their business quickly while they hurried to finalise preparations for war (Men. fr. 23,9/34–117) seem to have been based on the assumption that the envoys would carry back news of the warlike preparations which must have been evident throughout the country (Menander specifically mentions the collection and stockpiling of food on a large scale, and the assembling of troops). In 359, the ambassador Procopius alerted the general Ursicinus to the movement of Persian troops towards the frontier (Amm. Marc. xviii.6.17–9), while Khusro's knowledge of Roman successes in Africa (Proc. *Wars* 1.26.1–2) very likely derived from the Persian envoy who was present in Constantinople in 534 and witnessed Belisarius'

---

[4] In this latter instance, Menander complains about the way in which their escort slowed them down and their guard severely curtailed their freedom of movement in the capital, but not about the fact of the escort and guard.

[5] Christensen, *Les Sassanides*, 414.

triumph (Zach. *HE* ix.17, vol. 2, p. 133/17–18). Although embassies could take a long time to complete their business, the remarks concerning speed of movement in the previous chapter are also of relevance here.

The fact that there is not more in the way of explicit examples of embassies gaining useful information should not lead one to minimise this particular source; the evidence discussed above about attempts to limit the opportunities available to foreign embassies for doing this shows clearly that it was an activity which was taken for granted. There are, however, grounds for thinking that the Roman government will have acquired more information about Persian affairs by this means than about those of northern peoples – essentially because the scale of diplomatic traffic between the two empires seems to have been greater throughout more periods of late antiquity. Undoubtedly the random survival of sources means that there are some embassies of which knowledge no longer exists, but the extant sources convey the impression that during much of the fourth and sixth centuries, when relations were often characterised by tension and conflict, diplomatic traffic between Constantinople and Ctesiphon was fairly constant, and that it is only during the mid-fifth (Huns) and later sixth centuries (Avars) that diplomatic activity to the north reached a comparable pitch. Yet even in the fifth century, when relations with Persia were more settled, one contemporary still found cause to comment on the unceasing movement of embassies between the two empires (Soc. *HE* vii.8.2), and there are sufficient examples from the fifth century to give this claim substance.[6]

In addition to those sent to deal with particular issues, embassies were also sent between the two empires to make formal announcement of the accession of a new ruler,[7] a courtesy not apparently extended by the Romans to any northern people, no doubt as a result of chauvinism and the difficulty in identifying a single ruler among many of these peoples.[8] Furthermore, the volume of exchanges would have been significantly increased as a result of the

---

[6] Possible commercial agreement in 408/9 (*CJ* iv.63.4); Marutha to Ctesiphon twice *c.* 410 (Soc. *HE* vii.8); Persian embassy demanding return of Christian refugees, *c.* 420 (*ibid.*, vii.18); peace settlements after the wars of 421–2 (*ibid.*, vii.20) and 440–1 (Proc. *Wars* i.2.11–15); Persian embassy with various demands, 464–5 (Priscus fr. 41,1); further Persian embassies not precisely datable (*ibid.*, frs. 47 and 51); Eusebius to Peroz, *c.* 483 (Proc. *Wars* i.3.8); Valash requests subsidies from Zeno, *c.* 484 (J. Styl. 18); Kavad demands subsidies from Zeno, then Anastasius (*ibid.* 20 and 23; cf. 8). If the story of Arcadius' request that Yazdgerd I act as guardian for the young Theodosius II (Proc. *Wars* i.2) is historical, then further embassies will have been exchanged in the first decade of the fifth century.

[7] Helm, 'Untersuchungen', 388 n. 3. All the relevant references (including John Eph. *HE* vi.22, not noted by Helm) are sixth century, but the existence of the practice in the fourth and fifth centuries has been claimed (E. Chrysos, 'Some aspects of Roman–Persian legal relations', *Kleronomia* 8 (1976), 1–60, at 41; Garsoïan, 'Le role de l'hiérarchie chrétienne', 124).

[8] The only possible example of this practice *vis-à-vis* a northern people is when Priscus (fr. 20,1) says that the accession of Marcian was announced to Attila (who was, significantly, an easily identified ruler); but the wording leaves it unclear whether this was a case of formal notification by a Roman embassy or simply news reaching him through unofficial channels.

practice adopted by the two empires of sending a 'minor' embassy to offer thanks for the good treatment of the members of a 'major' mission and to follow up any additional matters arising (Men. fr. 18,6/1–8; 20,1/1–3; *De Caer.* i.89). Although literary references to it are restricted to the sixth century, Menander remarks that this was a long-standing custom, and its use in the fourth century has indeed been confirmed by the inscription on the seal-ring of an ambassador of Shapur III.[9] Again, however, there is no evidence that this practice was employed by the Romans in their dealings with any northern people.

These differing levels of diplomatic traffic are to a great extent a reflection of the varying degrees to which the empire's neighbours had progressed toward centralisation of power. Persia was a centralising empire whose underlying stability permitted the development of regular diplomatic practices with the Roman empire and whose cultural heritage gave an important place to ceremonial; these features in turn encouraged the development of mutual respect between the two empires, of which diplomatic protocol such as 'major' and 'minor' embassies and notification of new accessions was one expression. None of the empire's northern neighbours during late antiquity approached the sophistication of Persia. They were all essentially still 'proto-states', lacking in stability and continuity, and unable to expect recognition as equals from the Roman government.

SPIES

'It has long been the practice of both the Romans and the Persians to support spies (κατάσκοποι) at public expense. These men are accustomed to go secretly among the enemy in order to examine their affairs accurately, reporting to their rulers (ἄρχοντες) on their return' (Proc. *Wars* i.21.11). This, the most explicit statement concerning the use of spies by the Romans in late antiquity, raises many questions. How long does Procopius mean by 'long' (ἐκ παλαιοῦ)? From where were these spies recruited and how were they organised? Were they formally a part of the army, or quite independent? How did they go about examining enemy affairs? These are the sorts of questions one would like to be able to answer in a comprehensive manner, but perhaps not surprisingly, given the inherently secretive nature of their work, the evidence is not without its problems.

Terminology has the potential to assist with the question of organisation, but it soons proves to be an avenue of enquiry beset with frustrations. One might reasonably expect there to have been a fairly clear terminological distinction

---

[9] K. Stock, 'Yazdan-Friy-Shapur, ein Grossgesandter Shapurs III', *StIr* 7 (1975), 165–82.

between spies, dealing with strategic information and wider issues, and scouts, more narrowly concerned with short-term tactical intelligence, even if the precise line of demarcation between strategy and tactics is not always easily drawn. Authoritative works of reference (which, however, concentrate on evidence from the centuries before late antiquity) do indeed appear to accept a broad distinction between *exploratores*, responsible for scouting and usually operating as units, and *speculatores*, penetrating deeper into enemy territory and hence working covertly and alone.[10] When one turns to the late Roman sources themselves, however, problems quickly become apparent.

The history of Ammianus Marcellinus includes many references to intelligence-gathering activities, some of which are consistent with the foregoing distinction. In describing the behaviour of the would-be usurper Procopius who was trying to assess public feeling towards Valens while remaining incognito in Constantinople during 365, Ammianus likens him to 'a very clever *speculator* who goes unnoticed on account of his unkempt and gaunt appearance' as he gathers gossip (xxvi.6.6). In this context, *speculator* clearly bears the sense of spy, while elsewhere *exploratores* engage in what are self-evidently scouting activities (e.g. xxxi.16.2). Yet Ammianus is by no means consistent in his usage. In other contexts, those functioning in scouting roles are termed *excursatores* (xxiv.1.2), *procursatores* (xxv.8.4) and *proculcatores* (xxvii.10.10); and if one takes *speculationes* to be the reports of *speculatores,* then sometimes he has the latter also undertaking work of a tactical, scouting nature (e.g. xiv.2.15, xxvii.2.2).[11]

This variety of terminology can readily be explained in terms of the literary canons according to which Ammianus was writing: 'war and warfare . . . are to be described in the literary manner appropriate for the broader cultivated audience; that is to say, without undue use of technical language'.[12] It can also be explained in terms of an interest in function, rather than organisation.[13] But even when one turns to the *Strategikon* of the late sixth century attributed to Maurice, a practical military handbook with no pretensions to literary refine-

[10] *DS*, s.v. *explorator* (R. Cagnat, 1892); *RE* VI, 1690 (Fiebiger, 1909); 2nd series III, 1583 (F. Lammert, 1929). Fiebiger, however, incorrectly equates *exploratores* with the κατάσκοποι of Proc. *Wars* i.21, who manifestly were spies rather than scouts. For a more recent discussion of *exploratores*, see Speidel, 'Exploratores'.

[11] The problem is further complicated by the fact that during the first three centuries AD, *speculator* was also the rank of an officer in the service of governors who dealt with the custody of prisoners and their execution if they were condemned, and the term persisted into the late Roman period as an administrative grade (A. H. M. Jones, 'The Roman civil service (clerical and sub-clerical grades)', *JRS* 39 (1949), 38–55, at 44, 48).

[12] Matthews, *Ammianus*, 280. Cf. A. Müller, 'Militaria aus Ammianus Marcellinus', *Philologus* 18 (1905), 573–632 (without, however, any specific comment on *speculator/explorator*), and E. von Nischer in J. Kromayer and G. Veith, *Heerwesen und Kriegführung der Griechen und Römer* (Munich, 1928), 470–1.

[13] Austin, *Ammianus on Warfare*, 118–19, 122.

ment, one still finds an annoying inconsistency in usage. Three terms feature in the context of information-gathering: *kataskopos* (κατάσκοπος), *explorator* (ἐξπλοράτωρ), and *skoulkator* (σκουλκάτωρ).[14] At one point, *exploratores* are defined as those who 'fearlessly spend time among the enemy, so that they are regarded as being of the same race' (ix.5/53–5) – activity appropriate to spies rather than scouts – while *kataskopoi* and *skoulkatores* appear to have distinct responsibilities under the general heading of scouting (ix.5/61ff.). Obviously one must expect changes in linguistic usage over the centuries, but elsewhere in the same work, one finds *kataskopos* and *skoulkator* apparently used as equally acceptable alternatives (i.3/36, ii.11/4, viiB.17/20), as also *kataskopos* and *explorator* (viiA.3/4).

The lack of a consistent terminology obviously does not prevent one from drawing together the evidence where individuals can be seen functioning as spies, but it does mean that terminology is of little help in trying to discern how they were organised. Another problem concerning the degree of organisation arises from what is known about particular individuals used as spies. In those instances where specific individuals can be seen undertaking activities appropriate to a spy, the individual in question has invariably been chosen specially for that particular task, and would normally have been engaged in other work of an unrelated nature. Libanius mentions that a friend Clematius, an *agens in rebus* (i.e., one of the officials responsible for supervision of the government postal system), entered enemy territory in 355 to observe Persian affairs (τὰ Περσῶν) and then reported back to the praetorian prefect Musonianus in Antioch (*Ep.* 430.7).[15] In 358, Julian selected one of his tribunes, Hariobaudes, to undertake an espionage mission in Alamannic territory (Amm. Marc. xviii.2.2). In early 359, Ammianus himself, a staff officer (*protector domesticus*), was sent into Persian territory to observe Persian troop movements (xviii.6.20–2). In 530, when the generals Sittas and Dorotheus in Armenia heard that a Persian army was preparing for an invasion from Persarmenia, they chose two body-guards (*doruphoroi* – δορυφόροι) to infiltrate the Persian camp and investigate further (Proc. *Wars* i.15.4–5). In 533, Procopius himself, usually employed as Belisarius' secretary, was sent to Syracuse, in advance of the Roman invasion of Vandal Africa, to gather information concerning the whereabouts of the Vandal fleet and other relevant factors (*Wars* iii.14.1–5).

What is to be made of these instances? It might be claimed that it was quite

---

[14] For the Germanic (Gothic) origin of this last word (cf. English 'skulk'), see E. Gamillscheg, *Romania Germanica* (Berlin and Leipzig, 1934), vol. 1, 392.

[15] Seeck took τὰ Περσῶν to refer to 'the movements of the Persians' (*Die Briefe des Libanius* (Leipzig, 1906), 111), *PLRE* to 'the Persian defences' (vol. 1, s.v. Clematius 2); so too Clauss, *Der magister*, 200. Seeck seems preferable, since Libanius goes on to suggest that the information helped forestall a Persian attack of some sort. Clematius may well have been one of those responsible for the news of Shapur's commitments on the far side of the Persian empire (Amm. Marc. xvi.9.3).

consistent for an *agens in rebus* to undertake a spying mission, but I accept the arguments of Jones and others that the *agentes* were not in fact a secret state police;[16] Hariobaudes was chosen for his mission because he spoke and understood Alamannic; otherwise these cases suggest an *ad hoc* approach. Yet Procopius' statement about *kataskopoi*, with which this section began, clearly implies that an organised approach to information-gathering had been in place for some time, which is certainly consistent with the empire's movement towards a more systematic approach to foreign relations generally during late antiquity (see pp. 33–48).

There are in fact a number of possible ways of resolving the apparent discrepancy between the individual cases noted above and Procopius' general statement. The first of these begins from the fact that Clematius, Ammianus and Procopius were close and trusted adherents of the person who sent them. This is also likely to have been the case with the two bodyguards in 530, since *doruphoroi* were a subdivision of the category of troops known as *bucellarii*, the personal retainers of a commander,[17] and Hariobaudes is described as being a man of 'known loyalty' (*fidei notae*). Procopius specifically comments on the dangers of disloyalty on the part of some *kataskopoi* (*Wars* i.21.12), so it is possible that the stakes at risk in these particular cases were considered so high that proven loyalty was felt to be a more important criterion than experience, or that secrecy would be better preserved by using individuals outside any normal operational structures. A second possible explanation begins from the fact that in almost every known case of spying activity in the late Roman period – the exception is Clematius acting at the behest of the praetorian prefect Musonianus – reports are made to generals, or to emperors acting in a military capacity. Yet the statement of Procopius with which this section began has spies reporting to the *archontes* (ἄρχοντες), 'rulers' or perhaps 'officials' (rather than to the *strategoi* (στρατηγοί), his usual word for 'generals'),[18] and he was writing in the mid-sixth century when emperors had not participated personally on campaigns for one and a half centuries and when there was a clear distinction between civilian officials and the military. Perhaps the *kataskopoi* to whom Procopius refers here were engaged in activities altogether separate from the

---

[16] Jones, *Later Roman Empire*, 578–82; W. Liebeschuetz, Review of W. Blum, *Curiosi und Regendarii*, *JRS* 60 (1970), 229–30; J. F. Drinkwater 'The "pagan underground", Constantine II's "secret service" and the survival and usurpation of Julian the Apostate' in C. Deroux (ed.), *Studies in Latin Literature and Roman History* vol. 3 (Brussels, 1983), 348–87, at 360–7. This is not to deny that they had some oversight of politically sensitive areas: A. Giardina, *Aspetti della burocrazia nel basso impero* (Rome, 1977), 64–72.

[17] O. Seeck, *RE* III, 934–9; Bury, *History* vol. 2, 77–8.

[18] In *Wars* v.5.3–4, Procopius does use ἄρχοντες of a lesser grade of general subordinate to an overall commander (στρατηγὸς αὐτοκράτωρ), but this cannot be the sense of the word in *Wars* i.21.11.

cases referred to earlier, activities which are hardly reflected in the surviving sources at all.[19]

In the light of all this, there is little scope for investigating organisational evolution and changes over the course of four centuries.[20] A certain amount can, however, be said about how intelligence was gathered by those engaged in spying. Ammianus' description of the demeanour of the would-be usurper Procopius, and the historian Procopius' remark about *kataskopoi* going among the enemy secretly, indicate that disguise of some sort was a prerequisite. Likewise, in the context of Heraclius' measures to preserve the secrecy of his plans for his Persian campaign in 622, George of Pisidia remarks that '*kataskopoi* conceal themselves in the crowd as if in a cloud, and remain difficult to discover' (*Heraclias* ii.116–17).[21] Once in enemy territory, much could be learned by careful observation, which is, after all, the idea lying at the etymological roots of *speculator* and *kataskopos*. The size, composition and strength of an army could be gauged, and the route it was taking assessed, while preliminary warning signs such as campaign preparations would also be observable. Indeed, Roman *kataskopoi* are specifically described as operating in this manner during Persian preparations for an invasion in the 340s: '[our] spies witnessed this business [viz., Persian preparations] with their own eyes, not guessing the news at a distance, but reporting it on the basis of direct observation' (Lib. *Or.* lix.101).

However, by emphasising direct observation in this case, Libanius implicitly acknowledged that intelligence reports were not always based on scrutiny at first hand. Spies undoubtedly also used second-hand aural information, as suggested again by Ammianus' likening of Procopius to a *speculator* gathering gossip (cf. Amm. Marc. xiv.1.6). That this should be so is perfectly understandable, for it greatly extended the range of territory that a spy could cover, while of course also introducing risks. Reliance on aural information – and the attendant risks – is well illustrated by Khusro's invasion of Lazica in 541. Khusro made a point of making it known that his preparations were for a campaign against the Huns in neighbouring Iberia, which is exactly what Belisarius' spies reported back to him (Proc. *Wars* ii.15.35–16.4). They can only have derived their information about the purpose of Persian preparations from what they *heard* and not from actually following the Persian army on its route northwards.

---

[19] This is an appropriate point at which to note that the available sources do not allow us to plot the administrative route taken by an intelligence report from the acquisition of the information by a spy to its receipt by the emperor (if it warranted being passed on that far). It is unclear, e.g., which official(s) in the imperial palace took delivery of incoming reports (the *magister officiorum*?).

[20] The only 'development' that is mentioned in the sources is Procopius' claim that Justinian disbanded the κατάσκοποι (*SH* 30.11–12). For the likelihood that he in fact only (temporarily?) reduced their numbers, see Lee, 'Procopius'.

[21] For a case of Persian spies in Roman dress, see Th. Sim. iii.7.4; for use of disguise in earlier Roman periods, see Riepl, *Das Nachrichtenwesen*, 469, and for the middle Byzantine period, see Shepard, 'Information', 278.

This brings us back to the concerns of Chapter 5, and allows us to extend that enquiry by considering more carefully where one might expect to hear such information. An obvious location for spies to frequent was military camps and garrisons. This was where the two bodyguards were sent in 530 (Proc. *Wars* i.15.5), and the *Strategikon* of Maurice advises a range of measures for uncovering the presence of enemy spies in army camps (ix.5/99ff.).

Another likely location was market-places. The anonymous military treatise known as the *Peri Strategias* explicitly recommends that spies enter enemy territory under the guise of trading, proceed to a market-place where many Romans and foreigners mix, and begin trading there. In this way, they may avoid detection and 'discover what the enemy is planning and how their affairs stand' (42/24–8). Since, however, the traditional assigning of this work to the sixth century is now much less certain,[22] the direct relevance of its evidence for our period must be placed in question. Nevertheless, a number of considerations point to this as being one way in which late Roman spies worked. In the first place, there are some more oblique indications in the late Roman sources. In a passage from the *Secret History* (30.12) which parallels that from the *Wars* quoted at the beginning of this section, Procopius adds the additional detail that spies made their way into the Persian palace itself under the pretext of trading, and one of the agreements between the two empires which restricted trade to specified locations on the frontier gave as its rationale the desire to prevent trade being used as a pretext for spying (*CJ* iv.63.4); the fact that this was acknowledged in an official agreement makes it all the more significant.

Moreover, merchants in general, especially those engaged in longer-distance trade, have always needed as much information as possible about current travel conditions and the wider political and economic situation of their suppliers and markets, and so have a natural interest in acquiring information similar to that which is also of interest to governments. The obvious place in which such information as merchants possessed was likely to be made known was the market-place, which has always played a crucial role in the circulation of information within pre-industrial societies:

> Markets have several important functions other than the obvious one of transferring goods from producers to final consumers . . . Possibly the most important . . . of these non-economic functions is communication. The assemblage of such relatively large groupings of population make the market-place one of the most important nodes in the communication network of a peasant society. The dissemination of information may be either formal or informal; official announcements may be made and notices posted, or gossip and news may merely pass from

---

[22] B. Baldwin, 'On the date of the anonymous *Peri strategikes*', *BZ* 81 (1988)[1990], 290–3; Lee and Shepard, 'Placing the *Peri presbeon*', 25–30.

mouth to mouth. The presence of buyers and sellers from other towns ensures that the news will be taken there. Professional traders travelling constantly from market to market in a circuit of market towns bring the latest information to each of the market-places.[23]

It is this informal dissemination which is of relevance here, and may be illustrated by another incident recounted by Procopius.

After Belisarius had reconquered Africa from the Vandals and had returned in triumph to Constantinople in 534, the soldiers left behind to garrison the regained province became dissatisfied with their conditions and planned a mutiny. It was their intention to murder the commander during a church service. When it came to carrying out their plan, however, they were over-awed by their surroundings and departed from the church with the deed unaccomplished. They resolved to make good their failure of nerve the next day when another service would be in progress (it was Easter). But again their consciences were aroused once they were inside the church and they departed sheepishly a second time: 'Entering the market-place, they abused one another openly and each called the other a coward and destroyer of the band . . . For this reason they thought they could no longer remain in Carthage without danger, since they had broadcast their plot to the whole city' (*Wars* iv.14.27–8). The clear implication is that it was because they had discussed the matter in the market-place that they had good reason to fear that news of their treason would become widely known. Procopius also mentions how the empress Theodora kept track of her enemies through a network of informers, and one of the places where these informers were said to spend much time was the market-place (*SH* 16.14).

In a world which lacked more sophisticated modes of communication, therefore, the market-place played an important role in the dissemination of news. As such, it was entirely reasonable that the market-place should have been a focus for intelligence-gathering activities in antiquity.

The other location specified as a focus for information-gathering in Persia was the royal palace itself in Ctesiphon (Proc. *SH* 30.12). In what ways could the royal palace have been a source of information? An important market certainly existed at Ctesiphon during the Parthian period (Strabo 743, xvi.1.16), which

---

[23] W. G. Lockwood, 'The market-place as a social mechanism in peasant society', *Kroeber Anthropological Society Papers* 32 (1965), 47–67, at 52–3. Cf. G. Sjoberg, *The Preindustrial City* (Glencoe, Ill., 1960), 289 ('the market-place . . . is a center for the dissemination of much news. Travelling merchants are frequently sought after, for they bear tidings from other cities and from distant lands'); P. Bohannan and G. Dalton (eds.), *Markets in Africa* (Northwestern University, 1962), 15–16 ('undoubtedly one of the most important points for the dissemination of information is the market-place'); and much other anthropological literature. For antiquity, cf. Riepl, *Das Nachrichtenwesen*, 324ff.

Talmudic sources indicate continued under the Sasanians.[24] Given the central location and importance of Ctesiphon in the Persian empire, such a market would have been a source of unusually valuable information. But Procopius makes specific reference to the royal palace, to which access was gained 'under the pretext of trading *or* by some other ploy'. This suggests that information of importance circulated in the palace itself.

Two possible sources of such information may be suggested. First, there were members of the Persian nobility with whom the king is known on occasion to have consulted in reaching decisions, including those affecting foreign policy (e.g., Amm. Marc. xxviii.5.6; Proc. *Wars* ii.3.54). The care which Khusro is reported to have taken in 541 in not telling many people about his real intentions in leading forces north to the Caucasus suggests that members of the Persian nobility may sometimes have been a liability in this respect (cf. Amm. Marc. xxi.13.4). Secondly, there were the scribes who made notes of the king's decisions and who dispatched royal orders to the provincial governors. The Arab historian Baladhuri noted that 'the orders and decisions of the King of Kings were recorded in his presence by the royal secretary and another official entered them into his diary, which was checked every month, sealed with the royal seal and kept in the archives'.[25] Such information as these individuals possessed could have gained circulation simply through loose talk, or could have been procured by bribery. In a somewhat different context, Agathias mentions those in the camp of the Persian general Mermeroes who 'received money from the enemy to betray their own people, and clandestinely communicated secrets' (ii.19.8).

In view of the fact that Persia sometimes gained information about Roman plans and made use of spies,[26] it is worth pausing to consider the reciprocal situation *vis-à-vis* the late Roman administration. In particular, the role of imperial secretaries (*notarii*) is of interest. It has been argued that their rapid rise to positions of power in court politics was a result of their access to highly

---

[24] Christensen, *Les Sassanides*, 387–8; Neusner, *Jews in Babylonia* vol. 4, 388.

[25] *CHI* vol. 3, 712 (V. G. Lukonin). This is a statement with reference to the sixth century, but the position of chief scribe is attested at the Sasanian court from the reign of the first Sasanian king Ardashir in the *Res Gestae Divi Saporis* s. 24 ('Mard, head of scribes').

[26] Procopius' statement about Persian use of spies (*Wars* i.21.11) is corroborated by oriental sources: the existence of a Sasanian military text entitled 'Commissioning spies' is attested in a later Arabic source (*The Fihrist of al-Nadīm* viii.3, tr. B. Dodge (New York and London, 1970), vol. 2, 737–8); the Arabic chronicle of Tabari, which is recognised as a source of great value for the Sasanian period, makes reference to the use of spies by the Persian king against foreign peoples (*Geschichte der Perser und Araber zur Zeit der Sasaniden aus der arabischen Chronik des Tabari*, tr. T. Nöldeke (Leiden, 1879), 60–1, 101, 277); and they are mentioned in Armenian (e.g. Faustus of Buzand iv.24) and Syriac sources (e.g. Zach. *HE* vii.5, vol. 2 p. 32/18: *gashusha*). There are also various references to the use of Arabs as spies: see the refs. in Kawar (Shahid), 'The peace treaty', 196–7, who observes that 'Arabs lived on both sides of the Persian–Roman frontier, and so the appearance of Arabs on this or that side of the frontier would not have aroused suspicions'.

confidential matters,[27] and one incident from the late sixth century certainly shows that they were regarded as a liability with respect to the integrity of imperial secrets. During particularly sensitive negotiations with the Persians in the mid-570s, the emperor Tiberius authorised the Roman ambassador Zacharias to offer special concessions, but he had the letter of authorisation written out by his general Maurice instead of one of the imperial notaries, so that there was absolutely no possibility of its contents leaking out (Men. fr. 20,2/118–25).

Nor was the palace in Constantinople the only location in the Roman empire where information concerning forthcoming Roman plans could be acquired. The Roman deserter Antoninus was able, prior to his flight to Persia, to delve into military registers (ratiocinia) where he learned not only the strength and locations of troops throughout the east, but also when particular units would be moving elsewhere (Amm. Marc. xviii.5.1).[28] If Antoninus, who did not hold particularly high rank in the office of the dux Mesopotamiae, was able to gain access to documents of this nature, then knowledge of future Roman military plans cannot have been restricted solely to the highest officers in the army.

This discussion of palaces, records and administrative staff serves to highlight another significant contrast between east and north. Markets at which Romans and northern peoples mingled certainly existed, but northern peoples essentially lacked administrative centres and apparatus which might otherwise have been a focus for intelligence-gathering in the way that Ctesiphon seems to have been in relation to Persia. The less complex levels of military organisation among northern peoples also made the task of acquiring information more difficult. Indeed, the general absence of urbanisation in the lands beyond the empire's northern boundaries means that information would have circulated less widely and with less intensity in those regions than was the case in Persia, making the job of would-be spies very much more difficult.

In the light of this, it comes as less of a surprise to discover that there are in fact few references to the use of spies by the Romans in the north. Only two specific instances are known to me from the northern frontier on the Continent during late antiquity. The first is that of Hariobaudes, sent by Julian in 358 to learn what was being planned by certain groups of Alamanni (Amm. Marc. xviii.2.2). The second instance occurs in Priscus' history. On their return journey from Attila's camp in 449, the Roman party saw a Hun who had been impaled on Attila's orders because he had 'crossed from Roman to barbarian

---

[27] K. Hopkins, Conquerors and Slaves (Cambridge, 1978), 189.
[28] The existence of written reports on the strength of units, at least, is confirmed by one of the third-century papyri from Dura-Europus: Fink, Roman Military Records, 234–9 (P. Dura 95).

territory in order to spy (κατασκοπῆς ἕνεκα)' (fr. 14/58–61).[29] No doubt this paucity of examples is partly due to the scantier spread of surviving sources dealing with the north, but I would suggest that this is also a reflection of their being employed less in barbaricum where conditions reduced their ability to function effectively. This view finds further support from the fact that Procopius' remarks about Roman spies (*Wars* i.21; *SH* 30) are made in the context of Persian affairs.

Late Roman Britain does provide one additional example of spying activities which deserves mention here. Ammianus refers to a body of men in Britain known as *arcani*,[30] whose task was to move about among neighbouring peoples (one presumes secretly, from their name) and gather information of impending threats; by 367, however, they had succumbed to bribery and were now passing information about the Romans to the enemy, with the result that they were disbanded (xxviii.3.8). Because he had already discussed them in an earlier book, now lost, Ammianus treats the *arcani* briefly here, and so raises more questions than he answers on this point. Nevertheless, he says nothing to suggest that similar bodies of men were used along the northern frontier on the Continent, while the fact that the *arcani* in Britain appear to have operated with some success until corrupted does not constitute a strong argument against the conclusion reached in the previous paragraph. The crucial point is that of size: the region immediately north of Hadrian's Wall was a fraction of the size of the regions immediately beyond the northern boundaries of the Continental empire, making the task of surveillance in northern Britain much more feasible.

The limited effectiveness of Roman spies in Continental barbaricum might also account for Roman attempts to establish and maintain outposts beyond the northern frontier during the late empire. The *Notitia* describes two units as being *in barbarico* beyond Aquincum and Bononia on the Danube (*Occ.* xxxii.41; xxxiii.48) – possibly the result of Diocletian's activities in 294.[31] Interestingly, one is a unit of 'lookouts' (*vigiles*). However, although it has been argued that these forces must have been deep in Sarmatian territory, the more natural and

---

[29] There is also a reference from the late sixth century to men being sent ahead of a Roman army operating north of the lower Danube to spy out (ἐπὶ κατασκοπῇ) enemy movements (Th. Sim. vii.4.8–9), but the fact that they were operating in a group of twenty and at night suggests that they should be classified as scouts rather than spies (cf. Veg. iii.6, p. 76/7–77/1, on *exploratores* working at night).

[30] Most British scholars appear to have rejected this emended reading of *areani*, as it appears in the MSS. However, W. Seyfarth has pointed out (Review of N. J. E. Austin, *Ammianus on Warfare*, *Gnomon* 53 (1981), 452) that the word *areanis* also appears at xxiii.6.32 in one MS where there can be no doubting the need to emend it to *arcanis*, so lending support to his adoption of the same emendation at xxviii.3.8 in the latest Teubner edition. Cf. A. Demandt, 'Die Feldzüge des älteren Theodosius', *Hermes* 100 (1972), 81–113, at 89–90 (their name corresponds to their function).

[31] Mócsy, *Pannonia*, 269.

persuasive reading is that these were bridgehead dispositions on the left bank of
the river.[32] Even if these forts were not deep in barbaricum, however, the unit
of *vigiles* could have used theirs as a base from which to carry out scouting duties
in force deeper into enemy territory.[33]

Less ambiguous are Ammianus' reports about the attempts by both Julian
and Valentinian I to establish forts in barbaricum. Julian successfully restored a
Trajanic fort (*munimentum*) beyond the Rhine in 357 (xvii.1.11–13), while
Valentinian tried to construct new forts (a *munimentum* and a *praesidaria castra*) in
the territory of both the Alamanni and the Quadi (xxviii.2.5–9; xxix.6.2–3),
though both attempts ended in disaster.[34] The locations of these structures are
unclear; only in the case of Valentinian's Alamannic fort does Ammianus
mention its location (*mons Pirus*), but it is not certain to what this refers.[35] The
implication in all three instances, however, is that they were not just on the far
bank of the river but deeper into barbaricum. As for their intended purpose, this
too is not specified. But Ammianus does says that the decision to build the
structure on Quadian territory arose from Valentinian's desire to protect the
frontiers, and the idea that they were to serve as early warning posts would be
consistent with this.[36]

A considerable number of Roman sites in barbaricum, constructed or
occupied during the late empire, have also been identified archaeologically.
Some of these lie on the far bank of the relevant river where they clearly
functioned as fortified landing places and bridgeheads.[37] However, at least one
such site, at Sponeck on a spur of the Kaiserstuhl with excellent vistas up and
down the middle Rhine, was clearly designed to serve as an observation post.[38]
Other sites have been found at varying distances from the river. Most lack
military fortifications adequate for the protection of Roman troops deep in
hostile territory. Proposed explanations for such sites include the suggestions
that they were trading stations, or structures built by the Romans on behalf of

---

[32] Brennan, 'Danubian bridgehead dispositions', 561–2; Johnson, *Late Roman Fortifications*,
192.

[33] Cf. also the units of *exploratores* posted on the Danube (*ND Or.* xli.34, 35, 37; xlii.29). In his
edition of the *Notitia*, Seeck classifies these units and the *vigiles* as infantry, which would rather
limit their mobility and hence capacity to patrol widely. However, *miles* (which the *Notitia* uses
in the titles of the units of *exploratores*) can be applied to a mounted soldier (Speidel,
'Exploratores', 73 n. 45).

[34] The fort in Alammanic territory may be the same as that referred to by Symmachus, *Or.*
ii.14,18–20; cf. J. F. Matthews, *Western Aristocracies and Imperial Court AD 364–425* (Oxford, 1975),
33 n. 1.

[35] Cf. Schönberger, 'The Roman frontier', 185.

[36] Cf. Dio. lxxi.20.2; Tomlin, 'Valentinian', 163.

[37] E.g., on the Rhine, Deutz, Rheinsrohl, Engers, Niederlahnstein, Zullestein, Mannheim-
Neckerau, Whylen; on the Danube, Celemantia (Iza-Leanyvar), (Nograd)veroce, Zader-Imsos,
Contra Florentiam (Dunafalva): details in Petrikovits, 'Fortifications'; Mócsy, *Pannonia*, 269–71;
Johnson, *Late Roman Fortifications*, especially Appendix 2.

[38] R. M. Swoboda, *Die spätrömische Befestigung Sponeck am Kaiserstuhl* (Munich, 1986), 117.

client kings.[39] One site, however, at Fels am Wagram, 5 kilometres north of the Danube to the west of Vindobona, has revealed the remains of a fourth-century Roman fortification[40] and might have been practicable as a manned post.

As has been observed by a number of scholars, other Roman sites deeper in barbaricum can only have had Roman troops stationed at them with the consent of the people on whose territory the structure stood; indeed this would seem to have been the eventual arrangement Julian reached with the Alamanni over his reconstructed Trajanic fort. Given that the empire did sometimes establish client-type relations with northern peoples, some of the other structures might still have functioned in an information-gathering capacity within such a framework.[41] This might, for example, account for the Roman site at Hatvan, 60 kilometres east of Aquincum on the Danube bend. Constantius II certainly established some Sarmatian tribes in a client relationship with the empire in 358 (Amm. Marc. xvii.12.20). It has been argued on the basis of archaeological evidence that Constantine pursued a similar policy earlier in the century. The archaeological evidence in question is that known as the 'Devil's Dyke' or the limes Sarmatiae, a system of linear earthworks encompassing a bank and a ditch which delimits a large area beyond the middle Danube comprising the Hungarian plain. These earthworks run east from a point just north of Aquincum, cross the Tisza River before turning south and rejoining the Danube at Viminacium.[42] Although there remains room for doubt about their attribution to the reign of Constantine, the main uncertainty concerns their purpose. They are not of sufficient height to act as a barrier to invaders, yet many features point strongly to Roman inspiration – their linear nature, the way in which they link in with the Roman defences on the Danube at either end, and the positioning of the ditch beyond the bank which indicates that they were designed to face away from the empire. It has been argued that they are a physical expression of Sarmatia's client relationship with the empire under Constantine, who undoubtedly pursued a policy of forward defence on the Danube.

If this reconstruction is valid, then the Roman site at Hatvan, which lies on the northern side of the limes Sarmatiae, could be seen as a Roman outpost established with Sarmatian consent, and designed to alert them and the empire

---

39 M. Kandler and H. Vetters, Der römische Limes in Österreich (Vienna, 1989), 231–47 (Barbaricum); L. F. Pitts, 'Roman-style buildings in barbaricum (Moravia and SW Slovakia)', OJA 6 (1987), 219–36.

40 Kandler and Vetters, Der römische Limes, 231–2.

41 Cf. D. C. Braund, Rome and the Friendly King (London, 1985), Part II, Section 3 ('The king on the frontier').

42 E. Garam, P. Patay and S. Soproni, Sarmatisches Wallsystem im Karpatenbeck (Budapest, 1983); Soproni, Der spätrömische Limes, 113–27 with Tables 91–2; idem, Die letzten Jahrzehnte, Chapter 2. Note, however, the reservations of Dittrich, Die Beziehungen Roms zu den Sarmaten, 79–84.

to impending trouble from deeper in barbaricum. Constantius' arrangements in Sarmatia in 358 are of interest in this context. He had forced the most trouble-some Sarmatian tribe, the Limigantes, to move to a location well away from the empire (Amm. Marc. xvii.13). When they began to move back towards the Danube in the following year, the emperor received advance warning of their movements and was able to take preventive action (xix.11). Perhaps an outpost such as Hatvan played a role in alerting the empire.

The experiences of Valentinian, however, show that as the fourth century progressed, northern peoples were becoming less willing to countenance such encroachments on their territory. No attempts to establish outposts in barbaricum are known after the fourth century. This in turn must have further reduced the empire's ability to gather information about them or their more distant neighbours with any consistency.

As for the information which northern peoples received about Roman troop movements, it is highly unlikely that any of them used spies in an organised sense, which is not to say that they may not sometimes have sent individuals on specific missions.[43] However, it seems more probable that such information reached them through the circulation of news via informal channels, such as occurred when the *scutarius* inadvertently gave away Gratian's plans to the Alamanni in 378. That particular case is not to be generalised into a paradigm, but the transfer of large numbers of Roman soldiers away from one sector of the frontier must have created considerable local upheaval, such that news that something was afoot would become more widely known. We are unable to gauge whether northern peoples received information about Roman troop movements more regularly than the Romans received news about the move-ments of northern peoples, but if this were the case it would be consistent with the greater organisational sophistication of the Roman army which, paradoxi-cally, made it more difficult to conceal moves on a large scale.

CONCLUSION

The aims of this third part of the study have been to investigate the means by which information was acquired and in so doing, to account for the variation in its availability between east and north. To this end, the role of formal infor-mation-gathering agencies has been investigated, as well as the informal diffusion of news by word of mouth. Given the nature of the evidence, it is not possible to gauge which of these two broad categories of information-source was generally the more important; indeed, they were interdependent in notable ways. In the first place, the available evidence suggests that the Roman

---

[43] Cf. Julian's detention of an Alamannic envoy in the mid-350s on suspicion of spying (Lib. *Or.* xviii.52–3).

authorities did not normally act on intelligence acquired through informal channels without first confirming it through the dispatch of spies (Proc. *Wars* i.15.4; cf. Amm. Marc. xviii.4.2). And secondly, it seems that information-gatherers relied to a significant degree on picking up information circulating by word of mouth within enemy territory.

It has become apparent that a variety of circumstances increased the availability of information in the east compared to the north. The more sophisticated degree of organisational complexity in Persia encouraged a higher level of diplomatic interchange with the Roman empire (with all the attendant consequences in terms of opportunities to gather intelligence and increase knowledge of one another), and also made the task of detecting military preparations and the like easier for envoys and spies, while the greater degree of urbanisation meant that information circulated more widely and intensely within Persia. By contrast, the relative absence of these conditions in the north meant that it was inherently more difficult to gather information there, no matter how energetic the efforts. Differing levels of urbanisation, together with the various socio-cultural and economic factors making for more intense interaction across the empire's eastern frontier, also meant that information was more likely to traverse the eastern frontier than the northern through informal channels. All these considerations provide a persuasive explanation for the difference between east and north which emerged from Part II, serving as further confirmation of that conclusion.[44]

It is not the contention of this study that information provides *the* key to understanding late Roman foreign relations. It is, however, an important dimension which has hitherto largely been neglected. This is unfortunate because the theme of information offers a valuable and novel perspective on the interrelationship between late Roman military-diplomatic affairs on the one hand, and socio-cultural patterns (in the context of frontier regions) and levels of organisational development (both within and beyond the empire) on the other. As such, it is a topic of investigation which, importantly and very appropriately, encourages the crossing of boundaries between subject areas which have not always been seen as possessing mutual relevance. Of course, the limitations of the surviving evidence dictate that many pertinent questions cannot be answered satisfactorily, but those that are able to be explored in some detail have significant implications, in particular for understanding the greater

---

[44] These considerations may also provide a further explanation as to why the Persians and Romans made increasing use of Arab allies against one another: the conditions making for ease of information-gathering and information circulation along the Fertile Crescent were largely absent from the Syrian desert, which, together with the celebrated speed of Arab raiders, made it much harder for either empire to anticipate attacks from that quarter; hence also the necessity of counteracting the enemy's Arab forces with Arab allies of one's own, who presumably were more attuned to meeting such attacks.

stability which tended to characterise Roman relations with Persia compared with the situation along the northern frontier. In the concluding chapter to his monumental study of the late Roman empire, A. H. M. Jones discussed various factors which contributed to the ability of the eastern half of the empire to weather the crises of late antiquity to which the western half succumbed, among which he noted the more stable nature of relations with Persia. Jones accounted for this in terms of the preoccupation of Persian kings with troubles of their own and the fact that (in implicit contrast to northern peoples) 'when peace was arranged, there was genuine peace: Persia was a civilised power which normally kept its bond and could control its subjects'.[45] The present study has suggested that the availability (or otherwise) of information is a further factor of importance which deserves to be taken into consideration in accounting for the difference between the eastern and northern frontiers, and hence for the divergent fates of the two halves of the empire during late antiquity.

[45] *Later Roman Empire*, 1031.

SELECT BIBLIOGRAPHY

PRIMARY SOURCES

(In general, the following list does not include details of classical authors readily available in one of the standard series of texts.)

Agathias, *History*, ed. R. Keydell (Berlin, 1967)

Ammianus Marcellinus, *History*, ed. W. Seyfarth (Leipzig, 1978)

Aurelius Victor, *Liber de Caesaribus*, ed. F. Pichlmayr, re-ed. R. Gründel (Leipzig, 1966)

Chronicle of Seert, French tr. A. Scher *et al*. (*PO* iv, v, vii, xiii: Paris, 1908–19)

Chronicon Paschale, ed. L. Dindorf (Bonn, 1832)

Codex Justinianus, in *Corpus Iuris Civilis* vol. 2, ed. P. Krüger (15th edn, Dublin and Zurich, 1970)

Codex Theodosianus, ed. T. Mommsen and P. Meyer (Berlin, 1905)

Constantine Porphyrogenitus, *De Caerimoniis*, J. J. Reiske (Bonn, 1829)

Dexippus, fragments, *FHG* iii.666–87

Elias, *Life of John of Tella*, ed. and Latin tr. E. W. Brooks (CSCO Scr. Syr. 7–8: Paris, 1907), 31–95 (text) and 23–60 (tr.)

Eunapius, fragments, ed. and tr. R.C. Blockley, *Classicising Historians* vol.2

Eusebius, *Life of Constantine*, ed. F. Winkelmann (Berlin, 1975)

Eutropius, *Breviarium*, ed. C. Santini (Leipzig, 1979)

Evagrius, *Ecclesiastical History*, ed. J. Bidez and L. Parmentier (London, 1898)

Expositio Totius Mundi et Gentium, ed. and French tr. J. Rougé (SC 124: Paris, 1966)

Ps.-Faustus of Buzand, *The Epic Histories attributed to P'awstos Buzand*, tr. N. Garsoïan (Cambridge, Mass., 1989)

Festus, *Breviarium*, ed. J. W. Eadie (London, 1967)

Fragmenta Historicorum Graecorum, ed. C. Müller (Paris, 1841–70)

Geographi Graeci Minores, ed. C. Müller (Paris, 1855–61)

Geographi Latini Minores, ed. A. Riese (Heilbronn, 1878)

George of Pisidia, *Poems*, ed. and Italian tr. A. Pertusi (Ettal, 1959)

Gregory of Tours, *Historia Francorum*, ed. W. Arndt and B. Krusch, *MGH Scriptores Rerum Merovingicarum* vol. 1 (Hanover, 1884)

Herodian, *History*, ed. and tr. C. R. Whittaker (Loeb, 1969–70)

Historia Augusta, ed. E. Hohl, re-ed. C. Samburger and W. Seyfarth (Leipzig, 1965)

Jesusdenah, *Le Livre de la chasteté*, ed. and French tr. J.-B. Chabot, *Mélanges d'archéologie et d'histoire* 16 (1896), 228–83 (trans.), followed by the text (numbered pp. 1–80)

John of Ephesus, *Ecclesiastical History (Part III)*, ed. and Latin tr. E. W. Brooks (CSCO Scr. Syr. 54–5: Paris and Louvain, 1935–6)

   Lives of the Eastern Saints, ed. and tr. E. W. Brooks (*PO* xvii–xix: Paris, 1923–6)

John of Epiphania, fragment, *FHG* iv.272–6

John Lydus, *De Magistratibus Populi Romani*, ed. and tr. A.C. Bandy (Philadelphia, 1983)

Ps.-Joshua Stylites, *Chronicle*, ed. and tr. W. Wright (Cambridge 1882)

Julian, *Works* vol. 1 (Parts 1 and 2), ed. and French tr. J. Bidez (Paris, 1924–32)

Justinian, *Novels*, in *Corpus Iuris Civilis* vol. 3, ed. R. Schöll and W. Kroll (9th edn, Dublin and Zurich, 1968)

Lactantius, *De Mortibus Persecutorum*, ed. and tr. J. L. Creed (Oxford, 1984)

Libanius, *Works*, ed. R. Förster (Leipzig, 1903–27); *The Julianic Orations*, tr. A. F. Norman (Loeb, 1969)

Malalas, *Chronicle*, ed. L. Dindorf (Bonn, 1831); tr. E. and M. Jeffreys and R. Scott (Melbourne, 1986)

Malchus of Philadelphia, fragments, ed. and tr. R. C. Blockley, *Classicising Historians* vol. 2

Marcellinus *comes*, *Chronicle*, ed. T. Mommsen, *MGH Auctores Antiquissimi* vol. 11 (Berlin, 1894)

Maurice, *Strategikon*, ed. G. T. Dennis, German tr. E. Gamillscheg (Vienna, 1981)

Menander Protector, fragments, ed. and tr. R. C. Blockley (Liverpool 1985)

Notitia Dignitatum, ed. O. Seeck (Berlin, 1876)

Olympiodorus of Thebes, fragments, ed. and tr. R. C. Blockley, *Classicising Historians* vol. 2

Panegyrici Latini, ed. and French tr. E. Galletier (Paris, 1949–55)

Peri Strategias, ed. and tr. G. T. Dennis in *Three Byzantine Military Treatises* (Washington, 1985)

Peter the Patrician, fragments, *FHG* iv.181–91

Philostorgius, *Historia Ecclesiastica*, ed. J. Bidez, re-ed. F. Winkelmann (Berlin, 1972)

Photius, *Bibliotheca*, ed. R. Henry (Paris, 1959–77)

Priscus of Panium, fragments, ed. and tr. R. C. Blockley, *Classicising Historians* vol. 2

Procopius of Caesarea, *Works*, ed. J. Haury, rev. G. Wirth (Leipzig, 1962–4)

Ptolemy, *Geography*, ed. C. Müller (Paris, 1883–1901)

Res Gestae Divi Saporis, tr. R. N. Frye, *Ancient Iran*, 371–3

Socrates Scholasticus, *Ecclesiastical History*, ed. R. Hussey (Oxford, 1853)

Sozomen, *Ecclesiastical History*, ed. J. Bidez (Berlin, 1960)

Symmachus, *Works*, ed. O. Seeck, *MGH Auctores Antiquissimi* vol. 6 (Berlin, 1883)

Themistius, *Orations*, ed. G. Downey and A.F. Norman (Leipzig, 1965–74)

Theodoret, *Ecclesiastical History*, ed. L. Parmentier, re-ed. F. Scheidweiler (Berlin, 1954)

   Historia Religiosa, ed. and French tr. P. Canivet and A. Leroy-Molinghen (SC 234, 257: Paris, 1977–79)

   Letters, ed. and French tr. Y. Azéma (SC 40, 98, 111: Paris, 1955–65)

Theodosius II, *Novels*, in *Codex Theodosianus*

Theophanes, *Chronicle*, ed. C. de Boor (Leipzig, 1883–5)

Theophylact Simocatta, *History*, ed. C. de Boor, re-ed. P. Wirth (Stuttgart, 1972); tr. M. Whitby and M. Whitby (Oxford, 1986)

Valentinian III, *Novels*, in *Codex Theodosianus*

Vegetius, *Epitoma Rei Militaris*, 2nd edn, ed. C. Lang (Leipzig, 1885)

Ps.-Zacharias Rhetor, *Ecclesiastical History*, ed. and Latin tr. E. W. Brooks (CSCO Scr. Syr. 38–9: Louvain, 1924)

Zosimus, *New History*, ed. L. Mendelssohn (Leipzig, 1887)

SECONDARY SOURCES

(In general, only items cited more than once in the notes have been included in the following bibliography.)

Adams, R. M., 'Agriculture and urban life in early southwestern Iran', *Science* 136 (1962), 109–22

Land behind Baghdad: a History of Settlement on the Diyala Plains (Chicago and London, 1965)

Heartland of Cities: Surveys of Ancient Settlement and Land Use on the Central Floodplain of the Euphrates (Chicago and London, 1981)

Admiralty, Naval Intelligence Division, Geographical Handbook Series, *Syria* and *Iraq and the Persian Gulf* (London, 1944)

Admiralty War Staff, Intelligence Division, *A Handbook of the River Danube* (London, 1915)

Anderson, P., *Passages from Antiquity to Feudalism* (London, 1974)

Andreotti, R., 'Su alcuni problemi del rapporto fra politica di sicurezza e controllo del commercio nell'impero romano', *RIDA* 16 (1969), 215–57

Austin, N. J. E., *Ammianus on Warfare* (Brussels, 1979)

Balty, J.-C. 'Apamée (1986): nouvelles données sur l'armée romaine de l'orient et les raids sassanides du milieu du IIIe siècle', *CRAI* (1987), 213–41.

Barnes, T. D., *Constantine and Eusebius* (Cambridge, Mass., 1981)

'Constantine and the Christians of Persia', *JRS* 75 (1985), 126–36

Barrett, J. C., Fitzpatrick, A. P. and Macinnes, L. (eds.), *Barbarians and Romans in North-West Europe* (BAR s471, 1989)

Blockley, R. C., 'Doctors as diplomats in the sixth century AD', *Florilegium* 2 (1980), 89–100

The Fragmentary Classicising Historians of the Later Roman Empire 2 vols. (Liverpool, 1981–3)

The History of Menander the Guardsman (Liverpool, 1985)

'Constantius II and Persia' in C. Deroux (ed.), *Studies in Latin Literature* vol. 5 (Brussels, 1989), 465–90

Boyce, M. and Grenet, F., *A History of Zoroastrianism* vol. 3, *Zoroastrianism under Macedonian and Roman Rule* (Leiden, 1991).

Brandt, R. and Slofstra, J. (eds.), *Roman and Native in the Low Countries: Spheres of Interaction* (BAR s184, 1983)

Braun, O., *Ausgewählte Akten persischer Märtyrer* (Kempten and Munich, 1915)

Brennan, P., 'Combined legionary detachments as artillery units in late-Roman Danubian bridgehead dispositions', *Chiron* 10 (1980), 553–67

Brock, S. P., 'Syriac historical writing: a survey of the main sources', *Journal of the Iraqi Academy (Syriac Corporation)* 5 (1979/80), 1–30

'Christians in the Sasanian empire', *Studies in Church History* 18 (1982), 1–19

Brown, P., 'The diffusion of Manichaeism in the Roman empire', *JRS* 59 (1969), 92–103

Bury, J. B., *History of the Later Roman Empire from the Death of Theodosius I to the Death of Justinian* 2 vols. (London, 1923)

Cambridge History of Iran vol. 3, ed. E. Yar-Shater (Cambridge, 1983)

Cameron, A. M., 'Agathias on the Sassanians', *DOP* 23/4 (1969/70), 69–183

Procopius and the Sixth Century (London, 1985)

Christensen, A., *L'Iran sous les Sassanides*, 2nd edn (Copenhagen, 1944)

Clauss, M., *Der magister officiorum in der Spätantike* (Munich, 1980)

Constantinescu, M., Pascu, S. and Diaconu, P. (eds.), *Relations between the Autochthonous Population and the Migratory Populations on the Territory of Romania* (Bucharest, 1975)

Crow, J. G., 'The function of Hadrian's wall and the comparative evidence of late Roman long walls' in *Studien zu den Militärgrenzen Roms III* (Stuttgart, 1986), 724–9

Dagron, G., '"Ceux d'en face". Les peuples étrangers dans les traités militaires byzantins', *TM* 10 (1987), 207–32

de Ste Croix, G. E. M., *The Class Struggle in the Ancient Greek World* (London, 1981)

Delmaire, R., *Largesses sacrées et 'res privata'* (Rome, 1989)

Demougeot, E., *La Formation de l'Europe et les invasions barbares* vol. 1 (Paris, 1969)

Diaconu, G., 'On the socio-economic relations of natives and Goths in Dacia' in Constantinescu *et al.*, *Relations*, 65–75

Dilke, O. A. W., *Greek and Roman Maps* (London, 1985)

Dillemann, L., *Haute Mésopotamie orientale et les pays adjacents* (Paris, 1969)

Dittrich, U.-B., *Die Beziehungen Roms zu den Sarmaten und Quaden im vierten Jahrhundert n. Chr.* (Bonn, 1984)

Dodgeon, M., and Lieu, S. N. C., *The Roman Eastern Frontier and the Persian Wars, AD 226–363* (London, 1991)

Drinkwater, J. F., *The Gallic Empire* (Stuttgart, 1987)

Dvornik, F., *Origins of Intelligence Services* (New Brunswick, New Jersey, 1974)

Eadie, J.W., 'Barbarian invasions and frontier politics in the reign of Gallienus', in W. S. Hanson and L. J. F. Keppie (eds.), *Roman Frontier Studies 1979* (BAR s71, 1980), vol. 3, 1045–50

Eggers, H. J., *Der römische Importe im freien Germanien* (Hamburg, 1951)

Fink, R. O., *Roman Military Records on Papyrus* (Case Western Reserve, 1971)

Firth, R., 'Rumor in a primitive society', *Journal of Abnormal and Social Psychology* 53 (1956), 122–32

Freeman, P. M., and Kennedy, D. L., (eds.), *The Defence of the Roman and Byzantine East* (BAR s297, 1986)

Frézouls, E., 'Les fonctions du Moyen-Euphrate a l'époque romaine' in J. C. Margueron (ed.), *Le Moyen Euphrate: zone de contacts et d'échanges* (TCRPGA 5, 1977), 355–86

'Les fluctuations de la frontière orientale de l'empire romain' in T. Fahd (ed.), *La Géographie administrative et politique d'Alexandre à Mahomet* (TCRPGA 6, 1979), 177–225

Frye, R. N., 'The Sasanian system of walls for defence' in M. Rosen-Ayalon (ed.), *Studies in memory of Gaston Wiet* (Jerusalem, 1977), 7–15

The History of Ancient Iran (Munich, 1984)

Fulford, M. G., 'Roman material in barbarian society, *c*. 200 BC–*c*. AD 400' in T. C. Champion and J. V. S. Megaw (eds.), *Settlement and Society* (Leicester, 1985), 91–108

'Roman and barbarian: the economy of Roman frontier systems' in Barrett *et al.*, *Barbarians and Romans*, 81–95

Garsoïan, N .G., 'Le role de l'hiérarchie chrétienne dans les rapports diplomatiques entre Byzance et les Sassanides', *Revue des études arméniennes* 10 (1973/4), 119–38

'Byzantium and the Sasanians', *CHI* vol. 3, 568–92

Gignoux, P., 'L'organisation administrative sasanide', *Jerusalem Studies in Arabic and Islam* 4 (1984), 1–29

Goffart, W., *Barbarians and Romans, AD 418–584: the Techniques of Accommodation* (Princeton, 1980)

Gregory, S. and Kennedy, D. (eds.), *Sir Aurel Stein's 'Limes Report'* (BAR s272, 1985)

Güterbock, K., *Byzanz und Persien in ihren diplomatischen-völkerrechtlichen Beziehungen im Zeitalter Justinians* (Berlin, 1906)

Harley, J. B., and Woodward, D. (eds.), *The History of Cartography* vol. 1 (Chicago and London, 1987)

Harris, W. V., *Ancient Literacy* (Cambridge, Mass., 1989)

Heather, P., *Goths and Romans, 332–489* (Oxford, 1991)

Heather, P. and Matthews, J., *The Goths in the Fourth Century* (Liverpool, 1991)

Hedeager, L., 'A quantitative analysis of Roman imports in Europe north of the Limes (0–400 AD), and the question of Roman–Germanic exchange', *Studies in Scandinavian Prehistory and Early History* 1 (1978), 191–216

Helm, R., 'Untersuchungen über den auswärtigen diplomatischen Verkehr des römischen Reiches im Zeitalter der Spätantike', *Archiv für Urkundenforschung* 12 (1932), 375–436

Hendy, M. F., *Studies in the Byzantine Monetary Economy, c. 300–1450* (Cambridge, 1985)

Hoffmann, D., 'Wadomar, Bacurius und Hariulf: zur Laufbahn adliger und fürstlicher Barbaren in spätrömischen Heere des 4. Jahrhunderts', *Museum Helveticum* 35 (1978), 307–18

Hunt, E. D., *Holy Land Pilgrimage in the Later Roman Empire AD 312–460* (Oxford, 1982)

Isaac, B., *The Limits of Empire: the Roman Army in the East* (Oxford, 1990)

Janni, P., *La mappa e il periplo. Cartografia antica e spazio odologico* (Rome, 1984)

Johnson, S., *Late Roman Fortifications* (London, 1983)

Johnston, R. J., *Geography and Geographers: Anglo-American Human Geography since 1945*, 2nd edn (London, 1983)

Jones, A. H. M., *The Later Roman Empire 284–602* (Oxford, 1964)

The Cities of the Eastern Roman Provinces, 2nd edn (Oxford, 1971)

Kaegi, W., *Byzantine Military Unrest, 471–843* (Amsterdam, 1981)

Kandler, M., and Vetters, H., *Der römische Limes in Österreich* (Vienna, 1989)

Kawar [Shahid], I., 'The Arabs in the peace treaty of AD 561', *Arabica* 3 (1956), 181–213

Kettenhoffen, *Die römisch-persischen Kriege des 3. Jahrhunderts n. Chr.* (Wiesbaden, 1982)

Kropotkin, A. V., 'On the centres of the Chernyakhovo culture tribes', *Sovetskaya Arkhe-ologiya* (1984) fasc. 3, 35–47 (in Russian with English summary)

La Persia nel medioevo (Accad. Naz. dei Lincei, Quaderno n. 160: Rome, 1971)

Labourt, J., *Le Christianisme dans l'empire perse sous la dynastie sassanide (224–632)* (Paris, 1904)

Lee, A. D., 'Embassies as evidence for the movement of military intelligence between the Roman and Sasanian empires' in Freeman and Kennedy, *Defence*, 455–61

'Campaign preparations in late Roman-Persian warfare' in D. H. French and C. S. Lightfoot (eds.), *The Eastern Frontier of the Roman Empire* (BAR s553, 1989), 257–65

'Procopius, Justinian and the *kataskopoi*', *CQ* 39 (1989), 569–72

'The role of hostages in Roman diplomacy with Sasanian Persia', *Historia* 40 (1991), 366–74

Lee, D. and Shepard, J., 'A double life: placing the *Peri presbeon*', *BS* 52 (1991), 15–39

Lemerle, P., 'Invasions et migrations dans les Balkans depuis la fin de l'époque romaine jusqu'au VIIIe siècle', *RH* 211 (1954), 265–308

Liebeschuetz, J. H. W. G., *Antioch. City and Imperial Administration in the Later Roman Empire* (Oxford, 1972)

'The defences of Syria in the sixth century' in *Studien zu den Militärgrenzen Roms II* (Cologne, 1977), 487–99

Barbarians and Bishops: Army, Church and State in the Age of Arcadius and Chrysostom (Oxford, 1990)

Lieu, S. N. C., 'Captives, refugees and exiles: a study of cross-frontier civilian movements and contacts between Rome and Persia from Valerian to Jovian' in Freeman and Kennedy, *Defence*, 475–505

Lightfoot, C. S., 'The eastern frontier of the Roman empire (with special reference to the reign of Constantius II)' (Oxford D.Phil. thesis, 1982)

'Facts and fiction – the third siege of Nisibis (AD 350)', *Historia* 37 (1988), 105–25

MacMullen, R., *Roman Government's Response to Crisis* (New Haven, 1976)

Corruption and the Decline of Rome (New Haven and London, 1988)

Maenchen-Helfen, O., *The World of the Huns* (Berkeley, 1973)

Matthews, J., *The Roman Empire of Ammianus* (London, 1989)

'Hostages, philosophers, pilgrims, and the diffusion of ideas in the late Roman Mediterranean and Near East' in F. M. Clover and R. S. Humphreys (eds.), *Tradition and Innovation in Late Antiquity* (Madison, Wisconsin, 1989), 29–49

Mellor, R. E. H., *The Rhine: a Study of the Geography of Water Transport* (Aberdeen, 1983)

Millar, F., 'Paul of Samosata, Zenobia and Aurelian: the church, local culture and political allegiance in third-century Syria', *JRS* 61 (1971), 1–17

'Emperors, frontiers and foreign relations, 31 BC to AD 378', *Britannia* 13 (1982), 1–25

'Empire, community and culture in the Roman Near East: Greeks, Syrians, Jews and Arabs', *Journal of Jewish Studies* 38 (1987), 143–64

'Government and diplomacy in the Roman empire during the first three centuries', *International History Review* 10 (1988), 345–77

Miller, J. I., *The Spice Trade of the Roman Empire* (Oxford, 1969)

Mócsy, A., *Pannonia and Upper Moesia* (London, 1974)

Morony, M. G., *Iraq after the Muslim Conquest* (Princeton 1984)

Musset, L., *The Germanic Invasions: the Making of Europe AD 400–600*, tr. E. and C. James (London, 1975)

Neusner, J., *A History of the Jews in Babylonia* 5 vols. (Leiden, 1965–70)

Newman, J., *The Agricultural Life of the Jews in Babylonia between the years 200 CE and 500 CE* (London, 1932)

Oates, D., *Studies in the Ancient History of Northern Iraq* (London, 1968)

Oppenheimer, A., *Babylonia Judaica in the Talmudic Period* (Wiesbaden, 1983)

Petrikovits, H. von, 'Fortifications in the north-western Roman empire from the third to the fifth centuries AD', *JRS* 61 (1971), 178–218

Pigulevskaja, N., *Les Villes de l'état iranien aux époques parthe et sassanide* (Paris, 1963)

Pohl, W., *Die Awaren: Ein Steppenvolk in Mitteleuropa, 567–822 n.Chr.* (Munich, 1988)

Potter, D. S., *Prophecy and History in the Crisis of the Roman Empire* (Oxford, 1990)

Purcell, N., 'The creation of provincial landscape' in T. Blagg and M. Millett (eds.), *The Early Roman Empire in the West* (Oxford, 1990), 6–29

Raschke, M. G., 'New studies in Roman commerce with the east', *ANRW* II.9.2 (1978), 604–1361

Rebuffat, R., 'Le bouclier de Doura', *Syria* 63 (1986), 85–105

Renfrew, C., 'Trade as action at a distance: questions of integration and communication' in J. A. Sabloff and C. C. Lamberg-Karlovsky (eds.), *Ancient Civilization and Trade* (Albuquerque, 1975), 3–59

Ridley, R. T., 'Notes on Julian's Persian expedition', *Historia* 22 (1973), 317–30

Riepl, W., *Das Nachrichtenwesen der Altertums* (Leipzig, 1913)

Safrai, S., 'The era of the Mishnah and the Talmud' in H. H. Ben-Sasson (ed.), *A History of the Jewish People* (London, 1976)

Schmid, P., and Zimmermann, W. H., 'Flögeln', *Probleme der Küstenforschung im südlichen Nordseegebiet* 11 (1976), 1–77

Schönberger, H., 'The Roman frontier in Germany: an archaeological survey', *JRS* 59 (1969), 144–97

Seeck, O., *Geschichte des Untergangs der antiken Welt* 6 vols. (Berlin and Stuttgart, 1895–1921)

Segal, J. B., 'Mesopotamian communities from Julian to the rise of Islam', *Proceedings of the British Academy* 41 (1955), 109–39

'The Jews of northern Mesopotamia before the rise of Islam' in J. M. Grintz and J. Liver (eds.), *Studies in the Bible presented to M. H. Segal* (Jerusalem, 1964), 32–63

Edessa, 'the Blessed City' (Oxford, 1970)

Shaw, B. D., '"Eaters of flesh and drinkers of milk": the ancient Mediterranean ideology of the pastoral nomad', *Ancient Society* 13–14 (1982–3), 5–31

Shepard, J., 'Information, disinformation and delay in Byzantine diplomacy', *Byzantinische Forschungen* 10 (1985), 233–93

Soproni, S., *Der spätrömische Limes zwischen Esztergom und Szentendre* (Budapest, 1978)

Die letzten Jahrzehnte des pannonischen Limes (Munich, 1985)

Speidel, M. P., 'Exploratores. Mobile elite units of Roman Germany', *Epigraphische Studien* 13 (1983), 63–78

Stein, E., *Histoire du Bas-Empire* 2 vols., ed. and tr. J.-R. Palanque (Paris, 1949–59)

Stephens, M., *A History of News: from the Drum to the Satellite* (New York, 1988)

Stratos, A. N., *Byzantium in the Seventh Century* vol. 1, tr. M. Ogilvie-Grant (Amsterdam, 1968)

Teall, J. L., 'The barbarians in Justinian's armies', *Speculum* 40 (1965), 294–322

Teodor, D. G., *The East Carpathian Region of Romania in the V–IX Centuries AD* (BAR s81, 1980)

Thompson, E. A., *A History of Attila and the Huns* (Oxford, 1948)

'Christianity and the northern barbarians' in A. Momigliano (ed.), *The Conflict between Paganism and Christianity in the Fourth Century* (Oxford, 1963), 56–78

The Early Germans (Oxford, 1965)

The Visigoths in the Time of Ulfila (Oxford, 1966)

Tocalis, T. R., 'Changing theoretical foundations of the gravity concept of human interaction' in B. J. L. Berry (ed.), *The Nature of Change in Geographical Ideas* (DeKalb, Ill., 1978), 65–124

Todd, M., *The Northern Barbarians, 100 BC–AD 300*, rev. edn (London, 1987)

Tomlin, R. S. O., 'The emperor Valentinian I' (Oxford D.Phil. thesis, 1974)

Waas, M., *Germanen im römischen Dienst im 4. Jh. n. Chr.* (Bonn, 1965)

Wardman, A. E., 'Usurpers and internal conflicts in the fourth century AD', *Historia* 33 (1984), 220–37

Warmington, B. H., 'Frontier studies and the history of the Roman empire – some desiderata' in D.M. Pippidi (ed.), *Actes du IXe congrès international d'études sur les frontières romaines* (Bucharest, 1974), 291–6

Whitby, Michael, 'Procopius and the development of Roman defences in upper Mesopotamia' in Freeman and Kennedy, *Defence*, 717–35

The Emperor Maurice and his Historian: Theophylact Simocatta on Persian and Balkan Warfare (Oxford, 1988)

Whitby, Michael and Whitby, Mary, *Chronicon Paschale, 284–628 AD* (Liverpool, 1989)

Whitehouse, D. and Williamson, A., 'Sasanian maritime trade', *Iran* 11 (1973), 29–49

Whittaker, C. R., *Les Frontières de l'empire romain* (Paris, 1989)

Wightman, E. M., *Gallia Belgica* (London, 1985)

Wolfram, H., *History of the Goths*, tr. T. Dunlap (Berkeley, 1989)

Wolska, W., *La Topographie chrétienne de Cosmas Indicopleustès. Théologie et science au VIe siècle* (Paris, 1962)

Wolska-Conus, W., 'Geographie', *RAC* 10 (1978), 155–222

Yar-Shater, E., 'Were the Sasanians heirs to the Achaemenids?' in *La Persia nel medioevo*, 517–31

Zöllner, E., *Geschichte der Franken* (Munich, 1970)

INDEX OF SOURCES

GENERAL INDEX

Abraham (envoy), 46
Abraham of Kaskar (Persian ascetic), 56
Abraham of Nethpar (Persian ascetic), 56
Achaemenids, 21–2, 50
Adamantius (envoy), 38
Adrianople, 77n, 133
Aemilianus (emperor, 253), 133
Africa, north, 4, 7, 111, 133, 162, 172,
    176
agentes in rebus, 172–3
agri decumates, 26, 66, 68–9, 90
agrimensores (surveyors), 86
Agrippa's map, 85, 86
Alamanni (*see also* Germanic peoples; northern
    peoples), 3, 26
    embassies, 41, 137, 167, 182n
    gifts from Romans, 41, 137
    invasions by, 134–5 (259–60), 135 (3rd c.),
        96, 136, 137, 152 (350s), 137–8 (365),
        133, 182 (378)
    knowledge of Roman plans, 131–3, 134–5
    lack of urbanisation, 26–7, 89
    language, 130, 173
    military organisation, 29
    political/administrative organisation, 27–9
    in Roman military service, 76n, 77, 130,
        131, 132–3, 162
    socio-economic character, 26–7
    see also Juthungi
Alamannia
    lack of roads, 89–90
    Roman forces in, 71, 87, 131–2, 133, 162,
        180
Alani, 123
Alaric (Gothic ruler), 56n, 138
Alexander (envoy), 38, 47
Alexander Acoemitis (ascetic), 55n
Alexander the Great, 21, 22n, 50
Alexandria, 56, 83
ambassadors, *see* envoys

Ambrose (bishop), 75
Amida, 58n, 95, 149n
    legionary base, 53
    merchants from, 62n, 64
    siege by Persians (502–3), 92
Ammianus Marcellinus, 128
    geographical knowledge, 6, 82
    as historian: avoidance of technical terms,
        171; sources, 6–7, 82, 107–8; strengths
        and limitations, 6–7
    intelligence mission, 172–3
    urban-oriented conception of landscape,
        89–90
Amoudis, 164
Anagastes (officer), 130–1
Anastasius (emperor, 491–518), 54n, 78n, 110,
    115, 169n
Anatolius (envoy), 38, 46
Anbar (Peroz-shapur), 20, 58, 157
Ancyra, 124
Andigan (Persian envoy), 111–12
Antae, 123
Anthemius (*magister officiorum*), 42
Antioch, 111, 148, 155
    capture by Persians, 23, 121n (3rd c.), 124
        (7th c.)
    as military base, 53, 91n, 92, 93n
    patriarch of, 60, 117
    as Persian objective, 23–4
    prosperity of hinterland, 155
Antoninus (deserter), 61, 63, 66, 109, 162, 165,
    178
Apamea, 118n
Aphrahat (writer), 148
Aquincum, 74, 76, 179, 181
Arabs, 4, 167
    embassies to, 39, 46, 47, 102, 167, 172
    military strengths, 52, 183n
    as Persian allies, 52, 115, 183n
    as raiders, 52, 53n, 54, 91, 94, 165, 183n